Under a TRIUMPHANT SKY

A Bike Across America Story

Steve Garufi

Mount Princeton Publishing

Printed in the United States of America
First Printing, 2014
ISBN 978-0692302897

Bicycle on chapter headers created using graphics by Cherie's Art

Cover and layout design by Susan Dunn, Grand Slam Design

Mount Princeton Publishing
P.O. Box 53
Salida, Colorado 81201
www.MountPrincetonPublishing.com

INDEBTEDNESS

How can I express my gratitude?

To Ron, Lisa and Chris,
Your contributions helped birth this work.
You completed my literary SAG wagon.
Our friendship is forever deepened.

And thanks to so many others.

My second dream is fulfilled.

CONTENTS

Many days
I longed to finish my bike ride across America,
with as much desire as a young child in early December
who wants the time between then and Christmas morning to be over.

And yet suspecting that when the trip finally ends,
sadness, like the death of a dream
or the cold wind that signals the beginning of a long winter,
may quietly pounce upon my heart.

CHAPTER I

ANSWERING A DREAM'S CALL

*Dreams are the bright creatures of poem
and legend, who sport on earth in the night
season, and melt away in the first beam of the
sun, which lights grim care and stern reality on
their daily pilgrimage through the world.*

Charles Dickens

I had a dream.

I was standing next to my bike on a beach with the Pacific Ocean at my back. Looking east, I had visions of rolling through desolate deserts, riding up the steep terrain of the Rockies, scrambling across the flat grueling distances of Texas, crossing the Mississippi and finally, heroically dipping my front wheel in the salty waters of the Atlantic.

Turning a dream into a reality is another matter. It takes planning, preparation, training, guts and money.

On the last day of January, my bike was stowed in the trunk of my old Honda Accord. I was on my way, driving west through Arizona on Interstate 8, headed toward San Diego. The land was wide and open, and beneath the bright blue sky was an arid country with salt brush, fields of yucca, creosote bushes and other desert flora that became a blur as I sped toward the first day of my mission. I drove with the windows down to take in the fresh air and the chill of the day. My car's radio was on the blink, so my entertainment defaulted to the meditative hum of the engine and the sound of the tires rolling down the highway. The next morning I would leave the little four-cylinder behind and begin to rely on flesh and blood to keep my dream alive. My muscles and my determination would rule the days ahead.

I guess by nature I'm a dreamer. I'd chased after dreams before, but it was hit or a miss with making them a part of my history. As a kid I wanted to be a pro baseball player. I studied the box scores in the newspaper, collected thousands of baseball cards and fantasized of the day when my own statistics would be listed on the back panel of a Steve Garufi card. I worked on that goal, playing little league into my teens. But, somewhere in the confusing haze of youthfulness, the dream went awry. As a teenager, I didn't think I was good enough for the high school team, and worse, I didn't even go to tryouts. Fear held me back. Fear of failure. Fear of success perhaps. Whichever it was, it was fear.

There were other grand schemes and adventures that I pondered, yet never pursued. But this one dream kept coming back to haunt me. The idea that I would one day ride a bike across the country stuck and wouldn't let go. I couldn't shake it. I still don't know why. Maybe I wasn't sure if I could live with myself if I didn't nail this one down and succeed.

The first time I thought about biking across America had been ten years ago. A friend and I had talked about travel books, and I said, "I would love to ride a bike across the country and write a book about it."

"It's already been done," she said flatly.

Intended or not, my friend effectively squelched the idea.

I figured she must be right. Who was I kidding? The last time I'd ridden a bike was when I was in my teens. And write a book? How would I ever write a book when completing a term paper in college was such an agonizing ordeal?

Still, the seed had been planted. It had roots. And it would grow to a near obsession. When I turned thirty-six, I knew that I had to make the trip and write a book about it. The dream became more insistent and considering all the years I had talked about doing this, if I didn't go now, then I needed to shut my mouth entirely.

It was time. Windows of opportunity rarely stay open for long. I would bicycle from the Pacific Ocean to the shores of the Atlantic. I was prepared to battle desert, mountains, loneliness, and those words that diminished my dream: "It's been done before."

Well, not by me.

I was still driving when I noticed the highway rose gently toward the Gila Mountains, a rocky and rugged brown-shaded range. Then just ahead, I counted twenty-five bicyclists riding the shoulder. As one, they pedaled in unison, hammering their way toward the crest of a road known locally as Telegraph Pass near Yuma. I smiled and felt a connection with them. If I lived in this region, I knew that I'd be out there riding with them. In a few days, I would be cycling in similar terrain north of here, both struggling and triumphing over adversity as they were.

A few hours later, I would cross the California state line and find my way to the coast. In San Diego, the freeway widened to five lanes on each side, and my nervousness grew with the intensity of the traffic. I had a bad case of the jitters. A devilish voice inside wondered how many things could go wrong on my route that stretched 2,500 miles into the unknown. Not only did I question my abilities to handle the challenges of the road, but I also had to ward off the demons within that lured me to the safety of home.

Will I have what it takes to complete this trip?

Will my body let me down?

Would I lack the fortitude to see the whole thing through?

Was I setting myself up for failure?

I had to dismiss those thoughts, push them aside, and not allow negativity to rule the day. Deep down, at my core being, I knew that I was ready. I would gut it out. I would succeed.

Why would I let worrisome thoughts intrude on my dream?

I was a strong and experienced cyclist. Years earlier, I had biked across my state of Colorado, a mountainous journey of over 550 miles. I did that high elevation trip in ten days. I'd been biking for five years, and although I never considered myself a pro or any kind of expert, I was seasoned with thousands of miles in the saddle. I found it important and helpful to break my plan down into a series of shorter, more defined rides. I concluded biking across America would be no different than riding across individual U.S. states, one at a time, in a succession of doable trips.

I'd worked hard for two months—planning, training, and handling a surfeit of details to prepare for this adventure. And I had my road bike checked to be sure it was mechanically fit and set to serve me reliably.

I had a professional counseling practice and clients that I couldn't let down, so I made arrangements to work while on the road. I'd allow counseling sessions over the phone with some and would make accommodations to care for them.

I had the good fortune to have my friend Jill do research online that included finding motels, locating bicycle shops and meeting other logistical needs that might arise on my route. She intended to be a reliable and a handy "go to" person who'd be willing to hop on the Internet when I was on the road and feed me information to get me out of jams.

So I figured out the time issues, the work constraints and flexibilities, my need to be physically fit, and I saved enough cash to cover the financial challenges, before I hit the road. Fortunately, everything almost magically came together just at the right moment for me to start this dream and make it come true. Nothing would stop me.

At a gas station in San Diego, I called my friend, Charles, who lives in Memphis, Tennessee. He planned to meet me once I made it to Mississippi.

"I grew up in California," Charles said. "What's your route?"

"Tomorrow I start in San Diego. Then I go through Julian,

Brawley and Blythe."

"Never heard of them."

"They're east of San Diego, in the southernmost part of the state."

Charles paused and then said, "So you're really following through with this?"

I could feel the fear in Charles' voice.

"As wild as it may sound, yes I am."

"I understand," he said with a sigh. "You know, I'm scared for you. Are you sure you're okay with going by yourself?"

"I'm used to doing a lot of things alone, especially biking," I said.

"What I'm thinking is professional riders have buses following them, but you don't have anybody to help you."

Charles had referred to SAG wagons, an acronym standing for "support and gear." Private tour companies have these wonderful vehicles that offer whatever help a cyclist might need—food, extra clothing, medical supplies, a charged cell phone and often a mechanic to fix flat tires and handle other mechanical needs. I'd considered using my Honda as a support vehicle, but the added expense was too much to make that happen. And where would I find someone who'd take the time off to follow me, while I pedaled for days, at a snail's pace, across the country? I had thought about paying for a tour group ride across the country, but they tend to be tied to a set schedule that I would find far too rigid. No, that wasn't my style. I wanted the flexibility to navigate my own route and at my own pace. I traced a route that would take me through Phoenix, central New Mexico, and west Texas to see special friends.

"And what about getting hit by a truck?" Charles asked.

I laughed. "That's just part of biking. I could get hit by a truck a mile from my house."

Charles's anxiety seemed to grow the more we spoke, but he only made me more confident in my planning.

"Look, I'm not trying to discourage you. You've biked for years and I believe you know what you're doing, but I don't know much about this. What if you run out of water?"

"That's simple. I carry plenty with me at all times. Most of the country has stores along the road for buying basic stuff like that."

"All right. This will be fun to track you and I've already told people at work. They've had all sorts of questions about how you're doing this. Please be safe and call if you need help, though I can't do much until you get out this way."

Soon I arrived in La Jolla, a trendy, upscale beach town north of San Diego. It was a short drive from the home of Krista, a friend who I planned to meet once she got off work.

I had a couple of hours to spend, so I found a spot to park near the beach. The place was busy with people strolling, some running and others taking their dogs for walks. Gazing off shore, I could see surfers on the water, catching waves and riding them until they curled and flattened. Several older couples relaxed on the beach, talking and taking in the scenery. I strolled on a pier, aware of each footstep as my bare feet pressed against my sandals. Sitting down on a bench, I tuned into the sounds of La Jolla with its rhythmic crashing of waves and the furtive squawks of a colony of seagulls, looking for handouts. The mellow California waves were steady and soothing, and my mind drifted peacefully as I stared at the ocean's horizon.

After driving a day and a half to get here, all my plans that would begin tomorrow seemed surreal. Was this really happening? I grinned and nodded in disbelief. Yes, it was.

My dream of biking across America.

Finally, I was answering its call.

CHAPTER II

WITH THE HELP OF SAN DIEGO ANGELS

*It is not the critic who counts; not the man who points out
how the strong man stumbles, or where the doer of deeds
could have done them better.
The credit belongs to the man who is actually in the arena,
whose face is marred by dust and sweat and blood;
who strives valiantly; who errs, who comes short again and again,
because there is no effort without error and shortcoming;
but who does actually strive to do the deeds; who knows great enthusiasms,
the great devotions; who spends himself in a worthy cause;
who at the best knows in the end the triumph of high achievement,
and who at the worst, if he fails, at least fails while daring greatly,
so that his place shall never be with those cold and timid souls who neither
know victory nor defeat.*

Theodore Roosevelt

Krista came out to greet me in the driveway as I arrived at her San Diego home. Blonde, blue-eyed, with shoulder-length hair, Krista is a lifelong southern Californian. And a treasured friend.

"Come in, come in!" she shouted, after giving me a hug.

"This is so nice," I said, as I noticed the elegance of her suburban neighborhood. An elaborate array of flowers and shrubbery were beside the house with towering palm trees on the corner of the property. Her home sat on a bluff at the end of a cul-de-sac.

"Oh, this isn't mine. It's my aunt's and I'm house-sitting. She's out of town long-term, and I'm saving money for now. Remember, I'm on a teacher's salary," she said, with a smile, "There's a pool in the back as well."

As I walked my bike into the foyer, her tiny dog barked frantically at my presence.

"Never mind her," she remarked.

With the bicycle leaning against the wall, Krista examined it. "So you're going across the country on this? Look at those tires. They're so thin." She pinched the front tire, only one inch in width.

"It's a road bike—designed for speed and smooth roads."

She leaned down to examine the bike's frame.

"That's a pretty red color. You'll be going thousands of miles on this thing. You and your bike on a big journey. Kind of like Don Quixote and his donkey."

That made us both chuckle.

"But you're not insane like he was," she added.

Krista made me tea and I got comfortable on a couch in the living room, but the dog continued to worry about me.

"She's just nervous to have a stranger here," Krista said. It was a strange-looking dog, small but with long hair. "She's half Shih Tzu and half Poodle. So they call it a shit-poo." Her dog kept growling at me until Krista scooped her up and held her while sitting in a recliner across from me.

"I'm amazed," she said, her eyes beaming with pride, "You're really doing this. When you called last week to confirm the day you were coming, I was like, 'Wow, you're really going through with it.' I have to admit that I still had some disbelief, but that's not the case anymore. Here you are, and your bike is right there!" she said.

I grinned.

"It feels good to see you doing this. Too many people never go for it, whatever it is, and I'm probably in that group."

"You? I'm not so sure about that."

"Believe me, I'd love to escape with you on a bike. Work is stressful. So much of a teacher's morale depends on how the principal runs her school, and the woman running it is new. She's a nightmare. None of the teachers are happy. I love being a teacher, but this school isn't so great to work under."

Krista sighed in frustration. "And then there might be budget cuts in this crazy California school system," she added.

"Awww, hang in there. You're still teaching first grade, right?"

"Yep."

"I could easily see you teaching first grade. You're good with people and especially kids. It would be fun to see you running your classroom with your students."

Her face brightened. "Thanks. Things will get better. Spring break isn't far and then there's the summer. I'm probably going on a cruise."

"Yeah? That sounds nice. With the time off they give you, you could bike across America too." I joked.

"Yeah, right. There's no way I could do what you're doing." She snapped her fingers, as if she remembered something, "I've been meaning to ask you: on an average day, how many hours do you ride?"

"Five or six hours usually. It depends."

"Will you have music with you?"

"No. At home, I have an MP3 player but I don't have a lot of music on it and I'd never wear earphones while riding. It's too dangerous. It's important to hear what's going on around me."

Krista shook her head in amazement. "So you'll have silence? Just the sounds of the road? I don't know if I could handle it. I'd go stir crazy without tunes."

I chuckled and shrugged my shoulders.

"So what do you think about while riding?"

I paused. Honestly, I didn't know. Her question stumped me.

"Well what do *you* think about when you drive your car?" I asked.

"Nothing, I have music. That's the point!"

I glanced up at the ceiling, mulling her point. "I'll have to think about what I think about. That might be something to consider."

"I'm not sure what I'd do without my music. I think you're brave, Steve, and I'm glad you're doing this. I plan to live vicariously through you," she said energetically.

"Oh, and don't worry about your car. This is a quiet neighborhood and as you noticed, this is a dead end street. I'll drive it around the block once in a while to keep the battery charged."

"You're the greatest," I exclaimed.

The plan would be to bike to the Georgia coast. Then I'd ship the bike to my home in Colorado, fly one-way to San Diego and drive home.

Since we had an hour before the time she had agreed to drive me to another friend's place, I lay on a pull-out bed, attempting to nap while Krista tended to other matters. All my driving during the past two days had caught up with me. With the lights off, I closed my eyes. The only sound was the refrigerator humming in the next room; it still felt like I was driving, the motion of the car moving and my position in the seat with my hands on the steering wheel. I wanted to rest but I was daunted by the fact that I'd be biking ... tomorrow.

Was I physically ready for this?

I could feel the tension in my neck, shoulders and wrists. For some reason, when I become nervous, it feels like there are heavy pieces of metal in my wrists. It's probably similar to the trepidation that comes before seeing the dentist or flying in an airplane. I knew everything would be okay, but once again, my nerves took a beating.

The hour elapsed quickly and it was time to leave. I moved my car from the driveway to the road, and then placed my bike into the trunk of her car with all of my belongings in the back seat. It was frightening to see how little I was bringing along, but I had to be meticulous about carrying as little as possible and only what was essential, for every item would contribute to a heavier bike.

We arrived at Jae's home, my second friend, who lived in an

older neighborhood that's closer to downtown San Diego. The small home she was renting was behind a tall iron gate. Jae came out to meet us. I introduced Krista and Jae. They had never met and quickly got to know each other as I ducked inside the car to pull out all of my necessities. It had become dark, and even with the car's dome light on, I still couldn't see if I had everything. *What if I forget something in here?* My stomach began to feel like it had butterflies, but I did my best and was fairly sure I had everything.

I stood beside them with my bike when Krista turned to me and said, "Now you be safe. And eat lots of Wheaties every morning, all right? That might have sounded funny, but I'm worried for you."

My grin grew large during her short lecture. "I'll eat okay. I promise."

"Oranges and peaches are good. Any kind of fruit will give you energy," she continued.

"Oh no, Steve is a picky eater. I know this for a fact. He hates vegetables, and I'm not sure he eats much fruit," interjected Jae.

The truth is, I do eat some fruits, such as blackberries, raspberries and bananas, but fruit allergies have given me allergic reactions in my mouth during my adult years. Apples, peaches and pears are especially tough on me.

"What about yogurt? Do you like that? That's a dairy product and you can add in whatever fruits you like, and it's easy to carry," said Jae.

"But what about utensils? I'd have to carry them. We'll see about that," I said.

"Plastic utensils. Bring them or grab them on the road," said Jae.

We talked more and they chatted about me as if I wasn't there, like two concerned sisters about to send their brother off to boot camp. Their caring and familiar voices had a calming effect. It felt good to have my friends—these two angels in San Diego—so invested in me and vital to my preparations. Tomorrow would be the commencement of the greatest journey of my life, and we all sensed that there was magic in the air.

Krista said, "I'm sorry, but I'm worried for my buddy. I'm not an athlete and I don't exercise like I should. All I do is walk my dog," She turned to me, "What happens if you get tired?"

"I can do two things. Rest or keep going," I said with assurance.

Krista fixed her eyes on mine, then nodded in bewilderment. "Maybe it's a guy thing and I'm a girl, but I don't get it. You're something else. Be safe, okay?"

"I will."

"And you've got nothing to worry about with your car. I'll take care of it. That's the least I can do."

It was time for Krista to leave. We hugged and I put my arm around her shoulders. "And one last time, you're being so helpful. I'll see you again."

It felt funny to say that. Whether I rode only two days or all the way to the Atlantic Ocean, I had to come back to San Diego to get my car. A quiet voice inside wondered: *when I return, will I come back with joy or disappointment?*

Jae walked me into her residence. It was a studio apartment— an artsy place with many of her paintings hung on the walls. Peaceful, enchanting music was already playing when we entered. I met Jae years earlier when we both lived in Manitou Springs, Colorado. She and her roommate helped me decorate my new apartment, and over time, I'd visit and occasionally they'd feed me like the stereotypical cooking-averse bachelor that I am.

Jae and I were hungry for dinner and we walked to a busy thoroughfare with many restaurants to choose from. We decided upon Chinese and reminisced as we ate.

My friend practically shouted, "I've heard you talk about this for years, and now you're doing it. Tomorrow! You're biking across America!"

"I know, it's crazy, isn't it? I've done so much planning," I said, as I rubbed the sides of my head. "All the work I've done to get to this point. I haven't had much time to rest."

Jae assured me, "I've got you set up for tonight. You'll stay in a spare room next door in my landlady's basement. It's cozy. I think you'll like it."

"That sounds great," I said, but I had to tell her more about the pressures I'd been carrying with me, "Throughout this winter, I'd say for about two months, I was in this preparation stage. I had all sorts of planning that I had to handle, but the worst was what was going on in my mind. When I finally started telling people around Christmas that I'd be doing this, the pressure was on: either I'd follow through or I'd look like a fool. I couldn't bear to be the type of person who says they'll do something, and then not do it."

"Come on, you're being too hard on yourself," said Jae, "Sometimes we can be our worst enemy. Would you treat someone the same way you treat yourself? You know what I'm getting at. You're probably graceful and understanding with others, especially when they're following their dreams and doing something out of the norm."

"Yeah, you're right," I replied. I ate a couple of fork fulls of my beef and broccoli, and then I grew a mischievous grin. "You want to see what I did to myself? I'll show you …"

"What?"

"Did you know I got shingles three weeks ago?"

Jae's eyes widened. "I've heard of that!"

"You want to see it?" Before she could answer, I was already raising my shirt. A red rash extended across my left upper abdomen like a sash. By now the color had faded in intensity, but when it first struck three weeks earlier, it had been a deeper shade of red with itchy white ends. Jae drew back, and put her hand over her mouth. "Ouch!"

"I think the reason for this was stress. I did a lot of research about shingles. Usually the elderly get it because they tend to have a weaker immune system, but younger people can get it if they're stressed out. Imagine the self-beating I put myself through when I first realized I had this."

Then I imitated myself with a mocking voice, "Hi. I'm Steve. I'm biking across America and I got so nervous about it that I got shingles."

Jae's face showed real concern. "Are you sure you'll be okay to go?"

"Yeah, the doctor said this was a mild case and I'd be okay to

ride. It doesn't hurt too much anymore, but it did for a while. At first, it
was a tingling in my chest and stomach, then I had a fever, and then just
beneath the skin it was really irritated. Anytime I used the muscle or if
my shirt touched the skin, it hurt, and I couldn't sleep on that side. It's
still sensitive, but it's definitely better."

"So are you ready?" she asked.

"I think so," I said with a nervous laugh, "Let me clarify that.
I'm as ready as I'll ever be."

"You have trained, right?"

"Yes and no. Remember, I still live in Colorado, and in the
mountainous part. Biking outdoors was out of the question this winter,
and the road I live on has been covered in ice and snow for the past two
months. It's impossible to ride outside."

"Oh."

"But yes, I've trained," I assured her, "but not in the way you
think. I've been at the gym five to six days a week all winter. I've mainly
done cardiovascular stuff, and I've worked hard. If you put me on an
elliptical machine, I could go easily for ninety minutes at a hard pace.
So am I in shape? Yes, but I'll admit it's nothing like the fitness you get
from riding. That's how I became interested in biking in the first place;
I was amazed at how strong and in-shape I felt from riding everyday."

"You'll be okay then," said Jae.

"We'll see," I interjected, "I'll be training as I go. My fitness
will improve and a lot of the pain you go through on a bike is all in the
head."

"I think that's like life."

"The 'all in your head' part?" I asked.

"Definitely."

Then a playful smile grew on Jae's face.

"Do you remember the first time you tried something like this?
You wanted to bike across Colorado. I'll never forget it."

"Oh no," I said, knowing what was coming.

"You hadn't done any riding or training at that point, but you
were like, 'Oh, I'll do it. No problem.' And what happened? I had to

rescue you!"

"Yes, I remember," I put my head down and laughed with her.

"No training whatsoever!" she reiterated. She was almost shouting again, as animated as a sister digging up dirt about me that only a family member would know.

The truth of the matter was, although I had biked across Colorado successfully four years earlier, Jae reminded me of another attempt when she saw me at my worst. That's right—before I would succeed in riding across my state, I would fail miserably. At the time, I was a novice, and having had no bicycle of my own, I rented one from a local shop. Starting at the Four Corners Monument where the borders of Utah, Arizona, New Mexico, and Colorado all meet, I rode off full of confidence and ignorance, and laden with gear. Only a few miles into my ride, I faced my first major ascent, and it nearly defeated me. I was totally out-of-shape and shocked at how tough cycling was. I rode about thirty-eight miles that day and then camped at a KOA campground that night. I had little to no experience camping in a tent, and my sleep was dodgy. I was completely exhausted. And demoralized.

The next morning, there was more grueling ascent to conquer, but I only endured a few miles before I quit and turned back. From there, I rented a truck, tossed my bike in the back, and drove one-way to Pagosa Springs, where I dropped off the truck at another rental site. That night, I slept at a friend's house and the following day I got a ride to Wolf Creek Pass, elevation 10,850 feet. This meant that I had completely avoided all the pain of bicycling up one of the nation's most challenging paved mountain passes. Instead, I started my ride at the summit and cruised downward with minimal effort for thirty miles. Pathetic!

After that day, I completed two days of respectable riding, but at the center of the state, my determination was gone. I called Jae, who drove one hundred miles to rescue and bring me home.

"You were sitting on the ground at that truck stop in Johnson Village and you looked like a lost puppy. You were dirty and unshaven, and I'll never forget the glaze in your eyes. You kept saying in monotone, 'That was hard. That was hard.'" Jae said.

I laughed and put my face in my hands, acknowledging every painful detail.

"You'd better be more prepared now. That's all I have to say," she ragged, pointing her finger at me.

I kept my eyes closed and nodded. "I am. You've got to believe me. That was six years ago. I'm not saying everything will be perfect, but ..."

"I know," said Jae, "You've biked a lot since then. You learned your lesson. But this is the real deal, starting tomorrow."

CHAPTER III

THE FIRST DAY

I do not think there is any other quality
so essential to success
of any kind as
the quality of perseverance.
It overcomes almost everything, even nature.

John D. Rockefeller

The next morning, Jae and I cruised on Interstate 5 in her black Nissan sedan, a fifteen year old car that seemed new because of how immaculately clean she kept it. With my bike and all gear in the back, we traveled north, first through downtown San Diego and then into the northern suburbs. From the passenger seat, I watched a plethora of vehicles weaving in and out of lanes to get ahead. It seemed like a routine day in the city, but for me, this was an extraordinary time in my life. This was the first day.

"Is it okay to eat in here?" I asked.

"Sure."

I grabbed a banana and a bag of trail mix, my chosen road

cuisine that I could munch on while riding. These staples of bicyclists are lightweight and can keep blood sugars steady for those muscling bikes for long distances. I could snack all day if I liked and keep moving.

"Have you decided where you're staying tonight?" asked Jae.

"Whatever I can find in Julian."

"A campground?"

"No way!" I said with certainty.

I had no desire to camp each night, with the hassles of finding a place to camp and lugging a tent, sleeping mat and extra gear. After a long day's ride, I always needed a shower and a soft bed, and a no-frills motel gave me just that. Risking having poor sleep on a cold night was not an option. My lodging plan was to stay away from popular hotel chains and find "mom and pop" motels that looked clean, safe, and most importantly, affordable.

As a clerk in an attorney's office, Jae was dressed in professional attire. She told me about her new job, and that she liked working there because there was always something different to do. She also liked her boss, who always took the time to express his appreciation for her work—a rarity these days.

There was a break in conversation, and in the silence my nerves began to creep up my spine as I considered the magnitude of what I was about to do.

Jae broke the silence. "By the way, do you know your final destination?"

"Jekyll Island, Georgia."

"What's the significance?"

"None that I know," I said with a laugh. "It looks like an easy spot to hit the beach in the southern part of Georgia."

"Georgia!" exclaimed Jae, "You're biking to Georgia. I still can't believe it. May God bless those legs of yours!"

"Why thank you," I said, while demonstrably rubbing my long and boney legs.

"I trust you're staying south?"

"Yep. A lot of people have biked across the southern part of the country at this time of year. No scorching heat, but still warm in Arizona, Texas and throughout the South."

"And you were here last year," said Jae, alluding to my two-week vacation in Tucson and San Diego. "You loved the weather. You should be a snowbird."

I checked my map and saw we were approaching the exits for Del Mar, California.

"Del Mar to Jekyll Island," I said, "My start and finish remind me of the novelty of the place a person is born. Whenever someone asks where I started, I'll say Del Mar. I thought it was inside San Diego city limits, but it's not."

Although I had never been here, I thought Del Mar offered the best way to get through the metropolitan region. The roads seemed like typical suburbia with slow traffic and less congestion, at least according to my map.

Within minutes we found our way to the beach at Del Mar. This was a quieter public beach than the one I visited yesterday. Two kids were playing with their Dad, and a few seagulls and other birds chirped and flew overhead. It was an overcast day, and around sixty degrees, with only patches of blue sky fighting through.

I lifted my bike out of the trunk, leaned it against the car, and stretched my back and calves. My clothing was mainly red—that's my color of choice—a red short-sleeved jersey, a red and white helmet, black cycling shorts, socks in red and black with red hot chile pepper designs, and my black cycling shoes. My Giant OCR3 road bike was also adorned in a striking bright red finish.

For this long haul, I had a metal rack installed above the back wheel. The rack held a square vinyl box—sometimes called a "trunk box"—for storage. I'd also purchased panniers—sometimes called "saddle bags"—that hung down on each side of the back wheel. Besides the pockets on my clothing, everything else I would carry would be in these containers on the back of the bike. In a short time, everything was packed and ready, including tools, extra clothing, and personal items.

"Do you have sunscreen?" Jae asked.

"Sure do."

"And? Did you put it on? I'm worried about your skin."

I laughed. "Look at the sky. I'll be okay."

"What about ChapStick?" she asked.

"I don't need that."

"Yes, you will. Your lips will dry and take a beating if you're out all day in this wind."

I smiled and took it. It was small enough to pack anyway.

Along with yesterday's warm welcome, I was grateful to have Jae at the beach to have someone to share this experience with. It would have been a downer, and perhaps more frightening, if I had started alone. I'd have more than enough solitude on the road. It was then that I apologized for my snarky comment about sunscreen, and in fact, I applied some to my face. She was right: you can get sunburned when it's cloudy.

Jae needed to get to work, but she offered to take the requisite photo of my bike and me at the beach. With the waves soft and easy, I walked the bike into the edge of the water, but had to run upward to avoid getting my feet wet. I got a rush! Then, in between waves, I stopped and gripped the handlebar while Jae hit the shutter button.

"I've got to go," said Jae, as she handed me my camera, "I'm nervous for you."

"All I have to do is make it to Julian. One day at a time."

Julian, California, fifty-five miles away and nestled in the mountains of east San Diego County, was my destination. This overcast February morning was just the start—an everyday bike ride east. It was Day One of my adventure.

We'd talked earlier and Jae said she wanted to meet me that evening in Julian. She knew of a great Italian restaurant that would fill me up with some heavy carbs for the days ahead. As we said good-bye, a large gust of the ocean breeze came in, chilling me to the bone. I grabbed my second layer from a pannier and put it on.

"Is it warm enough?" Jae asked.

"Not really," I said with laughter, "But if it's fifty-five degrees here, then it's probably twenty-five or maybe even fifteen in Colorado. I can handle it."

And with that, Jae was gone.

I took one final gaze at the vastness of the Pacific and reflected on what I was about to do. If I completed this mission successfully, my efforts would end with the view of another ocean. Still, I thought, no matter where this bike ride ends, whether at the Atlantic Ocean or somewhere sooner, I knew and felt a measure of success to reach this point. Many have a desire for adventure, to do something as wild as this, and never get the chance. Gratitude reverberated deep within me.

Another rush of nerves followed after the gratitude, prompting me to check the bike one final time, but by now, I had already done enough checking and preparing. I laughed at myself. There is that point in one's frantic planning, like the kind you do for a long-distance vacation, when your paranoia becomes silly. You worry that you forgot something—you didn't turn off an appliance or that you left a door unlocked—and then there's that point where you tell yourself you have to let go. It's time to leave and enjoy the present moment.

For me, the journey beckoned. It was time to ride.

As I straddled my bike, I felt both excited and anxious. There would be no hesitation now. This was my time. This was my dream and reality.

I clipped my shoes into the pedals and launched my heavy steed into a leisure pace, gliding along adjacent to the beach. Given the full weight of my bike, my cargo and me, I took control by holding tight to the handlebar grips, feeling the strength of my legs pushing the bike forward. I felt strong. But I knew that later that day my muscles would be burning because I had cycled minimally during the past five months, no matter what I had done at the gym.

Immediately, three bicyclists sped past and left me in the dust. Clearly, they were not smelling the roses. They looked like hot shots—I'm not criticizing them—but they had trendy, sporty outfits and nice high-end bikes. It was a little humbling, but I did my best to laugh it off, knowing that my bike was like a ton of lead compared to their carbon hustlers, and my ride would last well beyond their accelerated jaunt.

I was under a mile into my journey, when I turned east on Del Mar Heights Road, a street lined with palm trees. Some of the homes had blossoming flowers and one in particular had lemon trees. The road ascended steeply. As I pedaled hard, I glanced at the cyclometer and noticed it wasn't working. While a perfect mileage reading would be unrealistic, I couldn't have mileage go undocumented, especially this early. With this contraption, there's a small magnet that attaches to a front spoke that triggers a sensor on the bicycle's front fork that registers speed, mileage and cadence. Fortunately, it was an easy fix. I walked the bike to the sidewalk and discovered that when I had put on the front wheel at the beach, I had placed it backwards. So, I dislodged it, refastened it frontwards, lifted the bike and spun it forcefully. The cyclometer worked and said I'd gone a hundredth of a mile. I gave a mock cheer for myself, proud of my small success. Now I could look at my device and smile at the miles I'd ridden or stare at it with derision at the distance left to go.

Back on the bike, I confronted that steep grade of pavement. I worked hard, with the ocean dropping away at my back. I kept waiting for the moment when pain or exhaustion would hit me like a brick, but it never came. The hill was only at a half-mile, at most, and at the road's crest, I was rewarded with a spectacular view of low-slung California houses with clusters of palm trees that gave them all a splash of green. Their beauty, so exotic and tropical, struck me. Biking across America has been pretty nice so far, I joked to myself. I pulled out my camera and snapped a picture, and upon glancing back, the ocean stood far on the horizon. I bid farewell to the Pacific, this time for good.

The road twisted and turned through the suburban landscape, as I crossed main avenues, passed shopping malls, local shops, gas stations and everything else that marks a place as normal. When I crossed Interstate 5, I found myself in an upscale area with well-manicured lawns, golf courses, costly condominiums and jungles of palm trees. Still, it felt like an ordinary knockabout ride. And it was, except this was special—my first day. I felt great. My legs were pumping fine and I felt fit and energetic. Grateful, my soul sang.

My planned route was intentionally made simple—the fewer turns and roads, the better. I would take Del Mar Heights Road to Carmel Valley Road to Poway Road to State Highway 67. Then I would head to Ramona and take State Highway 78 to Julian. Carmel Valley Road was perfect, with light traffic and plenty of shoulder. I was just logging eleven miles when suddenly, it seemed, the road led into a way-too-quiet neighborhood with massive homes. Confused, I checked the road signs and learned I was no longer on Carmel Valley Road. I could have sworn that I didn't make any turns. And so I turned back and eventually found Carmel Valley Road, but I was at a complete loss with finding Poway Road. Finding my way was maddening, because I knew what may have happened. Sometimes road names continue with a "turn" at an intersection, and it's easy to miss the sign, or roads have their names changed when they cross into a different municipality. I've also read that sometimes the winding layout of suburban roads is intentionally designed to confuse unwelcome visitors or would-be burglars or criminals. Whatever was the case, I was mad and biked with no clue about where I was or where I was headed. Eventually I stopped at an intersection of two streets with unfamiliar names, and again studied my map. Then a man with black hair and sunglasses glided up on a mountain bike and we stood together at the traffic light. He looked to be in his thirties, with a few days' worth of stubble on his face, and seemed approachable.

"How do I get to Poway Road?" I asked, motioning uselessly at the map.

He took off his sunglasses, looked out toward the road, and squinted. Then he pointed back to where I'd just come from. "It's up this road. You'd make a right at the highway and go for a while."

"My end goal is Julian. I just want to get to Highway 67," I interjected. I'm certain that my frustration must have surfaced in my tone of voice.

"Julian? Okay," He thought some more. He put his finger to his mouth as if I had asked a difficult math problem. At least I felt vindicated to see even he, a local, couldn't give me a quick answer.

"Believe it or not, I'm biking across America. This is my first day," I added, "I've been to San Diego before, but not this part. These roads are crazy!"

"Yeah. They're a little confusing if you're not from here," then his voice grew confident. "I got it!" He pointed with authority at our intersection. "Just go up this road. Continue uphill and it turns into Scripps Poway Parkway. That'll take you all the way to 67 and then you're on your way to Julian."

"Thanks!" The traffic light changed, and the mountain biker and I parted ways. "Have a good ride," I shouted. Moments after he was gone, I realized I should have gotten a picture of him, but I did make a mental note of this anonymous man, the first stranger to help along the way.

The ascent on this new road was my first major challenge. It was a tough uphill, forcing me to take my time. I clicked the bike into "granny gear," a common bicycling term for first gear in both the front and back. It's ideal for steep climbs, when you're going slow. The pedaling is as easy as it can get—so easy that maybe your grandmother could even ride in it. Unless you're a professional racer, most riders go slow on a major climb. It doesn't feel easy. The key is to keep a steady pace and not become overwhelmed. I toiled up the hill, and my breathing got heavy. No doubt, I was training here. Eventually the road crested. Relief.

Soon, the road became Scripps Poway Parkway and after crossing Interstate 15, I took a break in front of a gas station and ate from a large bag of peanuts and Fig Newtons. It felt good to be handling things well. Returning to the bike, the weather was breezier and the blue sky and clouds fought it out, with the clouds winning.

Scripps Poway Parkway is a major four lane road, and I was very much still in the heart of suburbia. As I slowed to a crawl for a red light, I realized too late that my feet were still clipped into the pedals. This is a moment when a bicyclist knows that his only recourse is to go with the flow, and fall. My bike swayed to the left and as I got to the point of no return, I instinctively extended my arm and my hand hit the pavement hard, breaking my fall . . . and possibly my wrist. I lay on the pavement, in the middle of the lane no less, in shock. *Can I get up? How badly did I hurt myself? Can I keep riding?*

I pulled my shoes out of the pedals and stood, feeling shaky, embarrassed and sore. I couldn't bear to look at the drivers behind and next to me. I told myself that none of these people knew me. They would continue on their way and while they may never forget the guy lying out in the middle of the street, they will never know it was me.

The traffic light was still red when I hopped back on the bike, and all I could do was shake my head with a grin. Once it turned green, I rode to a nearby grassy spot in front of some shops. While I thought I had enough cycling experience to take on a cross-country tour, I had just learned something painful about my new shoes.

For five years, I had used inexpensive pedal straps that accepted any kind of shoe. With straps, one can simply insert their feet regardless of their type of shoe—sneakers, dress shoes, sandals, barefoot, etc.—and begin riding. But today was my first long ride with what is known as "clipless" shoes. These are shoes with a special hook on the bottom that mechanically clip into the pedal. With the cyclist's feet firmly positioned on the middle of the pedal, one's legs and the rest of the body can do more work, usually increasing one's pedaling power. You also get more firepower because you can push down on them and pull them back up to the top of your stroke, nearly doubling your output. For years, other bicyclists had raved about how much they appreciated clipless shoes, and two months earlier, I finally gave in and purchased the specialized pedals and shoes. At home, I had only biked a short distance to acquaint myself with inserting my feet in and out of the clips. The important factor, I learned, is to be sure to unclip my feet from the pedal whenever I anticipated a full stop.

When riding, a bike rider's momentum is moving forward, which makes it unlikely that the bike will tip to the side, but the hazard of losing balance is greatest when one's bike is stationary, especially when one's shoes are still clipped in. Although I had done it many times on today's ride, the key was to get into the habit of *consciously* unclipping my shoes well in advance of coming to a stop, so I could plant my feet to maintain balance.

Now safely on the grass in the shopping area, I inspected myself and the bike. I seemed to be okay except for a modest scrape on my left leg above the knee. My wrist was in some pain from breaking my fall, but I had had worse injuries in the past, and I believed I would be okay. I laughed again at myself. Thank goodness the drivers who saw me were long gone.

I continued east on Scripps Poway Highway, which soon transformed into a thoroughfare more conducive to speed. A concrete barrier lined the middle of the four lanes with fewer intersecting streets. I enjoyed a full-size shoulder much of the way, and I was leaving the suburbs behind. Ahead, small mountains covered in greenery highlighted the views as the road ascended. For four miles, the road was gaining in elevation as I traveled east and away from the ocean. This highway had become my toughest workout of the day and my body was feeling taxed. At one point, a pretty scene of hills and mountains afar caught my attention, and it was an excuse to stop, rest, and take a picture.

Then it happened again. *Wham!* And I was back on my side. I really needed to get used to these shoes!

I rose to my feet and had small particles of gravel stuck to my side, but a few swipes got them off. Fortunately, all was okay. No broken bones, no more damage, and just another bruise to my ego. At least this time, cars were few and the shoulder was wide enough that I hadn't fallen into the lane. I had no idea who might have seen this ugly spill. A sobering thought hit me: imagine how tragic it'd be if I didn't make it out of San Diego because I broke some bones on the first day. That would be an equally awful and hilarious story to tell for the ages. And so, I lectured myself again: *Learn your lesson. Anytime you're coming to a full stop, be mindful to immediately undo your feet long before you've stopped!*

Sometimes I can be absent-minded, but the experience made me think of a child who must learn the hard way to not place their hands on a hot stove. The fear of another humbling fall had locked me in; I would never again forget to unclip my shoes before stopping.

I reached State Highway 67, and by now, it was afternoon. The sky had become completely overcast, with a chilly breeze that made the fifty-five-degree day feel colder. So far, I had had a tough day's ride. I pulled over to take a breather and put on two more layers of clothing, including winter gloves over my cycling gloves. I drank liquids and chowed down on a snack. I also took a kind moment to congratulate myself for unclipping my feet well ahead of time. I stretched and paced on the side of the road, preparing for what was coming: more uphill.

As I pedaled with intensity, the road rose steadily into forest and hills. To a driver of a car, a modest grade may not seem like much, but the vagaries of roads are felt more on a bicycle. Gravity was working against me. My cadence remained steady as I continued in granny gear, with the physical demands wearing on me like never before. My legs felt like rubber bands. My breathing became short and labored. I consciously tried to take deep breaths, yet my lungs would have none of that. I rode slowly in the seven-to eight-mile-per-hour range for miles, staring at the front wheel and zoning out. All I heard were the sounds of the bike chain making its churlish loops and of cars passing me. An occasional gust of wind chilled the bare skin of my face.

When working hard, bicyclists must take the time to hydrate. Some feel compelled, however, to keep gripping their handlebar to remain as focused as possible on reaching the goal. Sure, take a hand off the handlebar and your bike might begin to wobble, but don't take a drink and your whole world might collapse. I must admit that I'm one of these stubborn ones, but with such a demanding workout, I forced myself to stop and gulp down vast amounts of water. It was at this point that I realized that I was out-of-shape and that my coast-to-coast ride might serve as both my dream come true as well as my fitness track.

A short while later, I arrived in Ramona and was gleaming with pride that most of my riding had been done with some measure of ascent. I granted myself a prolonged break. At a bank inside a local supermarket, I joined a long line to cash a check. With my helmet in hand and long hair all over the place, I approached the teller. She smiled, took my check and deposit slip, and typed away.

"So you've been out riding, huh?" she asked.

"Yep. I'm biking to Georgia," I said, with a shy grin.

A quizzical look crossed her face. She didn't follow up with a question. Maybe she didn't fully hear me or believe me. And I had no energy to elaborate. Besides, I'd probably be skeptical of myself too.

On a bench in front of the supermarket, I rested and kept chomping on my trail mix. It was the mid-afternoon, and I had another twenty-two miles to Julian. The sky was more gray, and the temperature seemed to be getting colder. At this point, I realized my mistake: I had started too late in the morning. Although I do most things early, for some reason, Jae and I took our time. We didn't wake up early, and she had to drag me shopping with her before we left. By the time I started at the beach, it was 10:30 a.m. On top of the late start, I became aware of another misjudgment: early February days are short and my riding time before dark is limited. With many lodging options on the main avenue in Ramona, I considered calling it a day. In retrospect, maybe I should have done so, but my ego wasn't in the mood to fall short of my first day's goal. I wanted to go for it. Off I went.

As I left town, I began once again to ascend, this time on State Highway 78, alas a two lane road with minimal shoulder. This made for a tight squeeze for two cars and a bike sharing the path. The usual rule of the road for bicyclists is to stay as far right as practical, and I kept my wheels either on the white line or a foot to the right, although some spots required that I ride just left of the line. Cars and trucks slowed and passed with care. While neon yellow and orange are probably the best colors, it's situations like this where my red bike and clothing are helpful to alert road-weary drivers that there is a bike ahead and that caution should be the rule of the moment.

The uphill was ruthless. It's true that I bicycle regularly in the mountains of Colorado and have conquered many major passes, but this range east of San Diego demanded respect. And who was I to argue with it?

I didn't want to stop, but found my body so exhausted that I had to pull over for a series of short breathers. At least the scenery was pretty with picturesque farms, complete with fields of crops and grazing cattle. Unfortunately, the sky was growing darker and grayer. With my luck, this was arguably the coldest day in the San Diego area this winter. The clouds showed no signs of breaking. Darkness would take over soon. There was no time to waste.

I was nearly depleted, but I kept riding, sometimes at a five-miles-per-hour snail's pace. I didn't anticipate that I would be in the middle of the biggest change in elevation, as Ramona sits at 1,400 feet above sea level and Julian is positioned at a lofty 4,250 feet. Another mistake. My goodness, I felt like an idiot that I didn't anticipate all the elevation gain I would have on this first day ... and at the end of the day too!

All that "beat-up" happening in my mind was unproductive. I had to keep pedaling. Cramps developed in my abdomen and my breathing became ill-tempered gasps. I forced myself to take long deep breaths and stare at the front wheel just ahead of me. I felt like an aggressive salesman who keeps getting "no" after "no" with each sales pitch, but the statistical rationale is that he is closer to hearing a "yes" with each encounter. As grueling as this bike ride was, I knew that with each revolution I was getting closer to the end ... as long as the wheel continued to turn.

I did whatever I could to get my mind off the physical discomfort. One technique I found useful was to intentionally think about all the blessings in my life—a mental list of things to be grateful for. I thought of Krista and Jae, and of the fact I live in the wealthiest country in the world. I thought of my family, this bike journey ... anything. That helped for five minutes, but like the dynamic of denial, the mental and physical pain came back even worse.

My body, in its exhaustion, screamed at me.

What are you doing?

It's too cold to be riding!

Are you sure you want to do this?!

I stopped briefly to take a swig from a water bottle. Across the street was a fruit stand that was still closed for the season. The negative mental chatter continued.

See? The fruit stand is closed. You made a huge mistake biking so early in the year. It's still winter!

What a battle that was transpiring in my head! Indeed, long distance bicycling is very much a fight for one's morale. I continued. I persevered. I even got a modest burst of energy. And the sky continued to grow dim, while the lights in the surrounding homes brightened. After a few more miles, I worked my way up to the top of a hill and found myself looking down into a valley. As I accelerated downhill at a speed of twenty miles per hour, I felt an adrenaline rush coupled with a surge of optimism. My cyclometer clocked forty-eight miles; only seven miles separated me from Julian. I'd gained a second wind and was ready to attack the final ascent to Julian, only 1,250 feet higher in elevation.

Darkness was looming by the time I arrived at the base of the valley and soon it would be pitch black. Had I carried a light on my bike, I could have continued on my quest to reach Julian, but I've never used them. I've seen some brave cyclists ride at night with bright lights and reflectors in front and back, but it's too dangerous for my style.

While forgiving myself for falling short of my goal that day, I vowed I'd never again allow darkness to halt my ride. From that point forward, my daily rides would start at the break of dawn.

In the heart of this valley is the village of Santa Ysabel. It seemed to be no more than a few buildings and homes at the intersection of two highways. I turned into the town's gas station and general store and pulled out my cell phone to inform Jae of my location. Unfortunately, there was no cell reception in this area. I called her workplace from a pay phone, but a co-worker said she had recently left and was headed to Julian. So, I used the pay phone again to call her and left a voice mail about my location. After five minutes, I called Jae a second time with the pay phone, this time giving the number posted on it.

The time passed, and I grew more concerned. How would I get to Julian? What if Jae doesn't learn that I'm in Santa Ysabel? It was then that I recalled that Jae had told me that her cell phone's reception in this region was poor. I did consider hitchhiking to Julian, but shut that down when I thought of all the lectures I received since my childhood about obtaining rides from strangers.

Then I had an idea. Since Jae would be taking this route to Julian, I placed my bike against a signpost on the edge of the road, trusting she would see it as she drove through. When no vehicle headlights were on the road, it was nearly pitch dark, but I was hoping—just hoping—Jae's headlights would shine on my bike.

I bought a coffee in a foam cup at the convenience store, and then sat outside on a wooden bench and gazed at the dimly lit highway. The coffee's steam warmed my face, and as I sipped, I felt the hot liquid warm my body. I began to relax.

Although apprehensive about whether Jae would find me, I felt resigned to the circumstances. There wasn't much else I could do. I used that pay phone two more times but only reached her voice mail. After about fifteen minutes, the man who worked behind the counter of the store came out and stood near me.

"So, you've been riding your bike in this cold?" he asked. I couldn't tell if he was surprised or impressed.

"Yeah. I started at the beach and was planning to make it to Julian."

"On such a cold day," he added.

I nodded and looked down with a grimace.

"I saw you walk in and I thought, 'This man is riding a bike today? He's either tough or crazy."

"Or both," I quipped, with a laugh. "Actually I'm biking across America and this is my first day. I've been in San Diego around this time and most days it's usually warmer and sunnier."

"True, but we're in the mountains. It's colder here."

I knew he was right, but I had to vent. "Last winter I spent two weeks in San Diego and nearly everyday it was sunny and in the seventies, sometimes the eighties!"

He chuckled but didn't say a word, then he leaned against the front door while smoking a cigarette. While I could make out his face, I could see that he was about my age. He had a mop of jet black hair and a button down shirt and he told me that he managed the store. He pointed down the street and casually mentioned that a casino had recently opened.

"Gambling was all fun and games, and I did a lot of it, until I started losing," he said, "Once I got married and had kids, that was it. When your family depends on you, you have to be responsible."

I understood and shared my own story. Gambling or any game of chance intrigued me as a teenager, and my friends and I would go to the local racetrack when I was a young adult. All it took was losing a week's pay on horse racing, and I was done with it.

"I live in El Cajon—that's a suburb of San Diego—and I commute up here. What did you think of San Diego?"

"It's a nice city. Like I said, I've been there before."

"They call San Diego the Finest City. It's a big and bustling place that can be very materialistic—all the negative things people think of about southern California—but the weather is nice and you're so close to the beach. The Mexican food is amazing. I think we have to be the fish taco capital of the world. San Diego is so many things. It has too many military bases to make it safe, and the new downtown is only 'hip and trendy' if you don't know better. But it's home and it's easy to live here. And trust me, we're much more relaxed than Los Angeles," he said.

"And you have palm trees!" I blurted. "What do you think about your sports teams? Are you a Chargers fan?"

"Don't get me going. The Chargers are always disappointing. They're usually good, but not good enough. They've never won it all."

"I think they won a title in the AFL in the 1960s," I interjected.

He took a hefty drag of his cigarette and then waved his hand down. "That doesn't mean anything," he said, "Come on."

I did have a strong opinion that I wanted to share. "I always loved the San Diego Padres uniforms when they were brown. They lost their soul when they got rid of their brown and gold colors," I said. "Now they're blue like their rival Dodgers. That's not right."

He laughed and didn't say a word, taking hit after hit of his cigarette.

"By the way, how long are you open?" I asked.

"Nine o'clock."

"I'm waiting for a friend who's on her way to Julian. I'm hoping she'll see my bike by the road. But I could be here for a while. Is that okay? I promise I'll keep buying stuff if I hang around here long." I said, with a laugh.

"Sure. You can have more coffee if you like."

Two cars pulled into the parking lot, neither of them Jae's, and with that, the man returned inside the store to take care of business.

More time passed. If it wasn't for the few lights in peaceful little Santa Ysabel, it would be pitch dark. My body squirmed on the rock hard wooden bench. It was far from comfortable, but a welcome thing to have my body in any position other than hunched over my bike.

I walked back in and got another cup of coffee. Back outside, I gazed at the dark sky. It would have been the right moment to be reflective and ponder the deeper things about life or this bike across America ride, but I was too dog-tired to think about anything like that. I merely stared into space, enjoying the night air. For another thirty minutes, I sat there. At peace. Content. I knew I'd have this memory and wondered how Day One would fit with the rest of my story.

Just then, Jae's black Nissan turned into the gas station. I sprang to my feet in excitement and ran across the lot. Both of my arms were extended straight up—one arm holding my cup of coffee and the other making a fist—an expression of victory. I did a clumsy, joyful dance by pushing out my elbows and swaying my body back and forth, spilling hot coffee on myself.

"You have no idea how good it is to see you," I shouted, once Jae's car door opened.

"Good thing I saw your bike. My headlights caught it and I

knew it was yours," she said.

"I would have made it to Julian, but it got dark."

"This is impressive though. That was a long drive," she said.

"Did you get my messages?"

"No," Jae said with despair, "I've been having troubles with my phone. I don't know what's wrong with it. It works sometimes, and then other times, I can't make or get a call."

Then I told her about my pay phone calls, with both of us laughing and sighing in relief.

"Do you realize how awful it would have been if you were driving around Julian in search of me? Meanwhile, I'm down here at this gas station with no way to contact you. I'm so happy," I said.

"You would have had to sleep in front of that store for the night," she joked.

We loaded the bike in the trunk and headed to Julian. I was in her car again, and this time her passenger seat felt so warm and even more welcoming than before.

We talked about our day. Hers at work was uneventful, and I reviewed the events of my ride. I told Jae about how I left way too late in the morning, and some of the other mistakes I had made. Still, I was happy and proud of what I'd done. The road to Julian curved back and forth, working its way upward. Although I knew a while back that I would need a ride, there was a pressing question bothering me: was I cheating by hitching a ride seven miles to Julian, and with such an elevation gain no less?

For better or worse, I tend to be purist with my bicycling. If I will say that I biked across America, then I don't want any undue assistance from cars. Still, this was a situation I couldn't control. I had made an honest mistake, and it wasn't like I was lazy or unwilling to ascend those final seven miles.

I turned toward Jae, who dutifully listened as I talked about this. "What do you think?"

"Not a big deal," she said.

"What if I was in a marathon and I ran twenty-five miles, but hitched a ride for the last one?" I asked.

Jae turned to me with an incredulous look, "I understand, but what you did was impressive. Don't worry about it. When you've biked a thousand miles from now, I doubt you'll be upset about this, and like you said, this was a circumstance that demanded a car ride."

Immediately, I thought about how tomorrow morning I could start in Julian and bike downhill to Santa Ysabel and then return up. That would indeed clear my conscience, but something about that option seemed petty and silly. It was then that I accepted this seven mile lift with peace.

Soon we arrived in Julian, a mountain town with tourist appeal. The town center was also a historic district, with buildings designed in Victorian architecture lining the main street. Horse-drawn carriage rides are available for visitors, bed-and-breakfasts lure city dwellers for romantic getaways, and its apple orchards and annual apple festival attract tourists from afar. Most nights I would stay in less expensive places, but in Julian, with no lodging options besides bed-and-breakfasts, I paid the extra money. Considering the events of the day, maybe I needed the lovely amenities of my lodging.

Jae and I celebrated the first day's success with dinner at Romano's Italian restaurant, a place buzzing with patrons. When the waitress was taking our order, Jae grabbed the first opportunity to boast about me.

"My friend is biking across America. This was his first day!" she exclaimed.

Her pride in me was infectious; I felt some pride in myself as well. We had an enjoyable dinner. My tasty meatball sandwich with crusted bread and french fries filled me to the brim. We had a good time, mainly reminiscing about the early days of our friendship.

We then talked about tomorrow's plans. "You're the last person I'll see that I know until I'm in Phoenix," I said.

"How long will it take you?" she asked.

"Five or six days. It'll depend."

"Are you apprehensive at all?"

"About what?" I asked.

"About anything. Being alone. Or being in the desert."

"Personally I like the desert. It'll be warmer."

Jae put her hands underneath her chin and said dreamily, "When I think of you going across the country by bike, especially in the desert, I think of poisonous snakes and desert-dwelling psychopathic hillbillies. I think of your Mom whom I've met—the whole Mom instinct that I have—and how I'm freaking out about what you're about to face."

I smiled and said, "The desert isn't so bad."

"You're probably right, but I think of the pioneer days. It was a hard slog to get through the desert. On a bike, you can probably go faster than homesteaders did in a wagon, with little fear of perishing from running out of water. Today, we just don't feel the anxiety of such terrain."

"My average speed usually comes out to about ten to twelve miles per hour. And there are cars on the route. If I'm desperate, there are people to help," I said.

"And where exactly are you going? How close will you be to the border? There are illegal immigration problems and all that. People crossing by foot."

"First of all, I have a road atlas I bought at Wal-Mart. I tore out the pages and have them stored in a large sandwich bag," I said.

"I like that," smiled Jae, seeming impressed.

"Now about the border. Tons of people drive on Interstate 8 everyday and that goes real close to Mexico for a while. I'm not worried about it. If you think about it, nighttime is when stuff tends to go down, and I'll be riding in daylight."

"Just be careful. Once you're farther east, it will be tougher for me to rescue you if you have trouble. But if you're desperate, I want you to call me," she said.

Last night Jae had joked and teased me about when she had to help me five years earlier, but this time she was serious.

Too soon, Jae said good-bye and returned to San Diego, while I enjoyed the niceties of my room at the bed-and-breakfast. The walls were covered in an old replica wallpaper—a beautiful floral pattern of white flowers with burgundy paint. A stain-glass lamp sat at the night table. A large print—two people walking in a field, highlighted in lavender and mulberry flowers—hung above the bed frame. The bedspread was burgundy, with another thick silver comforter underneath. The bathroom was artfully decorated as well. I got beneath the sheets, and my tired legs melted into the cushy bed mattress. My achy shoulders and hips, both trashed, at first didn't seem to know how to react to the comforter wrapped around them. As I began to fall asleep, trepidation nagged at me about tomorrow's ride. Would my body recover? Would there be more and steeper mountains to climb?

I had visited Julian on only one previous occasion, but I wasn't acquainted with Highway 78 east of Julian. My map showed switchbacks and a green area marked as mountains. Although I knew that a low desert was beyond those mountains, I expected the worst—more climbing to start. Oh, how I dreaded that prospect!

CHAPTER IV

DESERT AWAKENINGS

I think the American West really attracts me because it's romantic.
The desert, the empty space, the drama.

Ang Lee

I I knew the beginning wouldn't be easy. My body would need to get some miles in before my bike and I were together on this dream. Yesterday had been my first day of getting into top-notch shape, and as I lay in bed, it felt like every muscle in my legs was sore. When I finally stood up, a burst of adrenaline kicked in and the excitement of where I was and what I was doing took hold. "Let's go!" something inside shouted. It was a strange feeling to be hungry and energetic and yet have cranky, tired muscles. I pressed through. Dressed in my cycling clothes, I went downstairs to the lobby.

A feast of my favorite breakfast foods awaited me. I wolfed down waffles with syrup, eggs and a handful of grapes. Whenever a complimentary breakfast was offered at the places I stayed, I took full advantage before waddling to my bike. Usually the modest spread would be named a "continental breakfast," which had items like cereal with milk, perhaps muffins or donuts, coffee and maybe more. But, like this morning, occasionally the hosts would go full bore and when that happened, I was never shy about filling up the tank. As my friends had already reminded me, good nutrition was not my strong point.

With my bike at my side, I hobbled to the street as the sun was coming up at seven o'clock. My lower back and hips were hurting and nagging me with each movement. And it was cold—only forty degrees. I bundled into three layers with big winter gloves pulled over my cycling gloves. I turned back for a final look at the B&B, a beautiful blue-gray Victorian-style home with white shutters and an all-American picket fence. And Main Street seemed so calm and pretty with only an occasional car breaking the serenity of the dawn.

Even though I had slept well, all night I cringed over the possibility that I would face more ascent. However, as I got ready this morning, any more worrying had become pointless. I had to deal with whatever was ahead. The thought itself made me smile. I arched my back and stretched my arms one last time, and then hopped on the bike. Pedaling slowly through Julian, my cell phone alerted me that a text had arrived.

"By now, I hope you've gotten your butt out of bed!" wrote Jae.

I laughed. At least her cell phone was working. And of course, I wouldn't repeat yesterday's late start.

Once moving, I forgot about the state of my aching muscles. No question—I was ready to go. Every cycling day is different, and this would surely be a new one. After a short distance from Julian's town limits, the first highlight was quite a change.

The road descended—a steep downward grade that had me moving quickly. The road curved back and forth, all the while I maintained a swift speed. I was giddy at how such easy riding required only token pedaling. The cold wind stung my ears, shocked the bare skin of my face and thudded against my helmet. It was painful, torturous almost, but how could I complain at moving twenty-five miles per hour? My wheels were spinning furiously and I was quickly racking up the miles. I pedaled harder to reach thirty-two miles per hour, but not for long. That kind of speed didn't feel safe. It's true that maniacs and competitive road cyclists reach speeds of fifty, sixty or seventy miles per hour in long descents, as fast as cars in some cases. And in fact, the average cruising speed of a professional cyclist is often in the range of twenty-five to thirty miles per hour. However, the consequences of crashing at that speed can be dire. A pothole or an oversight of any kind can suddenly become tragic. In no way did I need to show off to anyone, least of all myself.

I tapped the brakes now and then as I flew down the hill. I tightened my grip on the handlebar and was on the alert for anything that might unravel this joy ride. I thought about bicyclists going in the opposite direction, with their legs burning like fire as they climbed this same hill that propelled me downward. I knew their pain. There was one more section of road curves when I reached the end of the extreme descent. I was now in the valley. My cyclometer told me I'd ridden eight miles. Anyone (and I mean anyone) could have sat on a bike and ridden this section without the need to pedal.

In this valley, the signs of humanity became less. There were isolated homes and ranches, and few motorists. The road had exited the mountains, the pavement as straight as an arrow through wide open desert. For five miles, the road continued with a more modest descent. A gentle half-mile hill required some work, and then at the top, the topography blessed me with more downhill—twice as much as I had just worked up. And then, it seemed, I was in completely barren desert. Like I was on another planet. For sure, I was altogether away from the San Diego metropolitan area. At thirteen miles, I approached a road sign for the Anza-Borrego Desert State Park. This was a good spot to stop and remove a couple of layers of clothing, as the temperature was warming. By now, my body had forgotten all about the aches and pains of yesterday. In fact, I felt strong and good, and dare I say, like I was having fun.

My route led me into a rocky canyon inside the state park ... and the downhill just kept coming. More easy pedaling. Gravity was doing most of the work. I erupted in laughter as I recalled that in the darkness of last night, I had worried that another steep mountain climb was in my future.

In Colorado, when you get on a bicycle for any distance, if you don't find a hill, a hill will find you. When you go for a long ride, there's usually a tough ascent at the beginning and then you're rewarded with the descent. My intuition had me trained to expect the inevitable climb, but on this day, it never came. Instead, yesterday I did all the hard work, and today I reaped the rewards, flying down this eastern side of the range.

The canyon spilled into an area with hills that were lush with desert plants. The morning light shined brilliantly on the yellow thorns of teddy bear cholla, a multi-armed cactus that appears to have furry ends. The cholla were complimented with ocotillos, a hardy plant with vertical spiraling branches, some on the verge of blooming their distinctive orange flower. It's often said that the desert is void of plant life, but this area was a jungle of resilient bushes and cacti. There was a turnoff for Borrego Springs and the headquarters of the state park, but I continued on State Highway 78, en route to Brawley. Finally, more cars were coming through on this two-lane road. A gray Subaru plastered with bumper stickers passed and honked. The driver stuck out his arm and offered a friendly wave and shout of support.

The valley widened and the road climbed gently. Then it took a sharp left turn and a stunning vista unfolded before me. I forced myself to stop; the scenery demanded that I take it all in. Amidst the unusual and peaceful quiet, it felt like a special moment—that I should take my time. The curve had brought me full circle and I was admiring the valley I'd just ridden through.

The land was vast in sand and in many shades of gray and tan. Various cacti, desert sage brush, and creosote bushes grew on the desert floor. Those massive cholla fields I passed earlier were miles ahead, still gleaming from the sunlight. More ocotillos stood in the foreground with soft beige mountains hunkered afar. Even the utility lines, often an eyesore elsewhere, marched toward the horizon with grace and elegance. As I gazed at this awesome spectacle, I felt so grateful to be on this journey—and that I gave myself this gift of a great bike adventure. My heart overflowed with joy.

I've always been a fan of the desert. Maybe I grew an affinity for it because I grew up in New Jersey, which is mostly green and overpopulated—the very opposite of the desert. I've dreamed of living somewhere where the space is so wide open that you could see for miles with no one in sight. The desert is filled with meaning and symbolism. Its harshness and its delicate balancing of life and death express mortality. Its emptiness, and one's ability to see for seemingly forever—eternity. And humanity's difficulty to live there—humility. It's both a beauty and a beast.

Onward I pedaled. I was encouraged that I'd gone twenty-three miles in a little over an hour. Two more miles ahead I saw another hillside of ocotillos and again, I stopped to take pictures. When I reviewed them through my camera's back screen, I was disappointed. Sometimes a camera can't capture the essence of nature's beauty; the photos didn't come close to showing the richness of detail. Still, with a big grin, I snapped more photos as I stood on the pavement with the bike between my legs. I stretched my hips from side to side knowing I had all the time in the world. Then as I resumed riding, there was a rumbling in the front of my bike. I looked down with a grimace, and saw the sight that cyclists dread. The front tire had gone flat.

There should be a name for the fear of flat tires, something like "Flat Tire Phobia." I'm pretty sure I inherited the condition from my father, who dislikes driving and has an awful fear of flat tires or his car breaking down. For that matter, nobody in my family is gifted mechanically. If something needed to be fixed, we'd pay a professional. Not once did I see my Dad change a tire with a jack. Instead, he always had a AAA membership card to take care of such annoyances.

Now, even with years of bicycling experience, and having fixed many flat tires, I still have apprehensions about it. Never do I feel confident. For me, there's something profoundly humbling about fixing a flat on the edge of a road, with the trepidation about feeling like a total loser if I can't fix it. I knew this would be a potential problem on this tour, and so before the trip, I practiced letting the air out of a tire, removing the tube and then replacing it. I'd like to think it paid off with providing me more poise for this inevitable moment, and this was my big test. It's one thing to fix a tire in the comfort of your home, at room temperature with soothing music and a cup of coffee by your side, but it's all different when you're outside, in the middle-of-nowhere, and you're sweaty and tired … and you *have to* succeed.

Explained simply, there are three components of a bicycle wheel: the hub, spokes and rim, the tire and an inner tube. When inflated, the tube fits snug inside the protective hard-rubber tire which does all the heavy work. When there's a flat, it's the inner tube that has been punctured and must be repaired or replaced.

I removed the front wheel from the bike, pried the tire halfway off the rim, and pulled out the tube. Some bicyclists are adept at repairing punctured tubes by locating the hole and gluing a patch on it. I don't do such precise work well and find it easier to just replace them. I was carrying four spare tubes for situations like this, and I'd buy more along the route as needed.

The process for repairing a flat bicycle tire isn't difficult. One needs to insert a new inner tube into the tire, secure the tire back onto the rim and then inflate it with a pump. There's no rocket science here. But, I had some trouble that raised my tension level. I couldn't get the new tube to fit snug inside the tire. Often bicyclists will put some air into the limp tube so it has shape and makes it easier to fit, but I've never liked that. With air in the tube, one has a greater chance to puncture it as one fits it in. This is called "pinching" the tube.

And so I spent about five long minutes anxiously working to get the tube set. It was tricky. By now, it was mid-morning and traffic had increased. It seemed like a lot of cars and trucks were whipping past me, as I crouched down like a baseball catcher and attended to the tire. Worrisome thoughts berated me as I worked with it. *C'mon, Steve. How do you expect to bike across America if you can't fix this tire?* Eventually, I got it done. The tire-tube-rim assembly was finished and I secured the bike by rotating the quick-release until it was tight. Then I walked my steed back onto the highway's shoulder and pressed down. The tire held its air. Fixing the tire was intense and I took longer than most cyclists, but I'd made it back on the road with flying colors.

Feeling like a winner, I aimed for the Atlantic Ocean. The road was flat and the riding was easy. The desert became more arid and nearly void of plant life. The sun warmed the earth to seventy-two degrees, and an occasional gust of wind tried to nudge me off balance, but I was fine as I rode in a straight line for over twenty miles.

This region of southern California is named the Imperial Valley, a land of barren mountains and desert near sea level. Roughly bordered by the Salton Sea to the north, the San Diego County line to the west, the Gulf of California (beyond the Mexico border) to the south, and the Colorado River to the east, it's scorching hot in the summer. But historically, this area has near perfect temperatures during the winter, with highs ranging in the sixties and seventies. As desolate as it appears in spots, its towns attract shoppers and tourists from south of the border, it roars with its Imperial Valley Speedway, and it is the winter home of the U.S. Navy's Blue Angels.

I passed ranches and irrigated fields of crops for the final fifteen miles into Brawley, and when I entered town, my cyclometer read seventy-five miles for the day. I'd rolled downhill from the mountains, paced along the flats and enjoyed it all. Heck, even the flat tire incident wasn't that bad in retrospect. I spotted a motel on the edge of town and checked in. At the front desk, I stood sweaty and tanned as the elderly clerk swiped my debit card and handed me a key. Other than quoting the rate, the man with a receding hairline and unfashionable shirt remained silent. It was awkward and I felt compelled to break the dead air, uttering, "Yeah, I biked here from San Diego. Took me two days."

"Oh," he said. I couldn't tell if he was disinterested or just a quiet person. Maybe it was his policy not to delve much into the lives of his guests. It didn't matter. I was elated that I'd ridden 123 miles in two days.

The motel room was on the cheap side, but everything worked and it was clean. I plopped onto the bed and grunted with each movement of my legs and ankles. Pretty much everywhere was sore. I felt dirty, and my clothing stuck to my body, especially my socks and shoes. It felt like the hot pavement had become part of me, an awful icky, sticky, congealed layer of sweat. Eventually, I reached out to remove my shoes and peel off my socks. Then there was a knock on the door. Outside was the motel clerk holding my debit card that I'd left at the desk. The smile on his face communicated his amusement, but he didn't say a thing as he handed it back.

A long, hot shower restored me . . . a bit. So many muscles still ached. I lay back on the bed, wanting nothing more than to lie there and watch TV. After two days of riding, my body had not fully signed on to this adventure, but I had to deal with it. The mental, emotional, physical, and spiritual parts of me were in this together; sometimes, one had to pull the others along for the ride.

I put on my spare t-shirt, shorts and sandals that I stored on the bike. It's amazing what clean clothing and scrubbed feet can do to improve one's morale. My feet were so relieved to be in sandals. With the bike safe in the motel room, I ventured out in search of lunch. On the main avenue, I walked with a confident strut and goofy smile. I tried to contain myself, but just couldn't hide my sense of pride around others. *Yes folks, I biked here using my own strength and determination—and not with the help of a car.* As I searched for a restaurant, I giggled a lot, knowing that I'd look weird to others who'd see me laughing at my inside joke. Eventually I found a place to eat and downed a big chicken sandwich and a side of fries.

Back in my motel room, I washed my cycling clothes in the bathroom sink and hung them to dry. This would become a daily ritual. I hadn't brought much to wear. For riding, I had one pair of black shorts made of that stretchy material made mostly of nylon and partially of spandex with a synthetic chamois inner-lining. I also had a longer pair of pants made of the same fabric for when it was too cold for shorts. Up top, I'd wear my short-sleeve jersey, and had two long sleeve layers as needed. I wore a pair of open-fingered cycling gloves, but had an extra-thick pair for cold rides. I brought two pairs of cycling socks and my clipless shoes. When I wasn't biking, my clothing choices consisted of one light weight t-shirt, beige shorts, two pairs of underwear, and a pair of comfortable sandals. I did my best to be practical in planning my clothing choices, balancing my needs and the amount of weight I could push along on the bike. My toiletries were stuffed into a gallon-sized plastic bag: travel-size items like deodorant, toothpaste, shampoo, conditioner, lip balm, razors, shaving cream and sunscreen. I also brought a first aid kit, bicycle tools, chargers for my phone and camera battery, a small notebook and a pen. If I needed anything else on the ride, I figured I'd buy it on the road.

At 7:30 p.m., I was already in bed and soon fell asleep. Inside, there was a feeling of anticipation, like the journey hadn't begun with gusto yet. It didn't seem like I was biking across America. These past two days had felt more like two difficult rides on a Friday and Saturday, like an ambitious weekend of riding in one direction, but nothing to the tune of a cross-country tour. This adventure enchanted me like nothing I'd done before, but the journey still didn't have its own storyline, an overarching theme. Would its meaning reveal itself before my wheels dipped into the Atlantic? Would there be anything to learn? What would be the hardest things I'd encounter? A while back, I read an article about bicycling across America, in which the author wrote one should expect and be ready to have hard days and meltdowns. I figured that was true, but I couldn't worry about it. My mantra was "one day at a time."

***

At 6:30 a.m., after ten hours of sleeping or lying horizontally, I finally got up. My legs still ached and the bottoms of my feet were sore, almost like they were burning. I should have given myself a long hot soak in the tub, but lazy me didn't feel like exerting any additional energy, and once I was in bed, it was all over.

Today's destination was Blythe, a town on the California side of the Colorado River and eighty-three miles away. When I viewed my map, I shuddered at the thought of pushing my bike, my gear and me that far along State Highway 78, a single-lane highway that travels through more empty desert. This would have been a great day to have a support vehicle to follow along, or had I been camping, I could have split the distance into two days. With no lodging along the way, I had a single solitary choice and that was to begin with the end in mind and go.

Outside Brawley, the scenery opened in an expanse. The sky began to lighten. The sun's glow rose above the horizon and made the clouds pink and purple, while the rest of the sky remained a dim blue, as if it too were waking up after a long night's rest.

I was riding strong and moving at fourteen miles per hour. It felt like the road was still descending, however slightly, for about ten miles. The landscape changed from irrigated farms back to desert. And then it became isolated. Nothing. Just sand. Light and dark shades of brown. It was serene and dreamy—mounds of sand that shifted with the wind and shuffled around the desert floor. I'd entered the Imperial Sand Dunes, a region of forty-five square miles that reaches south into Mexico. As I was enjoying my reverie, I began to hear noises and people. I discovered that this lonesome place wasn't so lonesome after all, as it was filled with dirt bikers, dune buggies and ATVs, all hopping around like Mexican jumping beans. Clusters of RV parks dotted the roadside. As the morning progressed, more cars and motorhomes passed me on the highway, shattering the sensation that I was in a remote wilderness.

Twenty-two miles into the ride, I stopped in Glamis. It's not much of a town and probably not incorporated. The place was more like a rest stop with two general stores and a lot for off-roaders to meet and greet. I took a breather in front of one of the stores, guzzled down a drink and bought a bottle of Powerade. On the porch, I sat down and enjoyed the shade when a man approached.

"Where you headed?" he asked.

"To Blythe, but I'm biking across America."

"No kidding?" he interjected.

This man with silver hair and a rounded face, wore a stylish dirt biking jersey that was neatly tucked into his jeans. He seemed impressed by me and my bike.

"How much does a bike like this cost?"

"Not a lot," I said.

"I'm curious because I ride bikes too, but more casually than you."

He introduced himself as Wayne, a man from Palm Springs. He said he enjoyed coming out to get some quality time riding dirt bikes with his teenage sons. He circled around the bike and bent down to examine my clipless pedals. Then he turned up and asked, "You're headed east?"

"That's right."

He grew a big smile and rubbed his chin. "To think of all that distance you'll be riding. What will you do when you finally reach the end? Will you have a party? Will you raise your bike with your arms like some people do? I'd probably have a big bottle of champagne and take a long swig."

"Honestly, I don't know," I said, modestly, "There's no point in thinking that far ahead."

"And you really went over those mountains out west, didn't you?"

I laughed. "Yeah, I did."

"Did you know people with motorhomes or old trucks sometimes have problems with overheating from the steep grades on those roads? It's common to see one broken down with smoke coming out of the hood."

That fact made me feel accomplished.

"So you're going alone?" he asked.

"I am," I said, matter-of-factly.

For years, I had known I would probably make this journey alone. Sure, I would have liked company, but who would go with me? I couldn't think of anyone. Most of my friends were busy raising families or had jobs with little vacation time. I couldn't wait around, twiddling my thumbs, hoping someone would come out of the woodwork to join me.

"You're lucky," he said, "What you're doing is admirable."

He seemed especially friendly, and I wanted to know more about him.

"So what do you do?"

"I did charity work in Africa for many years—helping organize medical services in poor and remote areas. We're back in the states now. I teach English at a college."

"Your experiences in the Third World have changed your perspective, haven't they?"

"Absolutely," he said with a tender voice. He patted his belly. He wasn't necessarily obese, but he had some extra weight in the stomach like many middle-aged men have. "You see this pot belly? This is a sign of wealth in Africa. In America, we worship thin people, beautiful people, celebrities on TV, and heaviness is looked down on. But that's not the case in many countries."

I nodded in appreciation. Then, one of his sons shouted at him from afar, and he said, "I gotta go."

I shook his hand and that was that. The noise of dirt bikes, dune buggies and ATVs continued for a while as I biked east, but eventually it faded in the distance. And, again, I enjoyed the pedaling, mile after mile. My conversation with Wayne had me thinking. It's not that I was puffed up about myself as it was, but my cross-country tour didn't feel like such a big deal anymore. How blessed I was to be doing this, when there are people in other countries who are starving and living in abject poverty, often amidst political and social injustice. I felt like a spoiled American, yet grateful. How could I ever be grateful enough?

We've all seen footage of starving children in impoverished countries. Commercials encouraging us to adopt a child and where you can send money every month. Or just the latest news about Haiti—one of the poorest places on the earth that's so close to the United States. The living conditions are dire for the common person. Surely, the contrast between rich and poor in proximity should make a person pause, and perhaps motivate them to do something about it. I've seen people get into huge arguments over so-called "First World problems." A couple gets in a huge shouting match over whether to buy patio furniture with blue or green cushions. Someone has to wait five long minutes in line for their five-dollar latte. Or a proud owner of a $50,000 Cadillac has a meltdown when he notices a small scratch in the bumper. I've been guilty of my own forms of petty complaining.

The mileage wore on. My mind went to auto-pilot. I began to think about venturing across this country. What does it mean, if anything? Will this story only be about a thirty-something guy doing something fun? Or will there be more? I thought about my relationship with my country. We have a storyline. I thought about the days in my lifetime that will live in infamy. I remember where I was during the Oklahoma City bombing, the horrific Columbine High School shooting, the 9/11 tragedy, even the Challenger explosion when I was in the eighth grade. I am so grateful to be a U.S. citizen. And to think I was born here. I didn't have to risk moving to a new country, nor did I need to learn a new language like my grandparents and great-grandparents did as Italian immigrants.

As I rode, I reflected less and pedaled more, longing for the end of the day. I'd ridden forty miles and had another forty-three to go. I was making good time, but still, I wasn't even halfway there. I tried to stop thinking about it and enjoy each moment. But the moments were tiring.

State Highway 78 turned north near a long, horizontal stretch of peaks known as the Chocolate Mountain Range. Occasionally a dirt road intersected the highway. One sign indicated that it led to the Colorado River, a short distance to the east. I thought about what fun it might be to four-wheel in a Jeep out there, but alas, I was on a bike. Ahead, the road's shoulder shrunk to a narrow strip. And I was getting hot. It was probably only in the seventies, but with so much physical exertion and the sun constantly beating down on me, it seemed hotter. Even with sunscreen, my skin felt irritated. This fair-weather Coloradan was feeling it. For all my supposed love of the desert, I experienced the lack of shade painfully. There was nowhere to take cover.

The road dipped up and down, and to use the tired analogy, it was like a camel's back. More like a camel's back from hell. The road was maddening for a bicyclist—short ups and downs that were constant with little shoulder and cars passing too close. It required a lot of work with constant gear changing. I sped down a hill, but didn't have enough momentum to make it up next without shifting to first gear. On and on this went for miles. I hung in there and turned my brain off. Then on about the twentieth wave, I rode down a hill, came up another one, and stepped up on the pedals to ride harder, when there was a snapping sound at the back of the bike. Suddenly, I lost all pedal resistance and the bike slowed. Just before it stopped, I unclipped my feet, successfully avoiding a repeat of the San Diego crashes.

Walking the bike to the dirt shoulder, I found that the rear derailer had broken and was hanging off the frame. This small contraption is the device responsible for changing gears. As the bicyclist controls the shifter from the front, the chain gives and takes slack and the derailer moves the chain up or down gears. It also functions in holding the chain firmly on the back sprocket. When it broke, I was out of luck and my bike turned into a useless piece of metal. For all practical purposes, it was no longer a bike.

All my hard work and just like that, today's ride was over. My only option was to hitchhike to Blythe. There was a decent amount of traffic on the road, and so I wasn't worried about getting a ride. Surely someone would show compassion to the poor bicyclist on the shoulder.

As good fortune would have it, minutes after I began thumbing, a pickup pulled over. Inside the truck was a Hispanic couple with a woman in the driver's seat. She smiled and said they were going to Blythe, and so I thanked them, set my bike in the bed of the truck and climbed into the back seat.

"We are going to Blythe," the woman repeated, as she pulled onto the highway.

"That's where I'm headed too."

I had to vent about what happened.

"A piece of my bike broke off. It's called a derailer. I can't believe it. Just rotten luck out there!"

"Ah yes," said the woman, and then she repeated, "We are going to Blythe."

Meanwhile, the man in the passenger seat was silent.

"I want to thank you again for the ride," I said.

Then there was an awkward gap of silence.

"Where do you live?" the woman asked.

"Colorado."

"Ahhhh," she blurted, as if she had been there before and had stories that she was about to tell me. I waited, but she didn't elaborate. More awkward silence.

The man uttered something in Spanish to the woman, and she replied in kind. It was then that I finally gathered that we had a language barrier. I chuckled at the situation. No, I couldn't vent about my unfortunate turn of events, but at least I had help.

A few miles ahead, we rolled to a stop at a federal border patrol checkpoint. As we waited in the line of vehicles, I leaned forward to see that my new friends had pulled out their resident alien cards. At the front of line, they handed their cards to a patrolman in routine fashion without speaking.

Now, I have been to many immigration checkpoints in my life. There's never been a problem with me calmly answering the questions about if I was a U.S. citizen, where I was born or where I was headed, before going on my way. However, on this occasion, the agent made eye contact with me and merely asked, "What about you?" Never had I been asked such a vague question at a checkpoint, and I panicked.

"I'm hitchhiking with these people. My ID's on my bike in the back," I explained nervously. "I was riding and it broke down—"

At first, he stared at me.

"Are you a U.S. citizen?" he asked, sounding annoyed.

"Yes, I am."

He waved us through as I laughed with embarrassment at that interaction.

The couple spoke to each other in Spanish as we cruised toward Blythe. They talked quickly and matter-of-factly, as if they were discussing what color to paint their living room walls, or what they should cook for dinner that evening. The woman drove fast, as though she had traveled this route many times. She drove courageously through the hilly terrain, with those pesky ups and downs becoming bigger and broader, sloping every one hundred yards or so.

I lay back on the head rest and thought about what had happened. I felt humbled to be riding once again in a vehicle. In two of the first three days of this trip, I had hitchhiked. It felt like my trip wasn't legitimate. So many emotions ran through me, and I was frustrated that I couldn't talk through some of this stuff. Part of me was incensed, and I wanted to somehow get back outside and ride that bike, not sit idly in the back seat of a truck.

The thirty-five mile drive to Blythe seemed long, and good heavens, it would have been grueling to bike through. We turned off the highway and zigzagged on dirt roads surrounded by farming fields. These locals obviously knew where they were going. Soon we entered Blythe, pulling into the parking lot of a gas station. I lifted my bike out of the back of the truck. The man got out to help, but I didn't need his assistance.

He shyly said, "Good-bye." I thanked him, shook his hand, and they departed. As they drove away, I realized I should have said "Gracias" or given them a twenty-dollar bill. Wisdom usually comes to me *after* the point when I could have acted on it. No matter. This couple were my heroes.

As I checked into a motel, I had pressing questions. Was there a bicycle shop in this small town that could fix my bike? Road bikes have specific sizes and styles of derailers. My Giant road bike could only have a Giant derailer. This is similar to auto parts: if you need a new transmission for your Ford, you can't buy and install one at a Honda dealership.

And how did I know this? Well, there is a history here. Oddly, another derailer had broken off similarly six months earlier while I was riding near my home. A bicycle shop didn't have the Giant brand-name part, and I had to drive thirty miles to a certified Giant dealer. To have one derailer break off is extremely rare, but to have two derailers break within a short time was strange and suspicious. Obviously something was structurally wrong. Now, sometimes it's wise to bring extra bicycle parts on long distance tours, but a derailer is not usually on that list. They might get out of adjustment, but rarely do they break.

Through the motel clerk, I learned that there was a bicycle repair shop inside a place named Fred's Kawasaki, a business that specialized in selling jet skis and other watercraft. She told me from personal experience that the shop was closed on Sundays, and so I planned to return to Fred's when it opened the next morning. I had to put my faith in this local shop, as the next-closest shop was thirty-seven miles away in Parker, Arizona.

I settled into my motel room feeling confounded. I knew I needed to stop thinking about everything: the broken derailer, how it would be fixed, and how it felt like cheating to hitchhike. On the latter, it still bothered me. And it was bothering me that it was bothering me. "What is it about me?" I asked. I know that I'm a fun and laid-back person. People often say I'm easy going; a "free spirit" is something I've been called many times. But there is also this rigid part of me—the unflattering term is known as being "anal retentive"—where I demand that things go my way. Sure, I knew today's situation was beyond my control, but still, two car rides in three days? I figured I'd cheated for forty-seven miles. Again, I thought about the crazy idea of—once I got this bike fixed—that I'd ride from Blythe back to the spot of the breakdown, and then return. Or perhaps I'd get a taxi to take me there. What craziness! Why couldn't I let this go? Somehow, I took solace that the drive to Blythe was in a northerly direction. That meant I hadn't gained any true west-east distance to the Atlantic Ocean. The logic made sense and I had to be satisfied with it.

There was one event that encouraged me to forget about things—the Super Bowl would be showing on television soon. The New York Giants were facing the New England Patriots in the grandest of American sporting events. Probably because I felt like an underdog myself on this adventure, I felt compelled to cheer for the Giants, whom the odds makers had as the heavy underdog against the undefeated Patriots. Well, the Giants won 17-14 with an improbable drive in the fourth quarter, capped by a spectacular catch by David Tyree and a touchdown pass from Eli Manning to Plaxico Burress. I felt connected to their joy. This was the underdog's moment. Maybe I would win as well.

***

Peeking at the sunny morning sky from my motel room window, I felt optimistic that somehow my bike would be fixed.

Sitting on my bike seat, I kept pushing off from the ground with my feet, slowly gliding to the bicycle shop on East Hobsonway, a main thoroughfare in town. I approached the entrance and read the sign with the shop's hours. It said the place was closed on Sundays and Mondays … and today was Monday. "Oh no!" I thought, "I've got to get this bike fixed today." There could be no more waiting.

Below the schedule was the owner's phone number. I called and a man answered.

"Is there any chance you'll open today? I'm riding across America, and I've got bike problems. If it's a matter of money, I'll pay more," I asserted.

"Greg's the guy who handles bicycles," he said kindly, "but I think he's out of town. We'll be open tomorrow."

"Okay," I said, feeling dejected. "I'll be here. Thanks."

The prospect of spending an entire day in Blythe was not appealing. Not that it seemed like a bad town. It reminded me of Brawley, which isn't too big, and yet there are enough services for doing normal stuff. Most people probably know Blythe as a place with food and lodging services that caters to Interstate 10 traffic between Los Angeles and Phoenix. The town has beautiful palm trees and the weather today was warm—perfect for enjoying a day off. Still, I wanted to go. I already had a bungled ride yesterday, and I just wanted to get going and have a better day. I'll admit that I was impatient. A day off felt like a huge waste of time.

As for the bike shop in Parker, Arizona, I had no way to get there, but I called anyway in hope of a miracle. Maybe they'd say "yes" and I could figure out a way to visit them.

"I'm in Blythe, and my bike has a broken derailer. Can you replace it?" I asked.

After obtaining information, the gentleman told me he didn't carry Giant brand parts and wouldn't work on my bike.

"Do you have *any kind* of derailer that could get me going?"

He politely, but firmly, insisted that he couldn't help me—the same response I got when the first one broke last year.

Feeling dejected, I resigned myself to being stuck in Blythe for the day, hoping Fred's shop could do the job tomorrow. In the meantime, I had to pound the pavement and find a way to occupy my time. Somehow, I turned the corner and I was feeling positive again. With the sun bright and the weather warm, I decided to make the best of things. If I had to spend my day in Blythe, then I would make the most it. I had read books about travelers who encountered people on their journey—people so giving and generous that it made a portion of their trip magical. Hopeful, and probably naïve, I figured I was due for such an experience. This was the fourth day of my journey, and excluding Krista and Jae in San Diego, I hadn't had any extended interactions with others. Sure, I had enjoyed a few conversations with strangers, and I'd never forget the Blythe couple that gave me a ride, but I was ready for something special. "Maybe there is a reason I am stuck here," I thought. This was an opportunity. I told myself I'd act sociable in restaurants. I'd sit in the town's Starbucks and be open to whatever happened. I'd call a few churches and see if any fellowship meetings, dinners or events were happening. Maybe I'd meet someone willing to put me up for the evening; I could save money and that would be an incentive to strike a conversation or two. Suddenly optimistic, I convinced myself to be open—maybe something noteworthy or special would happen.

But as the day went by, nothing panned out.

During lunch at a restaurant, I got shy and didn't strike up any meaningful conversations. The Starbucks was empty. When I called area churches, I only reached voice mail systems and no one called back. In the end, I wound up talking with friends on my cell phone while I stood in the parking lot of a strip mall. By mid-afternoon, I had given up and checked back into last night's motel. At least I could keep the bike in my room, instead of lugging it beside me wherever I went.

At the motel, I took a nap, sat by the pool and watched TV. And while I did, my mind ran wild with worry. *What if I can't get a new derailer?*

The bicycle shop in Parker already turned me down. What were the chances that this small bicycle repair shop in Blythe would help?

There I was lying on the bed, a headcase. I tried to get a grip in the battle between the laid-back Steve and the one who thinks way too much. Regarding the latter, thinking can be good or bad. Take fantasy football. As I manage my team during an NFL football season, I'm always looking way ahead at future weeks and considering which players will be my starters and fill-ins. I constantly analyze the possibilities: if so-and-so gets hurt, are my back-ups adequate? Often I study prospects and figure what I'd do in different scenarios. Most don't happen, but even if only one-percent of them did, I already had a plan and would know how to act.

With this derailer problem, it felt like I was doing the same thing, and it obviously wasn't productive. It was ruining my peace. I didn't know whether this nearby bicycle shop could fix my bike, and already I was thinking of every worst-case scenario and agonizing about what I'd do. Upset, I called Jae.

"There has got to be a way to fix the bike," she said. "My dad was an auto mechanic, and there was always a way to get something running. I bet you a mechanic could weld a derailer on. Or tinker with it to get it working."

I sighed. "That wouldn't work. The derailer is a special part."

"At least be open to possibilities. There's usually a way."

"No, you don't understand. It's not like that at all."

"You've got to be open," she insisted.

Maybe Jae was right, but I sighed once more in frustration. The prospect of a failed bike tour across America, only four days into the journey, seemed like a real possibility. It tormented me. I dreaded the possibility that the trip could be over. If this bike shop couldn't replace this derailer, then what would I do? Sure, I could ask Jae or Krista to rescue me from San Diego, but would they? They both have normal jobs and can't just leave at a moment's notice. And if they did bring me back to the coast to fix this bike, would I return to Blythe and start again? It just seemed like a convoluted plan.

Now, I call myself a born-again Christian, and I can attest that God has done some remarkable transformations in my life—things that have changed my very being. However, there is often the day-to-day stuff that fogs this reality for me, and my Christian practice becomes a "going through the motions" type of thing. You say you believe in something intellectually, but it's radically different to feel it in your gut and live like it. Christianity teaches me that God loves me deeply and passionately more than any being in the world. Like a generous father who gives good gifts to his children, he is ultimately in control—that he knows best, that he'll guide me, and that his redemptive work for my soul is free for the taking. My main job is to seek him. To be close with him. God wants to have an intimate relationship with me, and through that experience, he changes me and gives me the strength and wisdom to bless others. He doesn't want me to fret, and when he's intent on accomplishing something, he doesn't get bogged down with details.

Well, on this evening, none of that truth mattered. All I knew was, there was a good chance this bicycle shop wouldn't be able or willing to install a new derailer. God couldn't do anything about it. And surely, I couldn't either. At the core, I felt like a loser—certain that things were bound to go wrong. Eventually, I went to bed and fell asleep, but my mind remained on overdrive with gloomy thoughts and worry-laden prayers. It was one of those situations when you have to let go, or try to let go, and let things fall as they may, even though your feelings are screaming and you want relief.

***

The next morning, I arrived at Fred's Kawasaki a half hour before they opened. After having breakfast, I sat down on a bench beside two towering palm trees with the bike beside me as I sipped on coffee. At the top of the hour, a man arrived on his mountain bike. He leaned it against the front of the shop and rustled with his keys.

"Are you Greg?" I asked, with anticipation.

"Yes, I am. I'll be right with you."

So this was the man whom my hope was in. Greg looked Hispanic, a muscular man in his forties with a head of thick black hair, graying on the sides.. He wore a casual blue hooded shirt and jeans. He performed what appeared to be his morning ritual of unlocking the front doors, opening the store, and moving out various jet skis on one side of the parking lot—a common sense way to advertise to motorists driving by. These he locked with a large chain. Then he walked a few bicycles out, and he locked those too.

"Okay, what can I do for you?" he asked.

I showed him the broken derailer on my bicycle. "I'm biking across the country," I explained. "I started in San Diego four days ago."

"Oh yeah, we get a few people every year doing that who stop by."

Greg examined my bike in silence. I stood beside him, waiting for him to tell me that he couldn't fix it. Without saying a word, Greg went behind the counter, wrestled with some parts, and came out with a generic derailer in a package. "I think this is the only one we have that will fit. Will this one be okay?"

"If you get it on my bike and it works, that's fine with me!" There was no discussion about the brand of my bike or the supposed derailer that was specific to my bike model. He was simply planning to install one with a "can do" attitude. I loved it.

For two hours, Greg worked on my bike in the back with contemporary Christian music playing. Not wanting to bother him while he worked, I waited in the front of the shop. During that time, only two customers came in, and he took short breaks to visit with them. Greg and I engaged in brief conversations as he worked. We talked about popular areas for bicyclists to ride and what it's like living in Blythe.

"You have no idea how hot it gets in this town. There is hot and then there's oh-my-this-is-like-an-oven hot. We'll get to 110 in the summer. Sometimes 120. Nothing prepares you for it. You just have to deal with it. Our hot is like winter for most people—you stay inside and only go out when you have to."

More time elapsed as Greg worked and my trepidation grew. I paced throughout the shop, looking at all the merchandise, two, then three times. It felt like that script from the old days when men sat in a secluded hospital room as they waited for the birth of their child. And the longer I waited, the more I anticipated Greg would make a defeated comment that he could not install the derailer. Then finally, he came out from the back.

"There's one bolt I can't screw tightly enough. How would you feel about going to the auto parts shop a mile down the road and buying me a one-sixteenths wrench? You can take my bike. I'd go myself, but then I'd have to close the shop."

Of course, I agreed. Greg handed me a twenty-dollar bill and requested I bring back a receipt. I rode to the store and purchased the tool, and ten minutes after I delivered it, the new derailer was installed. I tested the bike in the parking lot as Greg watched, and it seemed to work well. We both knew this was probably a temporary fix. I'd need to get a brand-name derailer installed when I got to Phoenix. I also wanted to learn why I had two derailers fail in six months!

I paid him at the front counter with a huge smile on my face. "I don't think you realize how much you've helped me. I was so worried that I'd be stuck here, and this shop has literally been a gift from God."

"No problem at all," Greg said.

Sometimes talking about religious matters is sensitive. Usually I shy away from it because of my fear of having a clumsy conversation or offending someone, but I didn't want to let it go with Greg. There was something different about him. He had a lot peace.

"Can I ask? I heard you were playing Christian music. Are you a Christian?"

"Yes, I am."

I smiled, "I figured you were. I just want to be clear that you've been an instrument of God. I was in crisis mode and it's a miracle that I can ride again."

Greg smiled. We talked with no one else in the shop, and I told him more about my story. He told me about his job, his family and his background. He went on telling me about personal challenges where he needed help and direction from God. He was raising a teenage son who was getting in trouble, making foolish decisions. It wasn't anything abnormal, just a phase of life that many of us have experienced. Soon, we were talking like old friends, encouraging each other as men.

We walked to the front, and before I left, he offered to pray for me. It felt awkward, but it didn't matter on this jubilant day. As he prayed, he mentioned various aspects of my ride including safety, wisdom, having physical strength and protecting me from discouragement. And then I returned a prayer in kind tailored about the things he told me about himself. By the end, it was obvious we had encouraged each other. Then we hugged and Greg sent me on my way.

Off I pedaled with newfound joy. I was practically laughing and hollering. It turned out something magical *did* happen in Blythe, but it wasn't based on my timing. It would be one day later—an eternity for an impatient guy like me. Yes, I had every reason to be concerned that my bike would not be fixed. Instead, I was blessed. I realized all of my worrying had been pointless.

For me, this was my biggest awakening. All this time I thought biking across America was solely my dream, but maybe God had put this dream in my heart in the first place. Maybe God wanted to come along for the ride. It was a classic "head versus heart" type of thing, and this knowledge had made a move to the heart. It was an exhilarating feeling. If there really is a God who created the world, who's all-powerful and who's guiding me on this trip, then I had nothing to worry about and everything to gain. Was this derailer an answer to prayer? A skeptic might say "no." All I knew was, my bike was fully working against extraordinary odds.

I guess you could call me a born-again bicyclist.

CHAPTER V

STOP AND SMELL THE SAGEBRUSH

Don't ask what the world needs.
Ask what makes you come alive, and go do it.
Because the world needs people who have come alive.

Howard Thurman

*I*f you try to ride your bike on the shoulder of almost any interstate highway, expect to be stopped by law enforcement and forced to dismount, as pedestrians, bicycles and other forms of non-vehicular travel are mostly prohibited. However, there is an exception to this general rule in the American West. When there is no reasonable alternative route between Points A and B, it is usually lawful for bicyclists to use such highways. In those cases, one must stay on the shoulder and avoid the traveling lanes. Before my trip, I contacted the Arizona State Police, who confirmed that it was legal to bike from Blythe into western Arizona on Interstate 10.

Even with that assurance, this was all new to me. My anxiety level rose as I biked on the acceleration lane east of Blythe. On the highway, cars zoomed past me at sixty, seventy and sometimes eighty miles per hour. It was frightening because if I were to be hit by a moving vehicle at those speeds, it'd be over, instantly. Yet it was also a rush to be so close to the edge of danger. I'll admit that it made me feel courageous. Like I was a bad ass on two wheels.

I pedaled steadily on the wide shoulder with two traveling lanes to my left. A tractor-trailer rumbled passed me with a loud whoosh, and with it an accompanying surge of wind that gave me a push forward. When a truck would pass, usually a vacuum of air rolling behind it gave me a surge of forward momentum. It was amazing to see how quickly I could increase my speed from this effect that bicyclists call "wind blasting." I found I'd be disappointed when big trucks courteously moved to the far lane to pass. Sure, they offered a larger margin of safety, but that courtesy didn't offer a wind-blast.

A short distance ahead, I approached the Colorado River. While pedaling on the bridge, I grabbed my camera from my back pocket. Keeping my left hand on the handlebar, I snapped some photos of the river with my right, all the while riding. I didn't want to stop; it just didn't seem right with cars whizzing past me and the shoulder somewhat narrowed. The river was wide and steely blue, with the sun reflecting on the calm surface. Maybe the current was fiercer underneath, but from my vantage point, it looked docile and welcoming.

Two more tractor-trailers wind-blasted me as I biked past the large welcome sign in Arizona. Then, a short distance ahead, I pulled over at a rest stop with tourist information about the region. Visitors were all over the area with picnic tables, restrooms and a pet run for dogs needing stretch time after being cramped in cars for long jaunts. As I got off my bike and leaned it against a bench, a family—a couple with their teenage son—got out of a minivan. Once out of the car, the father approached and asked about my journey. We got to talking.

"We're from Germany and vacationing. Your country is not like ours," he said, "Germany is about the size of Montana, just one of your states, but what you're doing is fantastic. I think that's what people call 'epic.' You are on an epic journey."

I nodded in amusement. Germans really do seem to travel

and get around. In fact, statistically they *do* vacation much more than Americans. It seems they show up everywhere. A sixth sense told me they were not American before I heard the man's accent. Usually, you can tell by their dress or appearance, like their odd-looking socks or sandals.

"Well, I want to welcome you to my country," I said, "I hope you have a good time. Where have you been?"

They'd visited various places in California, with Disneyland their most recent destination. "Now we want to see the landscapes. We're going to the Grand Canyon next, and then the national parks in Utah," he said.

I gleamed and felt some jealousy. I told them all about Arches National Park and the beautiful red rock scenery of southern Utah. It was a simple and friendly connection as we read visitor information together.

Soon I returned to the interstate, and by now I felt good about being there on a bike. Sure, vehicles passed at faster speeds, but I had a shoulder as wide as a car. Even when cars passed in the right lane, there was a rumble strip between us, and many courteously moved to the far left. Also, the road's sight lines were well-engineered and curves were gradual. My hunch was it was safer to bike on this highway that caters to machines of enormous speed and seeming indestructibility, than other roads thus far. After all, the congested streets of San Diego's suburbs squeezed me much closer to passing cars, and with a higher traffic volume too. In the past, most problems I've had with motorists have been where there was proximity among us. Closeness is an obvious factor in raising the risk of collisions between cars and bikes. Also, in busier areas, drivers are more apt to become angry and impatient at a cyclist's presence, where they might be tempted to slam their horn, yell or do something antagonistic. I've witnessed these things first hand. But out here on Interstate 10, drivers probably become bored with the scenery and my presence was something to look at. Perhaps I was a source of amusement: *Wow! A guy is riding a bike on the highway. Can you believe that?*

In some respects, there was more to see on the interstate than one might think. Litter to my right kept catching my eye. Most litter was ordinary. Things like aluminum cans, packaging for food, household items, fast food wrappers and cups. Pretty much anything. Ahead I spotted a large bright green teddy bear sitting underneath the guardrail. A tenth of mile ahead, I spotted another stuffed animal, a smaller one that was pink, with other plastic toys nearby. Being a counselor who has worked with troubled children, teens, and severely dysfunctional families, I confess that I thought the worst about those teddy bears and toys. Some abusive parent may have tossed them without any compassion for their kids. Maybe my professional experiences have jaded me; I tend to think the worst, and only think better when I see it.

I saw more litter. Odd things like tennis balls. A pair of sneakers. A crushed cell phone. All this trash had explanations. In fact, every piece of litter has a story—how it got there, who used it, or even the manner it was used. Maybe the road debris is a reflection of all the people who pass me that I'll never know.

Then ahead, about thirty feet, was a dark snake. I shrieked. It was too late to stop or negotiate around it. I braced as I got closer, then relief came when I realized that it was frayed black rubber from a busted tire. I laughed. I was well-aware that snakes could be on the road, especially in the desert, but I never saw any. If positioned just right, however, these rubber fakers scared me more than once.

The highway began to ascend from the desert floor. Ahead, I had another upgrade that would take me over the Dome Rock Mountains. The name sounded intriguing, but the range appeared ordinary from what I'd seen so far—dirt in earthy shades of brown, and no trees. The road curved a few times as the grade became steeper. Another huge semi passed me in the right lane—and a major wind gust carried me forward with extra speed. I smiled and wondered if those truckers realized just how much their heavyweight behemoths were helping me along my way.

I leaned forward with my shoulders hunched over. My upper legs were feeling the burn. Warm sweat poured out of me, drenching my shirt and making it stick to my skin. I unzipped my cycling jersey as far as it could go—half way down my chest. I was in "the zone" and enjoying my pace, my strength and my steel partner underneath me. I wasn't the only one working out on this ascent; so were those massive tractor-trailers. One lumbered at thirty-five miles per hour. Then another passed even slower.

The crossing point in a mountain range is commonly known as a pass. During America's settlement days, mountains were frequently viewed as loathsome obstacles to overcome en route to destinations. Hence, passes are the lowest point and/or the most passable point to get on the other side of a range. Today, our scenic mountains aren't considered quite as formidable as in the days of oxen and wagon trains. Modern day vehicles accelerate easily over such passes. However, as a bicyclist who was sensitive to any kind of hill, I felt the brunt of cycling up this pass. Eventually I reached the high point and enjoyed wonderful speed on the other side.

I sped into the next valley, a region that my map referred to as La Posa Plain, and the town of Quartzsite. I'd read that the population of this small retirement village balloons every February, when hoards of visitors descend for a month-long event focused mainly on rocks and gems collected from nearby quarries. I got off the interstate at the first exit and stopped on a bridge overpass to get a better view of the town. Palm trees stood like stately beacons, with what appeared to be a sea of campers and motorhomes. RV parks were everywhere. Tall signs of fast food franchises and other services jutted up from the frontage road. Jagged brown mountains stood in the background. I snapped pictures of the scenery; it was pretty, in a modern twenty-first century kind of way. Then I descended into the melee.

That day, I decided to stay in Quartzsite after a modest twenty-one mile ride. After the whirlwind of emotions from that morning's bicycle repair, it felt like I ought to take it easy. I didn't do much in Quartzsite, and in fact I avoided the rock quarry festival. I merely ate a large Mexican dinner at a restaurant and visited the library so I could get online.

In the final hour of sunlight, I wandered in a desert area near my motel. Watching the sunset and enjoying the warm evening, I marveled about being back on track. I still couldn't believe everything had worked out. Also, today I crossed into a new state. Granted, California's far southern section is narrow and didn't require much biking in the grand scheme of things, but it was a milestone. My route had me going through eight states, and now one was in the bag and there were seven more to go.

As sundown fast approached, I got a call from my friend Mark. I must say I am blessed with so many friends—and this is an old friend—a hard-working and successful sugar beet farmer in Minnesota. The extravert in me has found so many ways of meeting people and staying in touch.

"Steve, where are you?" he asked.

"Western Arizona."

"Oh good, I've been thinking about you. How the heck have you been?"

I told him about the snag in Blythe, but all in all, I was doing well on this fifth day of the journey.

"Do you have any big revelations about life?" he said, jokingly.

"Not really."

"Awww come on," Mark chided, "I remember when you told me about this last year. You said it was part of a mid-life crisis. You told me you had big decisions to make."

I laughed. "Did I say mid-life crisis? I don't remember. I think I said that it was probably a perfect time in my life to go."

"And that's very true. Are you having a good time?"

"I'm not sure what I'm having. Every day is different. I've had good and bad days. Since Blythe, I've been pretty happy. And it's warm—seventy-five degrees."

"Well that's good to hear," he said, "Listen, work gets me so busy. I don't want you to take it personally if you call and I don't call you back. Please keep calling to give me an update once in a while. It doesn't have to be long. And even when I'm busy, as you know I'll usually answer the phone, talk to you for a minute, and then let you go, but at least that's something."

A good friend, he is. I assured Mark I'd keep in touch.

***

The next morning, I stood at an overpass ramp on the west side of Quartzsite and waved good-bye to the town. Then I returned to Interstate 10 and began to ascend another pass—this one was named Plomosa Pass. More climbing, followed by a descent. Near the bottom, the land teemed with saguaros throughout the hillsides. They were everywhere and stood like beauties, saying, "Look at me!" Mountains and buttes were in the distance, a backdrop to highlight the beautiful landscape.

Eventually I exited onto U.S. Highway 60. Until the early 1970s, when the final stretch of Interstate 10 was built beyond this point, those traveling from Los Angeles to Phoenix had to take this two-lane highway. But today the road was remote and quiet, as though it had been made for bicyclists.

The land flattened. The saguaros and other cacti grew sparse. Now, large mesquite filled the desert floor. Small brown mountains were in the distance to the north, maybe thirty to forty miles away. No roads. No signs of humanity. Nothing. Who knows who's been out there recently? It looked like a captivating place to camp in solitude ... or hide from people like a frontier sheriff and his posse. It was a territory ripe for exploring, maybe for the first time. The imagery of the Old West captured me, with cowboys, Indians and new settlers of all kinds. Envision traveling through this land by foot or with a horse, without roads, relying on the storage of water you're carrying, and without the comfort of knowing a gas station and supermarket is within reach.

I pulled away from that siren's call and headed toward the small town of Brenda, another hamlet that mainly hosts retired snowbirds for the winter. It seemed like a tranquil place. An elderly couple walking near the shoulder waved and said "hi" as I went by. I returned in kind. Then, another couple enjoying the comfort of their lounge chairs by their home, gave a friendly wave. I grinned and gave a "thumbs up" gesture. Within minutes, I was out of Brenda.

Today's sunny seventy-degree weather seemed perfect for biking, and for some time it was. But eventually, the unrelenting sun began to get to me. Perhaps the greatest nuisance was how it made my forehead sweat and my sunscreen melt together to form a pool of nastiness that found its way into my eyes. Some collected on my eyebrows, fogging up my sunglasses. No matter how much I wiped my shades, perspiration gathered on them and I would ride blind. So finally I wiped off all sunscreen, trading the risk of sunburn for a clear view.

A southbound crosswind slammed against my side, and I held tight and crouched down to lower my center of gravity. Highway 60 traveled through more empty terrain, though not quite as desolate as the grainy black and white images seen in old western movies, with no signs of humanity and plenty of errant dust. Enough homes and campgrounds dotted the landscape so that I could get help if needed. The mileage began to add up. The temperature got hotter. Again, I had no shade.

At the junction of Highway 60 and 72 is Hope, which consists of a gas station with a convenience store, an antique shop, a church, and an RV park. The town was so undisturbed that it reminded me of those atomic bomb towns built only to be blown to smithereens. The silence was deafening. I quenched my thirst with a bottle of chilled coffee and stood in the shade in front of the store. There was one other person, a gray-haired man wearing a baseball cap who was pumping fuel in his truck that was pulling a small camper. We made eye contact, and as it happens often in rural areas, we were drawn into conversation.

"Where are you headed?" he asked.

"The other side of the country," I said with pride.

"Where'd you start?"

"I left San Diego on Friday."

"That's where my home is. My wife and I spend a lot of time here in the winter to be with family. Only takes about four hours to get back."

Four hours? I smiled at him incredulously. Everything I'd gone through in six days could be reduced to four hours driving. Oh, the irony of being a cyclist! On an average day, I expected to bike about sixty to seventy miles, equal to an hour of driving on a highway. In the case of man versus machine, machine wins. Or does it?

"I wouldn't mind having a bike right about now. These gas

prices are ridiculous. You don't need to fill that thing up," he said, pointing to my bike with a grin.

I laughed. "There are pluses and minuses. Right now, anytime I want to go somewhere, I have to ask myself, 'Do I really have the energy to make it?' You can get in your truck without any thought and go a lot faster."

He nodded and said, "You must be in top shape."

"I'm getting there," I said, humbly.

And then, he left in his truck. And although he didn't drive fast down the road, it seemed fast from my cycling perspective. Speeding into the dust.

East of Hope, my map showed another climb over the Little Harquahala Mountains, but it was only a modest hill named Granite Wash Pass. The range was treeless. Desert brush populated the ground with saguaros and palo verde trees. I biked past a bend and suddenly ocotillos filled the land, many twenty feet tall. The scenery delighted my senses. The vastness of the expanse. The delicate shading of colors. Even the taste of the wind scoured clean by the sands. I don't know what I liked most, the imagery or the peace. I was simply enthralled.

I felt like I was in the honeymoon of my tour. I was in a good zone and feeling happy. I was trusting God's providence with everything, not only keeping me safe, but also keeping my adventure alive and kicking no matter what obstacles arose. Sure, these emotional highs don't last forever. There are peaks and valleys in life. Still I was enjoying each moment with unusual joy. It surprised even me.

Beyond the pass, I entered the McMullen Valley, a wide-open expanse with mountains afar in most directions. I went through Harcuvar, a town that appeared abandoned. I passed the ruins of a closed and dilapidated motel. Then another. Then I passed a deserted café. This highway was probably a bustling place before the interstate was built, but today, it's a humble thoroughfare that's been pushed aside and ignored by the engine of progress.

Three more miles brought me to a town where a welcome sign read, "Salome. Where She Danced." How graceful! At first, I imagined the slogan relating to a beautiful bride dressed in Victorian garb or a Mexican flamenco dancer. Inside the town limits a sign explained the legend of its naming. When Salome Pratt, the wife of the town's co-founder, first stepped onto the hot desert sand in bare feet, she jumped up and down to ease the pain, and her husband joked that she had danced.

The next town with lodging was fifty-five miles further down the road. Although I was confident I could make it, I chose to call it a day. I didn't want to rush past this peaceful little town. There would be other sections of this journey where I'd want to get more miles under my belt and speed through. For now, I'd stop and smell the sagebrush.

I checked in at the town's lone motel. A number of palm trees on the grounds rose like towering ornaments. True, palm trees don't grow naturally way out here, but that didn't matter. The warmth. The beauty. I breathed it all in until it became part of me.

The motel's parking lot resembled a classic motor inn. I could imagine my grandparents driving up to this place in their 1953 Buick. And to give the true classic feel, my room contained badly outdated interior design and fixtures—stuff that reminded me of my grandparents' generation. The heating unit looked like it may have come from the 1950s, if not earlier, and the tile was falling apart in the shower. The furniture was made of ordinary wood—probably in the same era as the heater. Yet all of the basics in the room worked and I was thankful.

Whether it was the mid-twentieth century design of my motel room or something else, my grandparents kept coming to mind. All of them are dead now. Wherever they are, would they look upon my adventure and encourage me to do this ride? Would they tell me to "seize the day" or to "go for it and follow your dreams"? My hunch is they'd think I was crazy. I could hear them now. Both of my grandmothers lecturing me about how preposterous such a trip as this would be, each in their unique and endearing way. Or maybe I'm wrong. Didn't they have dreams of their own that they followed or failed to follow and later regretted? Maybe they'd be my best promoters.

After settling into my room, I had lunch. I ended up at a

restaurant across from the motel. Inside the joint, the old time theme lived on with an area that reminded me of a western saloon or tap room with stool seating. I sat on the side in a booth and a waitress handed me a menu. It was a quiet place with no music. It felt awkward, yet casual and relaxed. Four older men talked politics. Another couple, a man and a woman across the restaurant, kept glancing toward me. Maybe it was because I was a stranger, or they don't see many peculiar long-haired guys eating by themselves. Then again, they weren't talking to each other and may have been bored. I ate a half-pound bacon cheeseburger with a side of fries. An amazing meal.

Then I explored Salome in the Arizona sunshine. My body was beginning to feel strong and was adapting to the daily grind on the bike. This was one of those days where I wanted to walk, explore and discover. I wandered to the east side, which consisted of a few roads running perpendicular to one another. Only 1,200 people live here, according to the latest U.S. Census. In one view, Salome seemed an undesirable place to live. Most of the houses were dumpy, like tiny square shanties. There really wasn't much to it. It seemed like the kind of town where most of the youth grow up and dream of escape, and then do. And yet, I still felt endeared to the village. I continued meandering. On one street, a bunch of dogs barked at me from front lawns. It gave me the willies. And no one seemed to be around. I wanted to like Salome. I wanted it to be something.

Eventually, I found my way back to the motel. I lay on my bed and watched TV, but only for so long. I was bored and thought I'd go for another walk. This time I strolled in the west and southwest part of town, and I found a grave—a special, solitary grave—placed beside the sidewalk on a residential street.

According to the monument, the grave belonged to Dick Wick Hall, one of the founders of Salome, who lived from 1877 to 1926. I had already read about him in tourist literature in the motel. He was a humorist and national columnist. He wrote jokes about living in the dry, isolated Arizona desert. To this day, the legacy of this man lives on. His humor may seem corny today, but his joking about "the Salome frog that was seven years old and couldn't swim" brings a smile to my face. In fact, the school mascot of Salome High School is the "Fighting Frogs." When Hall was alive, he was touted as Arizona's most famous humorist, kin to Will Rogers, the colorful social commentator and motion-picture actor.

Hall had a deep affection and appreciation for the desert, and especially loved this particular valley, the McMullen Valley.

He once wrote: "This valley, about fifteen miles wide and forty miles long, lying between the Harquahala and the Harcuvar Mountains, appealed to me strangely the first time I came to it, not only its abundant warmth but the wonderful peace and quiet of it, which only a dweller of the desert can understand and appreciate, where I can get acquainted with myself and maybe find the something which every man in his own soul is consciously or unconsciously searching for—Himself."

A writer with a goofy personality who loved this region. Dick Wick Hall was my hero. Maybe he could be my mentor or role model. I echoed his love and appreciation for this land, and I felt a kinship with him.

I paid my respect to his grave. A cross shaped in rocks was etched into the concrete cover. A few Queen of the Night cactus stood behind the tombstone, with one large and magnificent saguaro standing guard. My eyes were drawn to the years of his birth and death, and I couldn't escape it. Dick Wick Hall was forty-nine years old when he died. I'm thirty-six, not that far behind. There's something about cemeteries and tombstones that have always moved me. They're humbling. They force me to think about life, and what's important. This grave I was observing could be like mine someday. Suddenly, I felt mortal.

And there was another issue that pressed in on my heart. I'm a big dreamer. To pursue my ambitions, I've had to take bold risks and do things that might be considered out-of-the-ordinary. Sometimes I've made decisions that went against conventional wisdom, especially based on my upbringing that defines success as graduating college, building a career and accumulating wealth with a robust 401K for retirement. There have been instances where I've been devastated by family and friends who withheld their blessing toward my efforts—relationships that are strained to this day. Sometimes I've had people openly work against me or discourage me with wounding words. Other times, their disapproval was telling through their silence. Such acts of omission can be just as heartbreaking. Still, I've never let these deterrents stop me from chasing my dreams.

At this point in my life, I don't allow anyone in my inner-circle who isn't outright supportive of who I am, the decisions I make and how I go about living. If there were people who may have thought that I was wasting my time for biking across America, they didn't matter. But, during weak moments, I can hear that voice from the pit of hell telling me that I'm doing it wrong. That I should be living like someone else based on others' values or expectations. Or, in this case, that I'm being irresponsible for doing a long-distance bike tour.

As I stood by his final resting place, I wondered if Dick Wick Hall would have encouraged me to embark on this adventure. I had no doubt. He would have laughed and urged me to ride like my heart's on fire.

Yes, I knew this trip was right. In fact, it was the most important thing that I could do.

CHAPTER VI

THE BIKE IS STOLEN

One of the greatest titles we can have is "old friend."
We never appreciate how important old friends are until
we are older. The problem is we need to start our old
friendships when we are young . . . Today is the day to
invest in those people we hope will call us "old friend"
in the years to come.

Grant Fairley

When the sun had peaked over the horizon, breaking the dawn and drawing long shadows across the land, I was leaving Wickenburg and moving on the shoulder of U.S. Highway 60. I was not quite willing to exert myself hard. Instead, I went slow and took things in with my senses. The crisp morning air. The sounds of the wheels rubbing on the pavement. A train rumbling in the distance. Road traffic was minimal with only an occasional car whooshing past.

And then there was descent. As I gained speed, I switched gears. With road bikes of my era, the gear shifters are right there on the handlebar, and you use your thumb or fingers to hit the button or pull the lever. In the days of my childhood, my ten-speed bicycle had controls lower on the frame. You had to adjust them by removing a hand from the handlebar, a trickier move for sure. I was riding at eighteen miles per hour, and I set the gears harder, then easier, then harder, then easier. Eventually, I got it just right.

Each morning I set the daily mileage tracker on my cyclometer to zero, and on my first check, I was at a mere five miles. Groggy and half-awake, I was upset with such short distance. I biked fast in small surges, and then I checked the tracker every minute, but that only made things worse. I couldn't believe how far I'd ride before it measured one tenth of a mile. So, to put my mind at ease, I set the cyclometer so it only showed the time; I'd have to hit extra buttons to read the day's mileage.

I stared ahead sternly. I've watched other bicyclists with this austere presentation, and they always look part-snobby and part-foolish. I laughed and told myself to lighten up. Slow down. Smile more. In fact, I decided I'd take my hands off the handlebar. Chuckling to myself, I folded my arms and arched my back, all the while pedaling. No, I didn't crash. When you're moving, it's usually okay to do it although you do have to watch for bumps. When riding slow, the chances are greater that the bike could swerve.

Up this road, about twenty-five miles ahead, were the edges of suburban Phoenix. Somewhere in that city was my friend Phil, the first person I knew since starting last week with Jae and Krista. I'd been to Phoenix twice and had positive experiences, and I was ready to be with more people. I also sensed I could go a long distance today—maybe up to eighty or ninety miles all the way to the east side of the city. Today could be a good day. My heart was happy.

Then, I did something I had never quite done before. I stopped, set my camera on a guardrail post, and using the timer, snapped a picture of me with my bike. This was the first and only bicycle I had bought as an adult. For five years, this bike had been my champion and companion—my bright red workhorse. The frame was a striking red, with the word "Giant" lettered in white on the frame. For me, this one was special; it had shared the road with me for nearly 6,000 miles. I thought about how I should have given it a name, like many people name their car or boat, but I never got around to it. I bought the Giant new out of the box for $700. Originally, I ordered a silver frame bike at the shop, but they sent a red one. The owner called and said, "Do you want it? I'll send this red one back, but it does look nice." After some thought, I said I'd go with red, and I'm so glad I did. Red became my main cycling color. It was on this bike when my love of biking came into full bloom. I chuckled when I thought about Krista's quip about Don Quixote and his sidekick's donkey. Maybe she was right. It seemed fitting that this bike would carry me across the country.

Mile after mile I continued, anticipating the first suburban developments of the northwest side of metropolitan Phoenix. The change came slowly. More gas stations. Suburban neighborhoods. The first shopping mall. Crossing a beltway. Then before I knew it, I was in the midst of the busy suburbs of Surprise, a town named by its founder because she said she'd be "...surprised if this town ever amounted to much."

My plan, at least in theory and effort, was to avoid congested areas. I set out on a route that would keep me on major roads: Bell Road eastbound, Scotsdale Road southbound and a frontage road that went east along the Superstition Highway, a mega-freeway on the east side. Just three roads would take me seventy miles across Phoenix. As I approached the intersection with Bell Road, the fury of cars intensified, and needing to make a left, I darted across the pavement and grabbed one of two "left turn only" lanes among a sea of vehicles. I rolled to a stop in front with cars behind me. Some bicyclists in this situation might have taken the crosswalk, but this true road biker follows the rules of the road. When the light turned green, I pedaled hard and was turning left in the middle of this huge intersection.

The view from my bike revealed a changing America. First it was San Diego, with its mass ocean and suburbs, then mountains followed by expanses of desert. Today, I was back in another city, the largest in the Southwest.

I continued for miles on Bell Road—two lanes on each side with a grassy median—and eventually I reached a cross street where three miles to the north was a bike shop that was also a Giant dealer. It was on my agenda to have the derailer examined and replaced with a name-brand part, but as I thought about it, I didn't want to ride even that short distance off my route. Plus, the derailer Greg had installed was working fine, and given that a derailer snapped off six months previously, who was to say a third wouldn't similarly break off? I told myself I'd save my money and take my chances. The decision felt right.

On a bicycle, I saw Phoenix with new eyes, and what stuck out the most were orange trees. The oranges were ripe and more than a few had dropped and were all over the pavement, like stray juggling balls. They grew in backyards, the road's median and even a parking lot of a supermarket. I couldn't believe it.

After more miles, Bell Road became busier and lacked any shoulder. I stayed as far right as I could in a lane-share situation with cars. Most vehicles slowed and edged to the left while they passed. Eventually, I made it to a red and white "Welcome To Phoenix" sign with a mythical bird stretching its wings. Then, another mile ahead, I stopped at a red light at a buzzing intersection with Route 101, an elevated highway. Cars and trucks were turning on and off all over the place. The light turned green and I rode ahead. As was sometimes the case, slippery gravel and sand was gathered in spots, and without a bike lane and the need to stay right, the stuff was unavoidable. I winced as my wheels went through it, and just ahead, I got another flat—again in the front wheel. I was so mad because I knew that kind of debris frequently causes flats. In the parking lot of an International House of Pancakes, I fixed the tire just fine—quicker than the first time.

Bell Road continued without any shoulder. Cars in the right lane passed me as courteously as possible, but it was becoming too close for my comfort. More patches of sand and gravel covered the road's edges. Then, the grassy median transformed into a fifth middle lane for making left turns into myriad stores, office buildings, and neighborhoods paralleling the road. My best-laid plan of a three road route was not working out, and so I devised a detour. I zigzagged on perpendicular streets with names such as Thunderbird and Greenway and numerical roads traveling north to south. As I traveled deeper into the city, the neighborhoods looked less safe. Stores had bars on the windows. Graffiti was strewn on the occasional building. And everything seemed older and dumpier. But at least I had more cycling space.

Nearing fifty miles of riding, it was time to rest. I could feel my attitude getting aggravated. Overall, my body felt strong, but I had to get off the bike, and soon. I felt like a kid who had enough energy to keep going, but who was cranky and in need of a nap. Besides, it was time for lunch.

I biked more miles, checking storefronts and restaurants. I needed a place where I could lock my bike *and* sit near the window with the bike in direct view. This was the big city, not Julian or Salome, and I knew I had to be vigilant about theft. I spotted a Taco Bell and decided that would be fine. No, fast food is not healthy, but after riding fifty-five miles, I could allow myself to gorge on anything I wanted. I didn't plan on eating a ton of food anyway. I locked the bike on a metal handrail in front of the restaurant's windows and sat at a table facing it. After thirty minutes of eating and resting, I got a text.

"Where are you?" wrote Phil.

"Taco Bell on Dunlap and 19th Ave," I wrote, "Taking a break. Will get to the eastern side of the city by late afternoon."

"Get out! That's where I eat lunch on workdays!" Phil replied. This was an extraordinary coincidence in this large, sprawling city of over four million people. Phil's workplace was less than one mile away, and if I had shown up one hour later, we might have met in person.

"My lunch break is in an hour," he wrote. "Can you stay awhile?"

"Sorry. I've got to keep moving," I texted.

The plan was to see Phil after his work day anyway. Sure, it would have been great to have seen my friend right there, but waiting forty-five minutes would test my patience. My body was pushing me to get going again—it's just a cycling thing. When I know I have more riding to do, it's difficult to sit on my hands. I become antsy. Something pushes me to get my bones moving. Whatever the reason, I was driven to ride soon and stuck to the original plan of meeting Phil in the evening when I reached Mesa or Apache Junction.

Outside, I unlocked the bike and pedaled out of the parking lot. Next door was a CVS pharmacy. It had been seven days since I shaved, mainly because I'd forgotten my razor and shaving cream. I was tired of looking like a dirt bag. So, I locked the bike on a sign post near the entrance, and went inside to buy my items … along with an unplanned impulse purchase of cherry pull-n-peel Twizzlers candy. I returned to my bike and tossed everything into the trunk box and was just about ready to go when I figured that I'd better hit the bathroom before taking off.

If you're not a cyclist, you might not have experienced the need to go and there's nowhere private to relieve yourself. I've seen competitive riders yank their shorts up and whiz while riding. That's definitely not my style. When I go hiking in the wilderness, I always carry a roll of toilet paper and I'm careful not to eat anything that will be explosive, if you know what I mean. I wanted to be on the safe side.

Leaving the bicycle locked to a sign post in front of the pharmacy, I went back to the Taco Bell, about 300 feet away. It was a short bathroom visit, and in fact, my trip was unnecessary. I had wasted no more than five minutes. Heading back, I saw that my bike had vanished. Were my eyes playing tricks on me? I quickly scanned the area. I squinted my eyes and then opened them wide as I jogged to the site. Yep, no bike.

Rarely have I had things stolen in my life, and I didn't know how I should react. I ran to the road to see if I could see someone riding away. Then I stepped inside the CVS, hoping an employee had somehow unlocked the bike and taken it inside—a long shot, for sure— but I couldn't think of anything better to do. When I told the workers that my bike had been stolen, they became infuriated for me, but nobody said they had seen anything. Fortunately, I'd had the forethought to hold on to my most important items: my wallet, cell phone, camera and of course, the clothes on my back. But everything else now belonged to some thief.

I didn't panic. Frankly, I wasn't that alarmed. In fact, I felt peace. I actually laughed and shook my head a little. *Okay God, what now? Is the trip over? Or will I get another bike?*

It was then that I texted Phil.

"Hold on. You won't believe this. The bike was stolen! Not joking. Come to the Taco Bell, I'll be here."

Then I called the police. The dispatcher asked a lot of questions, then assured me she would send an officer.

A few minutes later, Phil arrived in his truck. He pulled up with the window down and distress written all over his face. "I can not believe it! I don't have the words."

"It's okay. I'm not sure what to say either," I said.

"Didn't you have it locked?"

"It was."

Phil and I stood and waited for the police, but since they didn't arrive right away, we went back to the Taco Bell. It was so good to see Phil, an old friend, and yet any "feel good" greetings were overshadowed by the stolen bike. Phil was dressed nicely in his work attire—beige cotton pants and a collared light blue shirt. His brown hair is longer than the average man, as it just touches his collar. I've know Phil for years, and in fact, everybody seems to like Phil for his affable personality.

At the counter, Phil told the manager, "This guy rode here from San Diego. He's bicycling across America, and his bike just got stolen right out there! Can you believe that?" The man's eyes widened and he shook his head in disgust. Eventually, Phil took his tray of food to a table, and I followed with a soda.

"You know," he said, "I'm really not surprised. This area has a lot of crime. I hear many stories like yours. Stolen bikes. Car break-ins. We even have a security guard watching the parking lot at work. I've loved living in Phoenix for so many reasons, but the crime is definitely a problem."

A man at a nearby table overheard us. He was sympathetic to my situation, and then his eyes tightened and said, "If I saw some druggie homeless person riding my bike, I'd tackle him and crush the guy's skull." Part of me understood his perspective; the other part cringed.

A half hour later a police cruiser pulled up, and Phil and I bolted from our table. A man with a crew cut, a smile, and all the garb of a sergeant, he acknowledged bicycle theft was a common problem in the city. Although no kind of bike lock is theft proof, my cable and lock were apparently a snap to get through.

"These guys will steal a bike in seconds, and it doesn't matter if it's locked. With bolt cutters, you can cut off a cable bike lock in seconds. There are other kinds of locks that are better, but not that much. If a thief wants a bike, it's his," he said.

I described the bike, and he wrote down the details, saying he'd enter my description into a computer database. If a bike like it showed up, they'd contact me.

"So realistically, what are my chances this bike will be found?" I asked.

"I'd say the chances are slim, but you never know. We do have an elaborate system. If something comes up that we're suspicious about, we'll do a search."

Phil chimed in, "But your bike is unique. You had those panniers in the back. Did you include them in your description?"

I hadn't.

"Now, a bike with those kinds of saddlebags would be perfect for transporting drugs," the sergeant interjected.

I laughed at that image. My precious road bike, being used as a drug mule! Knowing that this was a pivotal point in my trip, the consummate chronicler in me wanted a photo of the officer. I asked him and he obliged; he stood in front of his cruiser with his chest out.

I was grateful to meet this friendly professional. The chances of my bike being found were miniscule. Even with their program, with all they're burdened with in this city, I didn't think any Phoenix police officers would be on the beat searching neighborhoods for my specific bike.

The officer shared more with us. "I always emphasize that people should register their bikes with their local police in case it's found. Also, check Craigslist, since a few have been recovered when owners have seen their stolen bikes for sale."

"I hadn't thought about that," I said.

As the officer was finishing his written report, Phil put his hand on my shoulder.

"Now, are you okay?"

"Yeah, I'm not that bad," I said.

"Well, for you I'm churning inside over this. I'm boiling that some low life would have the audacity to steal your bike right from under your nose."

Phil turned to the sergeant and said, "Steve's from out of town, but I live here. We've had car break-ins even with a security guard on the grounds!"

The officer nodded, conceding that's also a problem.

I asked, "What about the Club? I have one of those—it's that metal bar under lock and key that you put on the steering wheel, making it impossible turn the wheel much."

"With the club they'll just smash it," said the officer.

"I always thought the Club helped, with deterrence at least," I said.

Phil interjected, "It'll deter the amateur blue-collar criminal, but not the pro."

"That's right," said the sergeant.

Then Phil said, "So, the key is to have a twenty-year-old vehicle that's a P.O.S. You know what that stands for. That's the best deterrent."

We all laughed.

Minutes later, an employee of the pharmacy came out to give us information that we didn't have earlier. It turned out that the store manager drove into the parking lot and had seen a man riding my bike. The manager remembered it because he thought to himself, "What a bright and colorful red bike!"

Other than the offender being white and male, there were no other descriptions. From the parking lot, he biked east on Dunlap. It felt good to know someone had witnessed the incident and had a clue about what happened. Like the officer said, the guy likely cut the bike lock cable and rode off. He probably watched me walk away and, once out of sight, he did his thing.

Phil had to return to work soon and didn't want to leave me stranded. He offered to drive me north to a Wal-Mart on Bell Road, so I could buy basic items such as hygiene supplies and clothing. I wouldn't replace everything right now, but would buy enough to regain my standing. Also, this store was located about a mile from a motel, so I could walk there, check-in and relax.

As Phil drove me in his truck, he was clearly distraught.

"I don't know how to say this, but I want to say 'I'm sorry' for what happened. This is my city now, and I wanted you to have a good experience."

"No worries. How many millions of people live here? Crime happens. That's just the way it is."

We pulled in front of the Wal-Mart entrance and as I was getting out, I thanked Phil for the ride and patted him on the shoulder.

"It's so good to see you, man!" I said.

Phil pushed his hand out with remorse. "Somehow, we'll work this out. I'll see you later."

Inside the store, I walked awkwardly like a newbie ice skater with biking shoes on the slippery floor. I hate shopping if only because I become some kind of shopping predator. I feel like I'm on a hunt, relentlessly seeking my prey. I know women love to shop as a way to relax and explore, like it feeds their souls. For me, I'm angry when I can't find what I want. I wandered with frustration from one aisle to another, picking up stuff, and then it occurred to me that with my bike, my cell phone charger was gone. Another thing to buy and empty the wallet. I was in the shoe department in search of a new pair of sandals when my cell phone rang. It was Mark in Minnesota.

"How's the farming business going?" I asked, holding my tongue about my bike drama.

"Not bad," he said. Mark began to tell me about the weather, which for him, is by no means small talk. It has a huge affect on his sugar beet crops. I listened for a few minutes, giving him a follow-up question to give him some conversational courtesy. Eventually the conversation was directed to me.

"Well, you won't believe this, but my bike was stolen two hours ago," I said.

"Really? Were you robbed?"

"No, I was in a restroom with my bike locked outside. I didn't see the guy."

Mark breathed a sigh of relief. "The first thing that went through my mind was you were robbed at gunpoint, or beat up."

I never thought of that, a consolation of sorts.

"So what are your options?" he asked.

"I don't know. I could end the trip, but that doesn't feel right. I could buy a new bike, but uhhhh, it's not like I'm made of money. I'm not sure what I'm going to do. This just happened at lunch."

There was a pause.

"Don't make any quick decisions. Let me speak to my wife and I'll get back to you."

"Sounds good. I really do have peace about this, but at the same time, I'm going crazy in this place. I have so many things to buy. And I can't stand shopping in these kinds of stores. I have no patience!" I shouted.

"Oh, I'm the same way. My wife says she's still training me, and it's been twenty-five years now, " said Mark, "You hang in there."

Finally, with a number of items purchased, I trudged down the sidewalk of Bell Road, that busy four-lane corridor that I had ridden on earlier. My shoulders got a workout from carrying two large bags full of stuff. Cars sped by, only feet from the sidewalk, each time whooshing past me and aggravating me one more iota. I felt like a transient as I carried everything, with an irrational fear telling me that the front desk clerk at the motel would turn me away because I looked like a bum. At times like this, I couldn't help but feel frustrated about not having a vehicle in this world dominated by cars and trucks. It was hard enough to bicycle everywhere, and now I only had my feet to get around.

In my motel room at last—I had no trouble checking in—I plopped onto the bed and stared at the ceiling. *Who would've ever thought I'd have a day like this?* I showered and did nothing but veg in front of the

TV. Later that afternoon, Phil had spread the news about the stolen bike on an Internet forum we both visit, and phone calls and text messages began to flow in from friends. Most were shocked, alarmed, and angry, and I found myself consoling them. It was an odd situation for people to be reacting so strongly, and yet I felt calm and accepting about the theft. If anything, I endured more annoyance with the shopping afterward.

I sent a text message to the owners of my gym, who were tracking my ride with push pins on a map of the U.S.A. Each day I had been sending them a text message with the start and end destination and my day's mileage. Most days I didn't receive a response, but I did get a message of concern when I texted, "Wickenburg, AZ to Phoenix, AZ. 55 miles. Bike stolen. I'll keep you posted."

I watched more TV and tried not to think about anything. The one hope I had was that Mark would call me later, and eventually he did.

"I talked to my wife and we agreed we want to buy you a new bike."

"Wait a minute. Let's talk about this," I said.

"No discussion. How about if you work for me during harvest time? You can make things up to me then. There's about three weeks in October when my farm is running full-time, and I mean twenty-four hours when we're harvesting sugar beets. Maybe you could come to Minnesota and help me. You can stay in our guest room, and we'd have fun too."

"Are you sure?"

"Steve, there's no way I can let your trip end like this."

His words resonated with me. I just knew my cross-country ride couldn't come to an end. I was swept with many feelings, but gratitude and humility were at the top. It was one of those moments when I swore that if I ever had much money, I would help others in the same way. Find people who have financial needs and give. Right now, because of this strong friendship, I was on the receiving end.

After the sun went down, Phil showed up at the motel and I shared the good news. Phil raised his arm with a fist pump.

"Steve, are you aware of how fortunate you are? Who is this friend? Most people don't have someone who'd buy them a new bike."

"Remember, I've got to work on his farm to pay him back, but yeah, I'm on the lucky side. No doubt about that."

"It's working out like I said. I knew your trip wasn't over. I just knew it."

Phil had more good news. "My mother offered her spare car tomorrow so you can travel around Phoenix. Now you can go to bike shops, buy yourself a new bike, and shop for things you need. It's an older Ford Taurus. It runs okay, but there's a few quirks with it."

"Believe me, any car would be nice. You're talking to a guy who biked here."

Phil erupted in laughter. "That's right!"

And so I was blessed by the generosity of another friend. First Mark. Now Phil.

Phil hung around for a while, just talking and watching television in my motel room when my cell phone rang. The caller was the officer who had taken down the report this afternoon. My voice raised with anticipation. Phil, listening intently as I held the phone to my ear, also got excited.

"Maybe they found your bike!" Phil declared.

"No, we haven't found it," said the officer, "One thing I didn't get in my interview is your mailing address. I need that to finish my paperwork."

Unfortunately, there were no leads. No one had any clue about where my bike was. Phil and I shook our heads.

***

The next morning, Phil had his mother's car parked in front of my motel room, and within an hour I was at a nearby bicycle shop. The manager was sympathetic when I explained my situation, but he wasn't hopeful about how he could help.

"Our selection is limited. With road bikes, usually we order what our customers want and it takes a number of days to get here, but let me do some calling around for you."

As he made calls, I paced through the store, admiring the new bicycles—their brand new tires having perfect, unworn tread. A new bike would be great. I was sad about the fate of my beautiful red Giant, but the prospect of a new bike called me like a siren.

The man hung up, approached me and said, "Go to Landis Cyclery on Indian School Road. I told them about your situation. They should be able to sell you something today."

I felt embarrassed to ask, but I had to: "Is it in a decent neighborhood?" I was more skitzy than usual. I didn't want the car I was borrowing to get stolen too.

He made eye contact with me and I sensed he understood my worry. "Uh, it's a fair neighborhood," he said matter-of-factly.

Fair? I didn't know how I felt about the word "fair," but I guess I didn't have much choice.

Thirty minutes later, I was inside Landis Cyclery at one of their three Phoenix locations. It seemed like the perfect bicycle shop. A few pictures from the turn of the century stood out, proof of the sign outside announcing they were in business since 1912. Jerseys autographed by professional cycling athletes hung on the wall. Hundreds of brand new bikes sat in the shop, including colorful beach cruisers with baskets on the handlebars, wide-tire mountain bikes and a separate room with a selection of sweet road bikes. They also had a variety of accessories, including jerseys, shorts, socks, shoes, water bottles, locks, tubes, pumps, bike seats, helmets, tools … you name it. And the workers were so professional and at ease. They knew I was coming, and an employee greeted and consoled me.

"I guess you're not happy to be here, right?" he asked.

"Yeah …" I said, as I looked around, "but I'm enamored by all these bikes!"

We went to the road bikes and discussed my needs as a touring bicyclist. The term "touring" is used for those who don't race, but pedal for exercise, having fun or going lengthy distances. A touring bike tends to be more comfortable for a person, with a frame that has what's called a "relaxed" geometry. The other kind of road bike has more aggressive tube angles, and is used for racing. All of its design, including the kind of wheels, the weight, the design of the frame and components, and the positioning of the seat are all geared for light weight and with minimal resistance. It's about optimizing speed over comfort. Competitive cyclists weigh everything in ounces to reduce weight. Over the course of a long race, like the Tour de France, such minute weight savings play a crucial role in outdistancing the competition, even by fractions of a second.

He had two bikes in stock that would fit the needs of my cross-country tour. Their geometry was a good fit for my body. I checked out the two bikes. One was a boring gray; the other was mostly black with some red and white highlights.

I tried unsuccessfully to hold back my disappointment.

"Nothing in red, huh? That's my color."

"No, but I understand. People can be particular about that."

"I'm definitely one of those types," I said with a snicker.

We discussed the advantages of each bike. The gray one offered better performance and speed, but he recommended the lower priced black-and-red road bike. "They're both good. And while it's true that this gray one gives more performance in general, because you're touring long distance, this Trek will carry the extra weight in your panniers better. Plus, it still has some sporty features."

It was named a Trek 1.2. Actually it turned out to be a huge improvement over my old bike, which had a heavier frame, defective derailers, and a back wheel that sometimes made a ticking sound that drove me crazy. This one had more gears in the back, a seat post made of lightweight titanium, and a frame that was more forgiving on bumps. It was also lighter than my Giant; I lifted the bike easily with the palm of one of my hands.

I bought it. I took a test ride in the parking lot, with the manager watching. He shifted the seat and handlebar a few times, so my shoulders were comfortable and my legs would be positioned just right to maximize each pedal stroke. Then I picked out accessories, including a back rack, trunk box, saddlebags, spare tubes, cyclometer, clipless pedals, and a new lock. Mark's generosity had paid-off ... literally.

Then I drove to big box stores to replace the other stolen items, including a first-aid kid, travel-size toiletries, winter gloves and more clothing. It felt like I was on a wild shopping spree.

In the evening, Phil came by the motel to pick up the car. When he saw my bike, his senses peaked.

"These are some nice wheels," he said as he grazed the bike frame with his hands, like the models on *The Price Is Right* when they stand next to a new car.

"Your other bike was fine, but this one is so clean and shiny."

"I know," I said with a grin, "This is a good bike."

"Oh! Before I forget, you won't believe this. I talked to a guy at work who's a cyclist and he told me about bicycle trails that go along the canals. You could have avoided all the congested roads and traffic if you would have known about them. I wish I would have known about them sooner."

"Me too."

"Will you be okay tomorrow?"

"Yeah. From here, it's a straight shot twenty-five miles east out of the city."

"So, do you want to grab a bite to eat?"

"You bet."

"But wait, what will we do about the bike?"

"I'll keep it in here. Obviously, we'll lock the door and I'm sure it'll be fine."

Phil and I ended up at a Chipotle Mexican Grill, a great place to hang out and talk. We've been friends for ten years. I figure that's long enough to think of ourselves as "old friends." We first met in Colorado Springs when he took interest in my hiking reports and photos of the Rocky Mountains that I display on my website, www.coloradoguy.com. Over time, we began to meet regularly, usually for morning coffee, in which we'd give each other updates on what we called "empire building." Both of us had tough jobs and were seeking ways to break out of the grind—maybe start our own businesses that gave us more freedom.

Five years ago, I saw Phil start a restaurant in Florence, Colorado that he ran for two and a half years. I saw the money he made, but it turned out he worked usually sixty to seventy hours per week. The work took a toll on his health and marriage, before he got out.

"My job is better now. Yes, it's a normal job, but they treat me well and they're paying for graduate school," said Phil.

Phil has witnessed me struggle with demanding counseling jobs. He's seen me endure through life's ups and downs. In fact, I'd say he's seen me grow up. And something can be said about a friend who sticks, one who doesn't veer off to parts unknown without a thought of friends left behind. He's genuine and I cherish our relationship.

As we chomped on our massive burritos, Phil wanted to learn more about my trip. "So tell me, how do you handle biking all the hills?"

"You go slow."

"Come on. That's not what I mean. It's hard. How do you hang in there? That's what I hate about riding a bike. I can't stand going uphill."

"No, really. You take your time. You put your bike in the easiest gear and you pace yourself. That's all there is to it. There's no magic— you pedal slowly and you tell yourself that it's okay to feel pain and that quitting is not an option."

"You make it sound so easy."

"Well, that part is."

"You know, in spite of hills, you've inspired me. I'm thinking about buying one of those cruiser bikes just for riding around the neighborhood."

"Go for it. The key is to have fun when you start. Don't worry about going far or going fast. If you get on your bike and you have fun, then you're successful. Don't compare yourself to me or anyone else."

I dropped my phone on the floor and had to wiggle under the seat to get it. I winced and grunted as I used a myriad of muscles that were sore. Today's day off was helpful, as my body was still adjusting to cycling as a full-time job.

Phil had a pained expression. "Are you sure you want to go already?" he asked, "Maybe you should take another day off to regroup and relax. I'm still floored by what happened. Just yesterday, your bike was stolen, and thirty-six hours later, you have a brand new bike."

That was a nice thought, but I was ready to resume my adventure. "The aches and pains come with the territory. If I only rode when I felt great, I'd never go," I said.

Phil shuddered at my words, then smiled, knowing that the open road was calling my name.

CHAPTER VII

MORE TROUBLE, MORE TRIUMPH

Anyone can give up, it's the easiest thing to do.
But to hold it together when everyone else
would understand if you fell apart,
that's true strength.

Unknown

*T*here wasn't much traffic on Sunday morning on Southern Avenue, a west-east road that ran parallel to the Superstition Freeway and would lead me east out of Phoenix. Few cars passed and accompanied me at intersections, which validated the notion that Sunday mornings are a good time to ride in populated areas. There is no rush-hour traffic, there are hardly any commercial trucks, and the only thing that one might come upon are travelers headed to church.

On these empty roads, my new bike rode like a charm. It moved quietly, like a new car, with no squeaks or ticks. Everything worked perfectly. My body was positioned better on the seat, with minimum stress on my back and arms. I had more power with each stroke of my legs. The tires were virgin. The wheels had especially shiny spokes. The gears shifted effortlessly. New is nice, I had to admit. As I moved along, I reflected on the theft. Maybe it was meant to be that my old bike was stolen. Would it have made it across the country? With the derailer problems and other troubles associated with its age, maybe it wouldn't have.

Southern Avenue went on for twenty miles with countless shopping malls, residential neighborhoods and townhome complexes. In Mesa, two cyclists chatted in a supermarket parking lot with their bikes beside them. I waved, and they waved back. The more I headed east, the more relaxed things became. I saw an increase in RV parks. Homes became newer. At one time, Apache Junction was a small town, an outpost in the Arizona desert, but now it felt like the far suburbs of Phoenix. With all the distance I covered, it seemed like these neighborhoods would make for a long work commute to downtown Phoenix. At twenty miles, I stopped at a convenience store for a quick rest. I had enough food, but it never hurt to find a bench, gulp down an Arizona Iced Tea (in their renowned aluminum can), and give my muscles a break.

Eventually, I entered U.S. Highway 60 at the point where it downgraded from an eight-lane mega-freeway to a four-lane highway. The Superstition Mountains stood tall on the left, with high-class gated communities and golf courses populating the hillsides. The road was busy though, and the shoulder was far from clean. An increase in asphalt pebbles required shifts in the front wheel and minor twists with my body. These bumps and debris aren't good for bike tires and cause flats. Still I kept moving, and after two hours I entered a groove, my body finally warming up.

At thirty-four miles into the ride, I stopped to admire and photograph the landscape of palo verde trees, chollas, saguaros and all the things that make the desert glorious. Right there, I said good-bye to Phoenix; another city was under my belt. Even though it cost a bike in the process, I had made it through. The town of Superior was my destination today, and if I continued to feel strong and ambitious, I thought maybe I'd make it all the way to Globe. Today was turning into a good day.

The numbers of passing cars dissipated with every mile, and I felt peaceful in my solitude. My mind wandered, alighting briefly, and quickly moving on. Tranquility on the bike.

That's when I heard the voice.

You are my son.

At first, I thought that it had to be something that I made up, but I couldn't get it out of my head. It wasn't an audible voice, but a message so strong that I couldn't ignore it. I kept pedaling in rhythm and stared past the front wheel.

You are my son. Those four words wouldn't go away.

Was my mind playing tricks? The temperature had warmed and the sun was fully out. Maybe the heat and tiredness was causing this. I've had some profound spiritual moments in my life, so I know they happen, but I tend to be suspicious of people who claim to have supernatural epiphanies all the time. Yet, the more I tried not to think about it, the more it stuck in my mind. God wanted to make a connection with me.

"So, I am your son?" I asked.

Yes. You are.

I was speechless. My dad came to mind; he's 69-years-old and living in New Jersey. Like most, my relationship with my Dad has had its ups and downs, but this voice was not disrespecting my father's role in my life. It was more like a proposition.

I will assume the role of your loving father, but only if you let me.

I didn't know how to react. Or what to say.

Was this more intellectual knowledge that needed to seep down and dwell in my heart? Sure, there's lots of talk in church contexts about being a "child of God," but does that really mean I have perks with him like the way a human father and son can have?

Yes. We need to be close. I want to guide you and use you. Come to me like a son would go to his father when you need help—your problems, your needs, your battles.

I felt frightened and thrilled; something about the whole thing hit me hard. Tears began to pour down my face as I continued riding. It still felt like part of what I was experiencing wasn't real. Nobody would believe what had just happened. I know I've experienced God's love before; this wasn't all new. Still, this was something that could change my life forever.

I couldn't cry too much, because it wasn't safe. I had to be vigilant about dodging things on the road. There was an increase in chunks of asphalt, rocks, and litter on the shoulder, and it seemed like there were flattened aluminum cans all over. My arms and hands felt the brunt of the bike's shaking over large cracks in the pavement. Suddenly more cars were passing me. Then, the shoulder narrowed on two small bridges that crossed washes, forcing me to ride close to the white line and uncomfortably close to traffic. It was then that I heard the sound, a high-pitched "*Ffffffff!*" The back wheel was flat.

I leaned the bike against a barbed-wire fence beyond the highway and got to work. Beyond was the sound of motorcycles ripping through the hillside, and a truck with dirt bikes in tow pulled off the highway and toward a opening in the fence. The driver asked if I needed help.

"Thanks, I'm okay," I said, while crouched down with the wheel. "This is the main disadvantage of my hobby." Then he waved and continued toward the motorcycle paths.

After replacing the tube and airing the tire, I had trouble placing the wheel back on the bike's frame, partly because of the bulky saddlebags that hung on each side. I could have removed them, but I wasn't sure that I could refasten them as tight as the shop employee had done. I jostled with the tire for five long, frustrating minutes, knowing an average bicyclist would probably get this done in seconds. The mechanically-challenged dork in me was coming out again.

Then a pick-up truck pulled over, and an older man got out and ambled toward me. "You need help? I've ridden a lot of bikes," he said with a lisp. He had gray hair—his face wrinkled and worn as such that my intuition told me the cause was from something other than age. A band-aid showed conspicuously on part of his mustache and left cheek.

"Yeah, this isn't fun," I said, with a laugh, "If you can hold the bike as I set the back wheel back on, that'd be great."

He did just that, and within seconds, I had it on. I thanked my aide and asked about him. His name was Brian.

"Where do you live?"

"Apache Junction."

"For how long?"

"Too long. No matter where I live, it's usually too long," he said.

I snickered and chose not to ask why, but I thanked him nonetheless.

"Hey, can I get your picture for memory's sake?"

He looked at my camera and his face became grim. "No! None of that," he said.

I put my hands up to show no harm. "I understand. No problem."

And like that, we said good-bye and he went back to his truck. It took about thirty minutes to resolve this flat tire—much longer than usual—but it was a small victory nonetheless.

I remounted and began to pedal. Before this flat, it had been only a half mile since that intense spiritual encounter.

"Okay God, where were we?" I asked.

As I gained speed, I sensed the back tire was softening. Had I not pumped enough air? I rode a short distance and ignored it, as if denial has ever been an effective strategy, but the tire was certainly losing air. Leaning it against a guardrail, I used my pump, but the new tube wouldn't hold any pressure. I sighed, knowing I'd have to go through the tube-changing process over again. This time, I did everything quickly. I squeezed the tire; it felt firm. Then I resumed riding. Within thirty seconds, I felt a rumbling vibration below. It was flat again!

Something was obviously wrong. Never had I experienced this kind of problem. My confidence was shaken, and I only had two remaining spare tubes. I glared at the bike with anger and confusion. *What the heck is going on?*

I called Dave in Farmington, New Mexico, a friend who I've biked with on occasions. He knew more about bike mechanics than I did. Dave didn't answer his phone, and so I left a voice message.

Then I called Phil. He wasn't a bicyclist, but at least he could help me clear my head. I didn't know if it was a problem related specifically to this new bike, or something simpler that I was overlooking.

"Let me do some research," Phil said. "Maybe it has something to do with the tire. It must be a different brand."

"I don't think that's a problem," I answered. "A road bike wheel is a road bike wheel. And it's the same size as my old one."

"Let me see what I can find," he said. I heard him typing. Phil found a cycling website that listed common reasons for when a bicycle tire won't hold air. "You must have proper air pressure," he read.

"Yep. That's not the issue here."

"Be sure the tube is not crimped or twisted at any point ..."

"Good advice, but I doubt that's the case."

Phil kept going. "Some people find that the tube is easier to work with if you put a small amount of air in it, enough to hold it in the tire. However, be careful not to put too much air, as you may accidentally 'pinch' the tube when fitting it in the frame."

"Yeeeees. I know that too," I blurted.

He read more things from the website. I realized Phil wanted to be helpful, but my frustration grew. I bit my tongue, aware that he was trying his best. He insisted that he keep researching, and I was at a boiling point as he read one irrelevant thing after another. It felt like he wasn't listening to me, and then I exploded.

"Listen, I've changed so many tires!" I shouted. "You're reading obvious stuff, and nothing on the (expletive) Internet will help!" I rarely swear, but all decency had flown out the window with my patience. Instantly, I felt bad for yelling and apologized. Amazingly, Phil remained patient throughout. What a friend.

"I understand you're mad. Hold on," he said, and then he continued reading, "It says, 'If the tube is not placed snuggly or lacks proper tire pressure, the tube might shift and is more apt to be punctured.'"

Another good point, but I knew this wasn't the case. Still, I had no suggestions. "I don't know what to do with this tire," I said.

While I was still on the phone with Phil, Dave called. After telling Phil I'd call him back, I switched to Dave and explained my problem.

"It sounds like something might be lodged in the tire and it's puncturing the tubes," said Dave.

"But I checked the tire thoroughly, inside and out!" I replied, as defensive and abrupt as I had been with Phil. Actually, what I said wasn't strictly true. I had checked the outside of the tire, but not the inside. "Hold on. Let me check something."

I examined the inside of the tire and found a small piece of metal lodged in the rubber. The light bulb went on. This was the culprit. I had overlooked one important factor. A flat tire commonly happens when a sharp object adheres to the tire, breaks through the rubber, and punctures the tube. Now, when putting a new tube into a tire, it's vital to inspect the outer and inner edges of the tire, to be sure the culprit is no longer there. This was my critical oversight.

Talk about embarrassment: In my five years of road biking and changing some twenty or more tires, I had never been aware of the possibility that the sharp object that created the flat *could still be in the tire*, waiting to puncture the next tube. Waves of humility went through me like never before. But elation overtook my embarrassment. At least I had this figured out. Despite all the time I wasted, it felt so good to solve this.

After thanking Dave profusely, I changed the tube a third time with a renewed burst of energy. I inflated the tire and it remained as hard as a rock. Then I texted Phil, "All good. Problem solved. So sorry for the outburst!" Phil text me back with congratulations.

My last task was to insert the back wheel inside the frame, something I had done twice during this escapade, once with the help of Brian holding the bike, the other by myself. As I jostled the wheel inside the frame, something looked wrong. There was a loop in the bicycle chain. I'd never encountered *this*. When placing the back wheel inside a bike frame, one has the extra task of wrapping the bike chain around the sprocket. If the chain is not coordinated properly, no pedaling can be done.

I fumbled with the greasy chain, but no amount of my tinkering would undo the loop. My jaw muscles tightened. The whirring sound of cars speeding by fueled my anger. It was another snag that I couldn't solve! The problem wasn't just a matter of solving the looped chain, as maddening as it was; this would be another substandard mileage day thanks to these mishaps.

I tinkered with the chain more, and nothing helped. In fact, I think I made it worse. Not knowing what to do, I called Dave again.

"Go link by link," he advised. "See if you can find a kink somewhere."

I tried as he suggested, and followed other advice he gave, but nothing worked. By now, my hands were pitch black with grease.

"Dave, this is ridiculous," I shouted, "I've had so many problems on this trip! I can't possibly have all these obstacles and expect to make it across the country."

Unable to ride, I considered my options. Hitchhiking fifteen miles to Superior was a possibility, but that would be cheating again, and it's a small town that likely didn't have a bike shop. I could return to Phoenix, where I'd have to assume that Landis Cyclery could fix the looped chain. Earlier, Phil had said that he had the day off and offered to rescue me if needed, but I didn't want him to drive sixty miles each way. I had burdened him enough.

So there I was, on the edge of the highway—in an area that my map marked as Florence Junction—rattled, confused, and disgusted, with myself and life. In my exhaustion, I couldn't put things into perspective, and the thought eked its way into my mind: maybe fate was leading me to end this trip. In five years of bicycling, I had never had so many profound bike-related difficulties as I'd had in the past ten days. I wasn't sure I wanted to continue if more problems awaited down the road.

Seeing no other option, I called Phil.

"I'll be happy to pick you up if that's what you want," he said.

I sighed in disgust, knowing I couldn't give up just yet. "Let me play with this chain for another ten minutes. If I'm still stuck after that, I'll call back."

I was verging on a meltdown, but I dug deep down and did my best. I forced myself to be patient and to forget all those nagging thoughts about how poor I am at mechanical tasks. I told myself that I had all day. Just take your time and figure it out. Yet, nothing worked.

I was about to call Phil, when two people in an ATV approached. A young man and woman hopped out and asked if I needed help. I smiled and laughed. "That's an understatement. Do you know how to unloop a bike chain?" I asked.

"Never done it, but I love to solve things," he said. "And I'm pretty good at fixing stuff."

I held the bike while he handled the chain with determination, as the woman stood beside me.

"We saw you over an hour ago," she said, "When I saw you again after all this time, we had to stop."

"You're so nice. Thank you."

As I watched him work on my chain, I began to grin. I thought to myself, "These two people are my angels. They'll get me back on the road. I just know it!"

The writer in me realized this encounter would make a great story someday about how I overcame. Already, I envisioned the joy I'd feel to be riding and moving again. I held the bike and waited for the inevitable declaration that he had fixed it.

However, he never said it. In fact, within minutes, he told me he didn't know how to fix it either. The gleam in my face vanished. Even my two angels couldn't undo the loop. They apologized and asked what I planned to do.

"I'll be okay. I've got a friend who'll come out."

And with that, they resumed riding their ATVs.

"Phil, I need you to pick me up. I'm not going anywhere," I said dejectedly on the phone.

While waiting for Phil to arrive, I planned, and I probably went overboard with my thinking and analyzing in ways that never do me well. After I would visit the bicycle shop tomorrow, I'd have to endure another trip through Phoenix and pretty much redo today's route. Now,

I'm the type of guy who hates repeats. When I drive to work or common places, often I find alternate routes just for the change. Not to mention, I was nervous about being back in Phoenix—all those people, all those cars. Today I rode well because it was Sunday morning, but what would it be like tomorrow? I pondered ways that I could get a ride back to Florence Junction once my bike was fixed. Phil had to work the next day, so asking him to shuttle me was out of the question. I remembered that my friend Brandi, who lived in Tucson, had mentioned she had tomorrow off and wanted to visit me on my trip. So, I called her and asked if she wanted to meet in Phoenix.

"Sure," said Brandi, "Joel might come with me. He wants to see you as well." Her boyfriend was also a friend of mine.

Make no mistake, I was eager to seen Brandi and Joel in any event, but this was an instance where I needed a favor too. It was one of those times where I didn't want my friend to think I was only contacting her to ask for help. Sometimes when I need a favor, I think of my friends and envision "favor cards" that I can use for them. If the person is a casual acquaintance, I might have one card to spend. If he or she is a close friend, perhaps I have 100 hundred cards. And there are different kinds of cards that can be used for different purposes. There are the friends you'd call if your car broke down and you were stranded at 2 a.m. And there are others that you'd feel comfortable to ask to help move furniture. Others might be the type where you can show up at their house door without an invitation. I pondered, "How many cards did I have with Brandi and Joel? Would they give me a ride?" But all this analyzing was madness. They were the types who'd help anyway they could, and the situation demanded that I ask. After all, I was doing this trip solo.

I explained the situation to Brandi as I paced near the road. "After we hang out, if you could drop me off at Florence Junction—it's kind of east of Phoenix—that would be great. Can you do it?"

"I'll check with Joel and call you back."

I didn't tell Brandi this, but if she couldn't help me, I figured I was done with this trip. For two hours I sat in the desert, walking and taking pictures of the various cacti. The temperature was about eighty degrees, a nice day for Arizona, but the dry air sapped my energy. Even with my sunblock, it felt like my face and arms were sunburning. I also felt anxious about dehydration, for I was down to my last bottle of water.

Finally Phil called back, saying he was in Apache Junction, ten miles away.

"My bike is just past the turnoff for Highway 79," I said, "I'll meet you there."

Soon Phil pulled up, and when I got in the passenger seat, the air conditioning felt wonderful. As he drove us back, I recounted the details of all the day's difficulties.

"It was crazy out there. I don't even know what to say. I've never had such a hard day on the bike," I said. I even told him about this message from God, which by now, had faded into the background, pushed aside by my frustration and sense of abiding incompetence.

Phil listened intently and watched the road as he drove. "It's funny that you had all those bad experiences right after your blissful moment with God," he said, "I don't think that's a coincidence."

I knew what he meant. I do believe that there is an intelligent evil in this world. One who steals, kills and destroys. One who seeks to crush our hearts and our hopes. This satanic spirit hates when people have an intimate connection with God and will do anything to break up that communion.

"That makes sense, because it felt like I had my butt kicked out there. Everything imploded on me. My attitude. My impatience. And all these problems with flat tires and a stupid looped chain."

"Exactly," said Phil, "and you didn't sound like yourself when you called. You're usually confident, and if anything, you're kind of fearless. Nothing stops you. But on the phone, you had this spirit of defeat and confusion. Somehow it got to you."

"I don't know what to say."

"I'll tell you this. It wouldn't surprise me if you were attacked spiritually. How long was it between God speaking to you and when you started having problems?"

"Probably about two minutes," I said, with a chuckle.

"That's all?"

I sighed. I was too frazzled to analyze whatever happened and stared ahead. My morale was in bad shape, and my confidence to handle mechanical matters was shattered. And it felt like it was only a matter of time before the next major problem struck.

There was some silence, then finally, I spoke. "I can't go on like this if I keep having all these problems."

"Maybe you need to take a break."

"Nah, I can't sit around. That'll mess with me more. I have been riding for years. I'm not saying I'm an expert, but I've *never* had so many problems."

"Steve, you need a breather. Are you hungry? Let's go somewhere," said Phil, and I agreed.

Onward we traveled west, back into the city. The plan was for Phil to drive me to a motel near Landis Cyclery. We wouldn't make it there in time because the shop's Sunday hours were shortened. The next morning, when they opened, I'd have them unloop the chain. But that other problem about the route was also swirling in my head. "I will tell you this, if I can't get a ride to Florence Junction after the bike is fixed, I think I'm done. I realize you're working tomorrow and can't drive me, and I'm not asking you to, but I don't want to ride through Phoenix again. That's not an option."

"So would your trip would be over?" he asked.

"Well ..."

I put my head down, not believing what I was saying. I am generally not a quitter, and I think I've developed strong anti-quitting muscles over the years. All in all, I felt like I was prepared for this trip. Physically, my fitness had already become strong. Financially, I had enough, although I had to be careful. And psychologically, I thought my "one day at a time" mindset was good. But all these snags were wearing on me. Three years earlier, I gave myself a challenge of biking a minimum of ten miles everyday, which I did for over five months. During that time, I had an occasional flat tire, but that was it—no other problems. It kept going through my mind that I had all these struggles in just ten days. Would they continue?

Phil's voice grew tender. "Look, at this point, I would totally understand if you stopped. I'm so impressed that you biked to Phoenix. How many miles have you gone so far?"

"About four hundred."

"See, that trips me! That's a lot of distance, and you're doing this all alone! I can tell you that I could never do it by myself. I'd go bonkers at these motels you're staying at alone. And then having your bike stolen would traumatize most people. As for what to do, you have to make this decision for yourself. Know that you could hold your head high if you stopped here. And if that's the route you take, then we'll figure out a way to get you back to San Diego."

I rubbed my forehead. I could barely keep my eyes open, let alone process his advice.

"I don't know … I don't know what to think," I said.

Eventually we stopped at a Del Taco restaurant in Mesa. In the parking lot, I went into the panniers of the bike and put on my sandals. Taking off my socks and shoes brought great relief to my feet, and instantly I felt more human and less angry. I took off my jersey and changed into my spare t-shirt. While my chest was bare, I showed Phil the shingles scars on my body with a grin.

"And that's another thing," he said, in lecture mode. "I would never have started a cross-country ride with that! I heard shingles is painful."

I laughed. "It was, but it doesn't hurt anymore. It's fun to show people to get a reaction out of them."

Inside the fast food joint, we were soon stuffing our faces and talking about things other than bicycling. By the late afternoon, Phil dropped me off at a motel about a mile from the bike shop and gave me one final exhortation. "Remember, you've got to make this decision in the morning. You're too tired right now. Get a good night's sleep and see what things are like in the morning."

That night, everything about my motel room was depressing.

The lighting seemed dimmer than usual. There was nothing interesting on TV to watch. I lay on the bed and stared at my bicycle with the twisted chain. My new bike was already dirty with sand and mud on the frame. It was a gloomy evening all right. I was upset about being back in Phoenix. I've visited this city before and had nice experiences, but on this journey, it felt like I couldn't escape. The devil on my shoulder told me I should fold, but if I did, could I live with that decision? Then it occurred to me: how would Mark feel? He bailed me out with this new bicycle. Granted, I would be working for him to pay for it later regardless of whether I continued, but this wasn't just about finances. I was confused and unable to get myself out of this funk, and I knew I had to call Mark to give him an update. Truth be told, I needed his insight.

"So how's life on the open road with two wheels?" he asked.

"Today was a rough day," I said, and I proceeded with the details.

"If you give up, I understand. I'm at an age where it's a big deal to go for a short run. I won't give you a hard time about that. But you shouldn't quit just because you have forty miles to ride over again. Maybe I say this because of my farming background, but sometimes when you make a mistake, you have to suck it up. Allow yourself to have a do over. I could tell you stories about farming—embarrassing mistakes I've made—and like you said, it's humbling. But you've got to say, 'Let's do a do over.'"

I knew my insistence that I not do a do-over was unreasonable. I was just frazzled over all the problems. My head was in a bad place.[1]

"I need to stop thinking about this and go to sleep soon," I said.

"You do. You sound tired."

Before I did that, I called Brandi and left her a voice mail. I was thinking so negatively that I convinced myself that she probably wouldn't show up—that she and Joel would have something better to do than drive from Tucson to see me. But Brandi returned my call minutes later. "Joel is taking tomorrow off. We both want to see you," she said.

---

[1]   Six years later, as I edit this manuscript one final time, I'm certain that I wouldn't quit over a forty mile do-over ride. I'm a different person now. However, this was the truthful story when it happened in 2008.

My voice rose with joy, "Yeah? You do? This will be great!"

We discussed the details, and we agreed that they'd meet me at the bike shop. After spending time together, they'd take me and my bike back to Florence Junction.

"We're excited to spend time with you," she said.

What a relief! Once more, in the depths of despair, a friend had stepped forward to assist me when I wanted to throw in the towel on myself and my dream. Friends push you to be the best and most you can be, and sometimes without realizing it.

The next morning, the folks at Landis Cyclery undid the loop in the chain in a matter of seconds. The employee demonstrated how to do it a few times, "Don't pull them. Work the loops in toward each other," he said.

"Loops? As in more than one?"

"That's right," he said, as he showed me. "There are two loops in the chain. It's similar to a tangled phone cord. If it's going one way wrong, there is a second spot. Even if you can't see it, if you really work it, you'll probably find both of them. The key is to work both of the loops toward each other, and usually they'll snap back correctly."

Theoretically it made sense and I hoped I learned the trick, but I assured myself that it wouldn't matter, since I'd be extra cautious with the chain if I ever had to mess with the back tire again. The staff was so kind and friendly, and they cleaned up my new bike.

I waited almost two hours before Joel and Brandi arrived at the shop in a bright yellow Toyota FJ Cruiser. I was thrilled to see them.

Brandi came up first and gave me a big hug. Then Joel gave me one.

"So how's Phoenix treating you?" Joel said with a grin.

I laughed. "Uh, that's not a good question."

We put the bike into the back of the SUV and got settled inside.

Joel has long blonde hair and is in his upper 40s. He looks like he could be a lead guitarist in a rock band. He's a devout "desert rat," who hikes and explores the desert in all seasons, particularly in southern Arizona near the U.S. and Mexico border. We've done some hiking together as well, including climbing Picacho Peak.

And then there was Brandi. She wore a big smile and looked happier than usual, perhaps since dating Joel. Brandi wore glasses, had short brown hair, and wore a pretty green top and jeans. She works full-time as a nurse.

"So what are we doing?" asked Brandi.

"I don't know," said Joel, "What *are* we doing?"

"We're just here to see Steve," she said.

"Awww," I uttered with a smile.

We ended up not doing too much. We mainly talked in their vehicle as we drove in search of a place to have lunch. As we cruised, I got caught up about the latest in their lives and I told them about my trip so far. Then we passed a line of orange trees beside the road.

"By the way, I want to say you live in paradise. Look at those orange trees!"

"Spoken like a true snowbird. It's February right now. You need to come in the summer," said Joel.

"I would. I love the hot weather."

"There's always a spare room at my place. You know that."

I sure did. "But really Joel, look how warm it is. It's February tenth and it feels like it's seventy-five or eighty. And there's orange trees! Can you believe that? There are freakin' orange trees growing on the side of the road. You know what fruits grow in the wild in my part of Colorado?"

"What?"

"Snow. That's it. Snow and nothing!"

Brandi started laughing in the back seat. "I need to get a picture of you while you get this animated."

And so I turned so Brandi could get an angle as I went on another ranting.

"Seriously, if you're down-and-out in Phoenix, you could eat oranges and that's good nutrition!" I shouted, "You could go for a walk and pull one off and eat it as you exercise!"

"No, you can't," replied Joel, "They're ornamental oranges. You can't eat them."

"Aw, they're like gourds? Those funny-shaped things in the fall?" The wind was knocked out of my sails.

We were having a good time, and we decided to find a Chinese buffet restaurant. Joel paid our way. How generous. In the restaurant parking lot, Brandi snapped a photo of me. Wearing my cycling attire, I stood with my hands on my hips, like a model posing.

"Your legs are more muscular," she said.

I didn't see a difference, but appreciated the compliment.

As our visit was ending and we traveled toward the east side of Phoenix, I kept saying how much I appreciated them driving me to Florence Junction.

"No problem," Joel said. "We drive this route on our way from Tucson to Phoenix anyway. It avoids the traffic on the interstate."

As we passed Apache Junction, the scenery replayed, with the Superstition Mountains on the left and saguaros and desert fields to the right. The area where I had my first flat . . . and the second flat . . . then the spot where I had the meltdown with the looped chain.

"Let's pass this area a bit. I don't want any bad vibes from this spot," I said. A half mile up, I directed Joel to pull over.

As I got my bike out of their SUV, Joel stood by smoking a cigarette, while Brandi had already sauntered into the desert to photograph saguaros. The mountains in the distance made for some pretty scenery too. Then I joined Brandi and we wandered together. But soon, it was time for me to leave. Joel was inspecting my bicycle and playing with the brake levers, then he handed it over to me and said with a big brother tone, "I want you to be safe, okay?"

I nodded and gave both of them strong, tight hugs, and then I took off. Thanks to the help of my friends, back on the road, I was alone and capable.

Emotions flooded through me.

Joy. Thankfulness. Awe.

"I can't believe everything turned out okay," I said to myself.

Was this the pivotal moment in my trip? I had problems in Blythe and was given a second chance. Then there was the stolen bike crisis. I survived that too. And now, a third time, there was more trouble and triumph. Would I really have quit without a ride from Joel and Brandi? I don't know. However what for them was a simple favor, given freely as friends do, had resuscitated this journey.

The truth is, I am a weak man who's driven to worry. I struggle with having confidence. I get trapped into negative patterns of thinking when problems arise. I also don't know as much about bicycle mechanics as I thought I did. But as I biked forward, it felt like I was destined to finish. Nothing could stop me. God would get me through.

Today's ride would be a short one, only fifteen miles to Superior, but the distance didn't matter. At one point, I stopped to photograph Picketpost Mountain, a former volcano and an enormous landmark from the road. With the bike between my legs and my feet down, I looked up and glowed with a huge smile. That big blue sky had its grip on me and wouldn't let go. I was cycling under a triumphant sky.

Starting at the beach in Del Mar, California

Highway 78 between Julian and Brawley

The Imperial Sand Dunes

Greg at Fred's Kawasaki in Blythe

Biking into Arizona via Interstate 10

The Dick Wick Hall grave in Salome

Me and my red Giant bicycle on the morning of the day that it was stolen

The motel clerk in Phoenix was so kind and sympathetic to me over my situation

The new road bike

A Chipotle burrito with my buddy Phil

Leaving Florence Junction and headed east

The Queen Creek Tunnel

Looking back at my route with Mount Graham in the distance

Snow highlighted the scenery as I biked out of Reserve, New Mexico

A lonely highway on the Plains of San Agustin, near the Very Large Array

My cycling friend Dave, the only person to bike alongside me on the journey

U.S. Highway 380 in eastern New Mexico

CHAPTER VIII

INTO THE LAND OF SOLITUDE

There are three ways to pedal a bike.
With the legs,
with the lungs,
or with the heart.

Mandible Jones, Carpet Particles

*D*awn is a special time. There is that point in the early morning when the pitch-blackness of night has broken, but there really isn't much light. The sky is a dark and vivid blue, and the temperature is cool. Everything is dim and muted. Any birds or crickets who clamored throughout the night have quieted. Dawn, what it represents, elicits the reflection of creative people. So many poets have written fluffy platitudes about it—things about the awakening, the birth to a new day and a time when the spirit is refreshed and hopeful. For us humans, if you're often on your feet and moving at dawn, it might be because you have a job with early hours or you happen to be one of those "morning people." Whatever the case, early risers usually agree that they did the right thing, because it leads to productivity. And for cyclists, all things lead to getting on our bikes and spinning our wheels.

As I brought my bicycle outside my motel room in Superior, this was the enthusiasm I felt at "o'dark-thirty." This, I hoped, would be the day that I'd start having longer cycling days, for Safford (102 miles away) was today's destination. I got on the two-lane highway and my zeal was squashed by hard, heavy breathing. In fact, I had no warm-up time for what was ahead. As soon as I left town limits, the road rose sharply at an eight percent grade, winding through a rocky canyon.

Taking it slow in granny gear, I stood up on the pedals and went three times with each leg in rhythm, then I rested for two precious seconds before the bike succumbed to gravity. I did that routine and anything else I could think of for three miles, with my legs in agony, my shoulders in shock and me sucking air. My thoughts—that part of the human body that's committed to self-preservation—tried to convince me that enduring this pain wasn't worth it, but I blocked them out. I told myself that at this plodding pace of four miles per hour, at least I was moving swifter than the average person walking. I tried to mentally list all the things I'm grateful for, but I just couldn't—not with all this distress. Instead, every wretched, evil, vengeful thought tormented me. There was arguing over contentious political topics, beating up people who've wronged me and replaying ugly childhood memories of bullies twenty-five years ago. "Stinking thinking" is what it's called in twelve-step recovery groups, and oh did I have it on this grueling climb.

At five miles, I approached the Queen Creek Tunnel, a concrete tube a quarter mile in length. Here, the canyon was too narrow and steep for the road to possibly work up the valley, and so the structure was built through the north wall of the canyon. Inside the tunnel, the lighting was funny. Was it morning? Evening? If one were stuck here and not facing the ends, it would be hard to tell. An oncoming car passed through; its engine rumbled loudly with the echo. It prompted me to pedal harder to get through quickly, but the topography worked against me. I was hardly over a crawl by cycling standards. A short distance out, I rested. I got off the bike, leaned it against a guard rail, and turned back to marvel at the architecture of this Queen Creek Tunnel. Considering the massiveness of the canyon wall, it's amazing to think of all the work that went into it, from engineers who crafted the blue print, to the people who dynamited the hole and kept it from crumbling down, and then the precise work of laying out the road.

It was now over an hour into my ride, and my blood was rushing so much that I couldn't stand still. I paced back and forth. I drank fluids and chomped on blackberries. And I admired the scenery of what my map marked as Devils Canyon. Magnificent red rock spires adorned the canyon's upper walls. There were pretty yucca plants on the roadside and growing precariously on cliff ledges. Two hawks soared above, one making a scolding call to the other as if asserting his authority over the domain. Steep climbs are rarely fun, but at least the dramatic change in elevation gave me wonderful things to look at.

Eventually I got back on the bike, and the uphill continued. For more miles, I was tempted to stop once more, or even better, turn around and travel back downhill. Surely, I could have sped backward to the motel without pedaling, but I had to press on. I had to attack this hill.

The temperature was warming. By now, the sun had risen fully. Ahead, a sign read, "6% downward grade, next twelve miles." I got excited, like a kid who knows the brunt of the school day is over and the recess bell will ring at any minute. But as I continued, there were more rolling hills. Sure there were some descents, but there was a lot of demanding climbing too. I couldn't believe it. Was that sign wrong? Where were all the downhills? With some anger and self-pity, I told myself that I'd send a complaint letter to the Arizona Department of Transportation for their deceptive sign. But right there, what could I do? Throw my bike down and have a temper tantrum?

There were other mental struggles as I fought those hills. I worried about flat tires. This new bike was performing nicely, but what if I got more flats? The better question was, *when* would I get my next flat? How would I handle it? Beside the road were power lines, and when the wind blew hard, the vibration of the lines made a high-pitched sound that was similar to a tire going flat. There were also birds chirping and noisy gusts of wind. Any shrieky sound like that had me checking my tires.

In a crest in the road, I passed an area named Top of the World, elevation 4,600 feet. Based on the name, I hoped I was at a high point of all this climbing, and a short distance ahead, I was. Finally, there were downward hills for miles. My wheels were devouring the pavement. In one grand descent, I was cruising at twenty-five miles per hour—about eight times my speed when I was grunting like a snail out of Superior. Part of me felt like I was cheating to be going this fast, but surely I had earned this. All the anguish from the morning climb melted away. In fact, when I'm speeding this fast, I feel so positive. Like anything is possible and dreams can come true.

The road bottomed in Miami—no, not the south Florida city with beautiful beaches—but the prospecting boom-and-bust town of Miami, Arizona. A few miles ahead, I entered Globe, Miami's larger sister city and the seat of Gila County. This region was founded on mining in the late nineteenth century, and it has one of the few copper smelters in the country that remains in operation today. It was founded on the frontier with much of the old western associations of gun fighting, saloons, gambling and prostitution, in part from the disproportionately bigger percentage of men who worked in the mines.

On the main avenue, I rested at a convenience store and bought a banana, crackers and drinks, feeling proud to have covered twenty-five miles. It was a good time to relax and people-watch as I faced the gas pumps. Two teens, a boy and girl, were having their car towed, and from what I could hear, it was because they had expired registration tags. A truck driver was delivering merchandise with a dolly. Other people entered and exited the mart. Then a station wagon rolled up to the pumps, and an older man with a cowboy hat entered the store with a boy straggling behind. When the kid saw me and the bike, he grew curious. He was cute for his age—maybe nine or ten years old—with a baseball cap and freckles.

"What are you doing?" he asked.

"I'm biking to Safford."

"Why?"

I chuckled.

"I'm biking across the country. Everyday I ride."

His eyes widened.

"Really?"

Then he darted inside, apparently to tell the man he was with. Minutes later, they were both outside. The man's name was Don, the grandfather of the boy.

"It does look like you're going far," he said, "In what direction are you headed?"

"East."

He smiled. "Last year I met a guy who was biking in the opposite direction. He was finishing in California. By then, he was riding fast because he had to get home and start a new job."

I understood.

"So why are you doing this?" he asked.

It was an easy question, but I didn't have an answer. I was dumbfounded. It was obvious that he didn't intend to stump me and was just making conversation. I hemmed and hawwed. Then I said, "I've always wanted to do it."

"And why did you chose to go east?"

"The wind is more friendly. Plus it's better to get the mountains over with."

I answered that one without hesitation. I knew better.

"Doing it for charity?"

"No."

I felt embarrassed to say that. A search on the Internet for other bike tours will show that many do it to raise money for charity or to spread awareness for a cause. For me, the preparation, including coming up with the financial resources to do this trip, was hard enough work. If I promoted a charity, I'd want to go all out and I don't know much about how to gain publicity. No, I wanted to keep this real. I was doing this trip for myself. I was the charity.

"Do you have a sponsor?" he asked.

"No, I wish," I said modestly, "To be honest, thousands of people do this every year. You'd have to be really special or lucky to find someone generous enough to pay for your trip."

"What about a corporate sponsor?" he contended.

"That's a nice idea."

"You could make a plea to a company," he said, "like a bicycle manufacturer or any big corporation. They usually have money budgeted specifically for public relations. Make a formal request with public relations departments, and if they like your proposal, they could make you a jersey with their logo and they could help you financially too. All the while, they benefit from associating with you and your cause."

I laughed. "You think a company would want to associate with me?"

"Sure," he said.

I could have argued with him, but I didn't say anything more. Personally, I viewed my bike tour as a vacation, even if it was a sadistic sabbatical that made tremendous physical demands on me for the next seven weeks. Why should someone pay my way? If I went to Hawaii and relaxed on beaches for a week, should I expect someone to sponsor me? And what if I dedicated that Hawaiian vacation to a charity? You know, I walked around the beaches "spreading awareness" for some charity by handing out leaflets. It would be absurd to expect to get financial support. Having said that, I would never discourage anyone from trying.

"Just the fact that you biked from Superior this morning is impressive," he said. Then he turned to his grandson, "The boy got his first mountain bike this winter and he's been riding it a lot."

The boy nodded. He looked up to me like a hero.

"Have fun on your bike. Mountain bike trails can be more wild and dangerous, so be safe," I said.

"Oh he is," said Don.

Then they wished me the best and went on their way. As they were driving out, the boy watched me through the window as if he wanted to join me. Maybe I planted a seed.

Miles ahead, I entered the San Carlos Apache Indian Reservation. Few homes or neighborhoods were visible from the highway, making it a different world from the bustling city of Phoenix or even Globe. The desolation was unsettling in some respects, but I'd gladly choose remoteness over roads with unrelenting traffic and little shoulder. The warmer weather was still pleasant: sunny with not a cloud in the sky. It was a perfect day for cycling.

After crossing the Gila River, I biked on another long and gradual ascent. At the top, mountains of all kinds—some brown, some gray, some pointy, some rounded—lay on the horizon. A nearby hillside had hundreds of saguaros that appeared like a silent army marching across the sands. Nature's beauty clashed with humanity's propensity to make a mess of things. Litter and glass, mainly broken bottles and aluminum beer cans, lined the highway's edge for miles. The shoulder was mostly clear, but I had to be vigilant about avoiding glass that might be ahead. My peripheral vision was constantly attracted to shimmering light of the brown, blue and clear shades of glass. The debris was so plentiful that it looked like people had a contest: find a clear spot from your car and toss your alcohol-related litter right there.

The sun's intensity grew as I continued through the desert. I knew it would be a tough day, and I put everything out of my mind. "Just enjoy the ride," I said to myself, "... if you can." I thought about my struggle to respond when Don asked me why I was doing this trip and I chuckled to myself. How could I not have an answer ready? I faced down and observed the cadence of my upper legs and bike frame. I do enjoy cycling—the pace, the impressive fitness it gives me and even doing it outside. But realistically, I find myself in physical anguish to go such long distances. In fact, I think I like cycling most when I'm done with a day's ride. Riding a bike is kind of like writing. Many writers don't enjoy the process of arranging words on paper that flow and make sense. Truly, it is a difficult activity, but writing becomes worth it when one's effort leads to a successful product. When one has completed a masterpiece—a novel, a collection of short stories, or that perfect poem—the feeling can be sensational and the pain is forgotten. For me,

I have a similar joyous feeling when my cyclometer reads that I've gone something like sixty, eighty or one-hundred miles in a day.

I heard the sound of a tractor-trailer about a mile off behind me. The engine noise grew louder and louder as it approached. Then it moved past in the center of the highway (to give me space) with a climactic swooping wind. The hum of its wheels on the pavement faded as it sped into the distance. Then, it was quiet once again. So much of biking across America is being in the middle-of-nowhere with nature all around you. It's just you and your thoughts, with perhaps the sounds of the wind and cars or trucks whooshing past.

My lower back started to ache, but I didn't feel like stopping. That would only prolong this ride. I went on auto-pilot with my legs working on their own. My sciatica flared up, a sharp nerve pain that shot down my right leg. By the sixty-mile mark, my lower right back had become so tight that I had to stop. Throughout my thirties, I've had to see a chiropractor for chronic back and neck discomfort, and being in the same stationary position on the bike was probably an aggravating factor. As I paced and stretched, I dug my fingers into my lower right back, the makeshift massage providing relief. I was tired—very tired—but I was getting used to it. By this point, feeling physically good was not a necessary condition for riding. On this day, the road was relaxed, my bike was operating well, and my tires were holding air. Thus, I didn't have much to complain about. Getting back on the bike, I reminded myself of the writing analogy as I pedaled and stared ahead at the shoulder: if I just hang in there, I'll be so happy with my accomplishment when this is all over.

Quickly coming to my vision was a large chunk of glass, and it was too late to avoid it. I dodged it with my front tire, but my back tire bumped over it with a squeak. I yelled an expletive and inspected the tire, but it was fine. Without stopping, I leaned back and put my hand over the tire; if anything was lodged on it's outer edge, my gloves should have caught it. Sure, I might have cut my fingers or hand, but in that moment the risk was worth it to learn immediately whether I'd have to deal with another flat.

As if I needed to be tested more, ahead was another challenge: roadkill. At first, I smelled it. It was the pungent scent of a dead animal—an awful stink. Then, I saw it. It was the remains of a carcass below the guardrail that may have been a dog. As I got closer, I instinctively held my nose. However, an oncoming car was near and I felt silly to be seen doing that, and so I stuck my nose under my shirt and held my breath. That seemed to work, but of course, I had to breathe in and get one last whiff before getting far enough away. Three miles ahead, there was more roadkill. This one, a dead deer, lay on the shoulder. Gruesome. Horribly stinky. At least in this case there were no cars and I went to the far side of the road to avoid the stench.

Riding on the reservation continued. Near Bylas I encountered two other bicyclists, a man and a woman, on the roadside beside fat-tire mountain bikes carrying lots more gear than I had. The woman was sitting, apparently resting.

"Is everything okay?" I asked.

Little did they know that I didn't have much confidence in my ability to help after what I had gone through in Phoenix.

"We're okay," the woman said with a European accent.

"Where are you headed?"

"Safford," replied the man. He didn't say anything else.

With all that gear, this couple had to be riding on a multi-day tour like I was, but I didn't feel like telling them about my mission. Maybe we could have traded notes about our experiences, but fatigue crushed my willingness to engage.

"All right, have a good one," I said, and then I rode off.

A short distance ahead, I couldn't believe what I had done. Usually I'm such a people person. Then again, they didn't ask me anything; maybe I had caught them during an argument. As exhausted as I was, I didn't want to start a conversation for risk that the interaction might be lengthy and drawn out, which would require more energy. Still, I felt bad. Opportunities like this are what make long-distance bike tours memorable. You never know how we might have helped each other, even if only with encouraging words. I continued riding, thinking perhaps they'd catch up to me and then we'd connect later.

Outside the reservation now and approaching Fort Thomas, I was at seventy-nine miles. Relatively speaking, I was nearing the end. Twenty-three more miles to Safford would be a cinch. In this small town, with a general store, grain elevator and intersection of two highways, I'd have my first confrontation with a vehicle. A tractor-trailer behind me honked its horn. I turned back and noticed it was an ordinary semi. I moved as far to the right as I could, although that wasn't much, with only one foot of pavement right of the white line.

The trucker honked again. Again, I turned back to assess the situation. Sometimes trucks have wide loads and that's something to be cautious about, but that wasn't the case here. He had plenty of room to pass me safely, especially if he moved a little toward the center.

He honked a third time.

Sir, you have enough room to pass me safely.

This was becoming a standoff, and I wasn't budging. I was biking legally and had a right to be on the road as much as anyone else, including him.

Then another protracted honk reverberated as the truck passed within inches of me. *What a jerk!* If that driver had pulled over, I may not have been able to control my anger. There would have been a fight—one that wouldn't have ended until one of us couldn't fight anymore. I stared ahead with my meanest face toward the side view mirror of that semi as it disappeared into the horizon. I was boiling. It was one of those instances when they say you should count to ten before doing or saying anything. I wished that truck would tumble down a cliff on one of these mountain passes.

In cycling terms, the act of a motorist passing a bicyclist too closely is known as "buzzing." Sometimes it may be done unintentionally or out of ignorance, but that wasn't the case here, especially with that antagonistic horn slam at the end. Buzzing can be a passive-aggressive way to "get even" with bicyclists. It's a tactic by drivers to express their frustration when they don't appreciate the hassle of slowing down to pass safely. Other times, it can be a way to make a statement that the driver doesn't think a cyclist should be on the road at all. Whatever the case, buzzing is dangerous and when done intentionally, it is reckless driving. Most states require motorists to pass cyclists with a minimum of three feet clearance.

As the intensity of the moment faded, I made a decision. If a tractor-trailer honks and there's not much shoulder, I'd simply pull over. Just turn the bike to the right, put my feet down, face the driver and wave with a smile. Kill him with kindness. My mission would not be ruined by a game of chicken with a trucker who could kill me or lure me into an ugly road rage incident. So many trucks had passed me by now, and almost all had been courteous. It wasn't worth battling the one "bad apple" in a massive hunk of metal from the saddle of my tiny bicycle. In any such fight, I was certain to lose. Pride had to take a back seat, and so I let the incident go.

The ride to Safford now seemed longer than it should, and my lower back continued to bother me. It seemed like I couldn't gain much speed in this flat valley. Eventually I arrived in Thatcher, with ninety-seven miles down and a short distance remaining to neighboring Safford. Highway 70 through the town had two lanes in each direction and a center lane for turning left.

Ahead, a car heading in my direction stopped in the left lane to make a left turn, mistakenly not using the center turning lane. Many cars waited behind it, no doubt frustrated at this driver's error. As I came closer, the car directly behind me in the right lane apparently didn't feel safe passing me, although there was plenty of room for both a car and my bike to share the lane. Thus, a miniature traffic jam formed until I passed this stationary vehicle on the left. As that happened, many cars passed and I received the brunt of one young man's frustration.

"Get on the sidewalk!" he shouted.

I turned to him, and I didn't smile or wave like I told myself after the trucker episode. It was hard to feel sympathy for someone who had to wait some extra seconds, when I had biked this far in seven hours. Again, I must repeat that it was perfectly legal for me to use the road. Some behind the wheel believe the myths that "bikes belong on sidewalks" and "the road is for cars only." However in most cities, it is illegal to ride a bicycle on sidewalks, and studies have suggested that it's twice as hazardous as riding in traffic. Additionally, bicyclists on sidewalks pose a danger to pedestrians.

At last I arrived in Safford, and found a lower-end motel on the main avenue with my cyclometer reading 102 miles. This was the second "century ride" of my life. Inside my room, I lay on the bed and didn't have the energy to carry myself to the shower, despite being so smelly and stinky. I merely turned on the television and watched it like a vegetable. After an hour, hunger pangs finally motivated me to get up and wash, and then I headed to a nearby Chinese buffet restaurant. There's something wonderful about a buffet, knowing you pay one price and can eat all you want. With the ride done, it didn't matter if I stuffed myself without shame, for I would be sleeping soon anyway. Spare ribs, a pile of spicy chicken, two egg rolls, cheese wontons, beef and broccoli, all under replenishing layers of rice. Add in a soft serve chocolate ice cream cone with caramel and nuts, and my stomach was in its own state of euphoria.

After shopping for tomorrow's supplies at a convenience store, I returned to my room, plopped onto the bed and sighed. After an initial energy burst from the delight of today's accomplishment, my body crashed. *Just put me in a casket and let me sleep forever.* I felt pathetic. My lower back was sore. My upper legs had a sharp ache. I couldn't do anything. Heck, I didn't *want* to do anything.

I considered tomorrow's plan to bike to Glenwood, New Mexico, about eighty-five miles. The most I had ever biked in a two-day period was 150 miles, and this two-day series would total 187. No doubt my stamina and mental toughness would be tested. I did my best to help my body recover; that meant going to sleep early and minimizing all physical activity. As a rule, I refrained from using my bicycle to explore towns once I finished a day's ride. If something interesting was not within walking distance, I didn't go there. No more riding . . . period. Why would I want to? I had to get off that bike for physical reasons, but also for my psychological state. If there was anything Safford had to offer outside of this four-lane highway by the motel, I missed it. It was a night like many others: ordinary, kind of lonely and close to a highway. For better or worse, this was how biking across America was shaping up for me.

I remained horizontal, too lazy to get beneath the bed sheets, and I gave myself instructions: *Don't move. Don't exert energy. Rest. You have a long ride tomorrow!* Soon I was close to dozing and I got myself under the sheets at 7:30 p.m. Through the gap in the curtains of the window, I saw the European couple with their bikes. They had the room next to me! I considered stopping by and greeting them; it seemed like the neighborly thing to do. Here was the chance to interact with them again, but the required effort to lift myself out of bed and walk next door was too much. Through the wall between us, I heard the woman cough—a constant hack that sounded like she was sick. I felt bad for her, and thought how sad it would be to see your wife struggling like that on a long distance bike tour. My overworking conscience asked again, "Should I knock on the door?" The physical side swiftly voted against it. At least the woman had her husband to care for her, I rationalized.

***

The next morning, I was gone early and tried to get into my cycling routine. Even though the road was flat beyond Safford, quite a contrast from yesterday's grueling climb out of Superior, my body resisted. Again, I was cranky and didn't want to go, kind of like a child who doesn't want to get out of bed, dress themselves and hit the bus stop to start their school day. I'm convinced there are neurological factors to this; the lack of energy makes me prone to think negatively. Maybe it's why a caffeine addict grows dependent on their morning jolt to get going.

Outside of town, I turned north on U.S. Highway 191 in what seemed like no man's land. My map indicated there was an ascent for eighteen miles into Tollgate Canyon, but first I was toiling uphill on the plains. There was nothing but yellow grass past the pavement: no homes or ranches for miles as the road stretched straight toward the mountain range ahead. As usual, my legs bore the brunt. While the scenery was different from yesterday, there was one similarity to this climb: I felt the temptation to turn back. Surely I would have if I lived in Safford, but I had to continue. I couldn't wimp out. It's a mixed blessing when you're committed to a goal. Your determination gives you peace, but you've got to endure the pain as well.

An hour later, I finally reached the mouth of the canyon. As I slowly gained elevation, I kept trying those mental tricks to encourage myself—anything to get my mind off the anguish. I replayed 1970s disco tunes and upbeat 1980s songs in my head. I dreamed about the celebration I'd have with friends when this cross-country tour was done. I envisioned music blaring with people having a good time on the dance floor, and of course, I was in the middle of it. I fantasized that between songs, I'd grab a microphone and tell everyone about the time I struggled up this pass in eastern Arizona, when I overcame weariness and made it to the top. In my own world, I was the hero this morning. Out of necessity.

I stared at the shoulder, watching the varieties of weeds slip by. I didn't know their names, but I was becoming an expert in recognizing the kinds. There were noisy bugs, some snapping their wings loudly. I noticed the rocks on the edge—some natural, some the result of the asphalt's decay. There were culverts too. And litter. Always litter. Some roads had signs about fines for littering, but I guess you have to get caught first.

After reaching the broad summit, as always the downhill drastically transformed my experience. I sped down, gliding weightless through the miles. As I rode, I pondered the nature of climbs. It takes hours to struggle up a pass and only minutes to descend. All that work, and then the quick, delightful payoff. It's like a Thanksgiving meal where you spend hours buying, preparing and cooking the food, and then the crowd spends half an hour eating it. Is it worth it? Of course. Especially when you do it out of love. It's the same with biking, but how I wished the descent was the longer of the two!

I sped toward a construction area, which narrowed the road to two slim lanes for traffic and no shoulder. No worries, though, because

Into the Land of Solitude

the speed limit was specially marked at twenty-five miles per hour, with stern warnings about speeding. Since I was flying at that pace, I confidently grabbed the center of the lane and rode with cars in front and behind. Finally, the road leveled into a valley in Three Way. This was another spot marked on my map that didn't appear to be a town; it was only a junction of highways. I took the road traveling east and saw a sign that read, "New Mexico State Line 20 Mule Creek NM 32."

Today's destination was Glenwood, New Mexico, about fifteen miles past Mule Creek. My cyclometer read thirty-nine miles; forty-seven more seemed reasonable. Then I got a better sense of the terrain I would be riding in, and knew loneliness would be my full-time partner for the remainder of the day. This new road seemed even more isolated than the one through Tollgate Canyon. This was a two-lane highway that traveled northeast toward mountains, and way up on the range, I could see a road with numerous switchbacks. Was that my route up there? With distress, I realized it was. Ahead would be a more grueling climb than the first one. I put down my head and charged the mountain like a bull ... at the humbling pace of eight miles per hour.

The road became dusty, windy and lonely. Depending on how much I allowed fear to intervene, this could be a scary ride. Few signs of humanity could be found in this region, and hardly any vehicles passed me—about one car every five minutes. Looking at my map, I could see why most people have no reason to drive here, since no major towns or prominent destinations exist on either end. The sun broke through and warmed the midday as I biked slowly into this land of solitude.

Bicycling solo across America was proving to be a lonely experience. Sure, I had many friends help me so far, and even when I was at a convenience store, I had some pleasant encounters. Still, it felt reclusive. I guess I wasn't surprised by this, but I think the barrenness of the land contributed to what I felt inside. A week before my trip started, a woman at my church suggested that I'd have many meaningful interactions with people. "You will be Jesus to the people you meet," she insisted. I liked her idea, and looked forward to making friends or helping others anyway I could. But after two weeks of cycling across

California and Arizona, I think I could have been Jesus to a lot more people and with less physical rigor if I'd stayed home and mustered the courage to knock on the doors of my neighbors. While it felt funny to think this way, my reality was that I needed people to be Jesus to me. I was the one without a car, roaming in unfamiliar towns and dining by myself in restaurants. There was a greater chance that I would be the one who'd have problems that required the help of another.

After two hours, I reached the top. My fitness was becoming exceptional. My legs were becoming trunks of steel. On the other side of the crest, the road went through forest. I enjoyed plenty of downhill grades, even though the slopes weren't as extreme as on the other side. Soon I hit the New Mexico state line and stopped briefly for a picture by the sign. The sky was becoming gray. The temperature was dropping. A new wind from the north had a bite that chilled me to the bone. I put on all three of my layers and pushed ahead.

Near sixty miles, I reached Mule Creek—not much of a town and no services besides a post office that was closed. More fatigue. Crosswinds that menaced me. And then there were more hills—this time a mix of ups and downs that made it difficult to cruise at a regular speed.

Eventually I reached Glenwood, with eighty-five miles logged and two major passes conquered, and I checked in at the only motel in town. Thankfully Jill, my online researcher, had called ahead to confirm its rates and vacancies. I was elated to be moving along, a torrent on two wheels for the past two days. To think, only forty-eight hours ago, I was with Brandi and Joel in Phoenix. How far I had come.

CHAPTER IX

TRAVELER IN NEW MEXICO

I've been absolutely terrified all of my life —
and I've never let it keep me
from doing a single thing I wanted to do.

Georgia O'Keeffe

New Mexico, when I think of it, has the remnants of a love story. I first visited the state at age twenty-three on a cross-country drive, and I fell in love with its wide open spaces, dreamy shades of sandy desert and captivating landscapes. I couldn't put it into words, but I felt that the state deserved its nickname: the Land of Enchantment. In New Mexico, there's a promise. The charm of peace.

On that visit, I stayed in Truth or Consequences and was swept in by its slower culture, the hot springs, and the fact that there was only one traffic light in the whole town. To live in southern New Mexico, where it's hot and dry, would be a dream come true. Three years later, I had everything packed in my car, nose pointed toward Las Cruces.

Within two days of my arrival, I met two New Mexico State University students who offered me a spare bedroom for weekly rent. I was elated. It was September; most days were sunny and summer-like. The apartment complex had a pool. As trivial as it might seem looking back, I felt I was set.

I had no job when I set out, but decided to move first and then find work. The job hunt was difficult. I was relatively fresh out of college with a bachelor's degree in political science, and I didn't know what I wanted to do or what I was qualified for. And Las Cruces wasn't a budding metropolis brimming with entry-level jobs. Quickly I became discouraged. I had no family or close friends in town, and after a short time, I left and was pretty sure I wasn't coming back. I had given up. Instead, friends to the north in Colorado Springs offered to host me and let me stay on their couch until I figured things out. They were friendly faces; I needed that. Within days of reaching the city, I found a job at a radio station, and that was enough to convince me to settle in Colorado.

Still, the power surrounding New Mexico reaches deep into my soul to this very day. The imagery. The impressions. Heat and desert, but not quite as hot and dry as Arizona. Mountains, but not quite as mountainous as neighboring Colorado. A rich Spanish history and heritage, settled in the late 1500s by Spaniards from Mexico, claiming the land for the Spanish Crown. The native lands of twenty-two Indian tribes with names like Apache, Navajo, Zuni and Comanche. It is underpopulated compared to the coast lands, with many regions destitute with poverty. There are the creative meccas of Santa Fe and Taos—artsy, liberal, and wealthy. There are conservative communities like Artesia and Hobbs that are rooted in ranching and the oil and gas industry. And then there's Albuquerque, the most populated city and economic nerve center of the state. There is also the chile growing industry that plays a prominent role to New Mexican culture. There is red chile, green chile, and when combined together on a dish, it's named "Christmas chile." In fact, the state government officially decreed the state question as "Red or green?"

These were my impressions of the state, and my heart embraced the romance of this Land of Enchantment. Although I've settled in

Colorado for sixteen years, I still find myself yearning for New Mexico's arid expanse, its isolation and its beauty. The lure and mystery of the state tugs at my heart, and I wonder, "What if . . .?"

***

After two long rides, I needed a short day.

A thirty-five mile excursion over Saliz Pass (elevation 6,435 feet) brought me into Reserve, a village with a population of only 387. It's size has no bearing to its local stature, as Reserve holds the distinction of being the seat of Catron County. I checked in at the sole motel, then strolled across the town's width in ten minutes. There was a grocery store, a bar, a bank and two restaurants. The courthouse was a humble brick building with an American flag flapping strongly and the New Mexico flag below. Plenty of trucks, covered in dirt and mud, were parked on the main drag. Either their owners were hard-working types or they lived on rugged dirt roads. Perhaps it was both. The hamlet seemed like an unpretentious mountain town that was not trying to impress anyone. Also, to give a true back-in-the-day feeling, there was no cellular service. In Reserve, the past holds on, and the future waits in the wings.

I debated where to eat and asked two men for a recommendation.

"We're eating there," one answered, as they entered Ella's Cafe. Their actions spoke louder than words. I followed.

The cafe was a homey place with country-themed items hung on the walls. My waitress was a pretty woman with brown hair down her back. She seemed like a pro—the way she welcomed me and called me "hon" when she brought me to my table. She gave me a menu and I told her about myself.

"You biked here? From where?" she asked.

"California."

"On purpose?"

I laughed and pulled out my camera. "I can show you pictures if you don't believe me."

"I do. You look like a biker," she said with a smile, "When I was younger, I was very active and ran on the track team and played soccer.

With the high school soccer team, we barely had enough girls for the squad, so you played the entire game. Those were the good old days. When you're young, it feels like you're invincible and you have extra reserves of energy that you can tap into. But right now, I could never do what you're doing. My body would drop. Chasing after my kids—my youngest being two—that's my exercise."

I laughed.

"Well, you'll get back into it," I said.

"There is one thing that I'm worried about. You came at the wrong time of year. Do you realize we're getting snow tomorrow?"

I waved my hand down and said, "We'll see. I'm not worried."

"I like your attitude," she replied.

She asked for my order and it didn't take long to decide. Once I read that they served a green chile bacon cheeseburger with guacamole, I knew what I wanted.

She jotted down my order and then said, "By the way, nothing ever happens in our dinky little town. You're a big deal."

"No way," I said, with a laugh.

"No really, you are."

"Believe me, biking across America is not that big of a deal," I said. She rolled her eyes like I was ridiculous, and then I added, "Wait. Are you saying *I'm* a big deal or my bike trip is a big deal?"

She paused for a moment, then said, "Both." Then she tended to another table.

At first, I figured she said it to stroke my ego and get a larger tip, but she was so kind and down-to-earth. I knew she meant it.

I thought about my "not a big deal" statement. It was one of those times where the words came out and I wasn't sure if I meant it. I put my feet up on the chair across from me, and I pondered.

This bike tour, so far, felt like an experience I had with climbing a mountain. I first gazed on a peak named Emma Burr Mountain (elevation 13,544 feet) in the Sawatch Range of Colorado just a few years ago. It is an obscure mountain with a base that's only accessible with a four-wheel-drive vehicle. The peak's name intrigued me—Emma

Burr. Who was this woman? Was she a child? Was she a nurse or doctor who served the medical needs of the first settlers? Did the name have to do with a mining claim? I couldn't find any information. On my first attempt, a friend and I began our climb, but we turned back when rain and thunder became a major threat. That fueled my desire to summit the mountain even more. The next year, with me full of excitement and anticipation, we went at it a second time and reached the top successfully. However, throughout the morning our hike felt ordinary; it was a "one step at a time" journey. The summit views were stunning and there was a sense of accomplishment, but there were no trumpets blaring from the heavens. While the "doing it" was ordinary, it was the "having done it" that made it special.

And that's what I meant when I declared that this journey didn't feel like a big deal. It was one day of riding after another, like any other cyclist who bikes on a daily basis, but I just so happened to be traveling in one direction. I wanted to explain this to my waitress, but the opportunity seemed gone, and I didn't want to turn this into a therapy session anyway.

My bacon cheeseburger was massive and juicy with a heap of diced green chile on top, requiring large bites to devour it. The onion rings were greasy and tasty with ketchup. It was great meal with a Pepsi to wash it down.

When I went to the register to pay, my waitress introduced me to a group of older men who were ranchers at a nearby table. She made a fuss over me; I'll admit the attention felt nice.

The waitress took my money, gave me change, then locked her eyes on mine.

"Remember, you're a big deal here," she said.

"Okay, you win," I said, with more laughter, "Sorry for arguing with you. I get it. Really, I do."

The next morning, I declared it a rest day. The cold air, steel gray sky and gusts of wind suggested it could snow at any point, although it never did. I ate at Ella's again. I tried the Mexican place too. And I visited the library twice.

After a full day off the bike, I was ready to go. Once the first light came, I rushed outside to assess the weather. Overnight, snow had graced the branches of trees, and afar, the highest ridges of the Mogollon Mountains had a fresh layer of white. The television forecast called for a fifty-percent chance of snowfall in the morning, before it would clear in the afternoon. I considered my options, and I searched for reasons to say "yes." The sky was mostly gray, but there was one small patch of blue near the horizon, and it was to the northeast—the direction that would lead me out. Also, despite the precipitation, the roads were clear of snow and ice.

I felt driven. I didn't want to wait around. And so I went.

Outside of Reserve, I pedaled into a winter wonderland of snow-covered signs, homes, and trees. Every single branch in the forest was highlighted in white, a magnificent spectacle. I laughed to myself—with half-pride at my toughness, and half-anxiety at my bullheadedness—that I was determined to ride my bike on a cold, thirty-eight degree morning.

It was a slow climb out of Reserve with plenty of road curves. There was no shoulder. But no cars, either. This was after all, Catron County, with an astonishingly low 0.51 people per square mile. At ten miles, I saw a solitary house on a hill surrounded by pinyons, and I wondered what it'd be like to live there. Would I like the solitude? Would it be beneficial for someone who enjoys writing? I went through Cruzville and Apache Creek—small villages with no services. At nineteen miles, I came to Aragon, which consisted of about twenty-five houses and no stores. On the roadside, there was an old and pretty building named Santo Nino Church with terracotta walls and red trim. I should have rested there, but I kept going. Soon after, snow flurries began to fall. Sure, most of the snow melted as soon as it touched me and the road, but it was magical. For parts of the morning, it was so cold that I endured that nasty "pins and needles" effect on the palms of my hands. Sometimes it hurt so bad that it was hard to grip the handlebar. Still, Mother Nature had given me a special gift, and I was grateful. While riding, I took pictures of the snowflakes coming at me, giddy with the experience.

Soon the snowfall subsided, and this desolate two-lane road wound upward. It twisted and turned in a deep valley with greenery. It was scenic and yet scary to be this isolated. There were no homes. No ranches. No people. Nothing. The toiling uphill continued for six miles. And then, in a crest in a road, I arrived at a sign that read, "Continental Divide, Elev. 7312'."

I savored this momentous event. The Continental Divide is a line of ridges, hills and mountains that divide river systems from the Pacific Ocean and Atlantic Ocean. Theoretically, if I poured water on the west side, it would flow downward through rivers that would reach the Colorado River and flow into the Pacific. Poured on the other side, it'd travel east toward the Rio Grande and flow into the Gulf of Mexico and Atlantic Ocean. Because the divide crosses the western section of the nation, I still had a long way to go, but I was happy nonetheless. For now, I was king of the hill. Or perhaps, king of the continent.

I got off the bike and leaned it against the sign. With snow on the edges, I stood in the middle of the road to avoid getting my feet wet. For five minutes, no cars passed. I could have reclined and taken a nap on the pavement, and I would have been safe. And with it as quiet as it was, if a car approached, I would have heard it coming miles away. In fact, it occurred to me that I hadn't spoken a word to anyone on that morning. It would be a lonely ride, but I had something to look forward to. Dave, my cycling friend who helped me by phone during the Arizona flat tire day, was on his way to meet me in Datil this afternoon.

I began my descent with joyful, effortless speed. Freezing wind startled my senses. The trees cleared and the land opened. I wondered how far I could see. Maybe seventy-five to one-hundred miles? This is what people probably dream about when they long to be alone and at peace amidst creation. Yet the remoteness still felt unnerving to me. It was the kind of territory that humbles humanity. Maybe when I'm in populated areas, at least there's a sense of security in knowing that at least *some* people are around, should I need help. I saw a house in the distance with a dirt road with two ruts. Does someone live there?

Is it abandoned? Whatever the case ... *wow!* This region would be an excellent choice for someone who doesn't need people. Or like them.

Eventually, the road flattened in a valley where much of the snow had melted. Seven miles ahead was Horse Springs, the next dot on my map. The town featured five homes near the road, with some older structures scattered in the distance. One building had about ten old cars beside it, most decayed beyond recognition. There was one rundown building that looked like a gas station and convenience store from a previous era. No vehicles were out front and the place didn't appear open, but a table and benches lured me to rest. With forty miles down, and twenty-eight more to go, this was a good place to take a prolonged break.

I paced and stretched my muscles. Hearing some noise in the building, I realized this store might be open after all. I pushed the creaky front door; it wasn't locked. Inside, the lights were off. The only illumination was daylight through the windows. Some items were stocked on the shelves. I turned and saw a man standing behind the register.

"Hi," I said quietly.

"You scared me," he said, "I'm not really open."

"Sorry about that. I'm on a bike and stopped at the table outside."

"That explains it. I'm used to hearing a car engine before someone comes in. If there's anything you want, I'll sell it to you."

I didn't need anything, but I wandered among the shelves anyway.

"So where did you bike from?" he asked.

"From Reserve today, but I started in San Diego two weeks ago."

"No kidding. Did you get held up by the snow?"

"Sure did. I spent all of yesterday in Reserve."

"And you biked here today? That's impressive. You've got my respect. And you're all alone."

"Well . . ." I didn't know how to answer him.

"Are you a loner type? Maybe you thrive on this."

I laughed. "Not really. I'll take quiet roads over busy roads any day. And I'm a fan of little towns like this without the pressures of city life. I could imagine being a writer, an artist or a guy who restores cars and works in a shed with no distractions out here."

"I know what you mean," he said, with a smile. "I own this place. It's closed during the winter months, but the gas pumps work all year round. I only came in because there was a problem with the pumps." Then he paused, as if uncertain of what to do. "I need to lock up the place. Do you want anything?"

"No, I'm fine."

He stepped in front of the counter and made an offer. "If you like, I can give you a tour of Horse Springs. It won't be long, because there's not much here."

Of course, I accepted.

We stepped out and he locked the door. Then the tour began. "As you can see, Horse Springs isn't much. I think eight or nine people live here," he said.

We went to the back and I saw a parked pick-up truck that I hadn't noticed earlier. He explained that his wife was waiting in the passenger seat, and after introducing us, he said to her, "This won't take long." Then we walked on a primitive road with wheel ruts.

"The town got its name when a horse got loose and the owner found it at a spring down the hill. A few hundred people settled back then." Then he pointed toward a small white building with a steeple. "My grandfather built that church," he said.

"No kidding? That's a beautiful structure," I said, "By the way, you're making my day. This is fun."

"That's nice of you to say," he said, "I spent some of my childhood here, and whether you like the place or not, the memories stick with you."

With each new site that he showed me, my new friend was making this place come alive with his stories. We returned to the store and on the other side was an old house—its white paint badly peeled—with sage doors and a shed beside it. "For years, I lived there as a kid.

That was my bedroom window. Back then my Dad owned the store, which was a bar. There used to be another gas station across the road, but you can't see any signs of that now. And that," he said with a smile, "is about all I can show you."

"This was great," I said, soaking in the interaction. "and the walking helped me use different muscles and relax tired ones."

"I'm glad you liked it. Visitors come this way in the summer for the mountains and peace and quiet. Hunting is popular as well."

At the end, noisy gusts of wind required us to shout so we could hear each other talking. He made me an offer.

"I could put your bike in my truck and take you to Datil."

Although grateful, I declined. I had to ride this myself.

We said good-bye, and as I watched his truck drive into the distance, I cringed when I realized that among the many pictures I had taken of Horse Springs, I didn't get a photo of him. And already, I had forgotten his name. So many people were etching memories into my heart: waitresses, store owners, motel clerks, even folks waving from cars. I'd probably never seen them again, but in some mysterious way, they remained with me.

Back to riding the bike, the highway stretched to the horizon across a whole lot of nothing. A sea of golden grass comprised this land that my map named the Plains of San Agustin. A mountain was hunkered to the north, covered with pinyons, junipers and pine trees, and snow on its highest sections. As I pedaled, the wind blew harder. The temperature finally rose to fifty degrees, but the wind chill negated any warmth I may have felt. The road was headed northeast, and westerly winds pounded me from the back left. At least the wind was pushing me however slightly, as it wreaked havoc on my face, neck, and exposed skin. My shoulders groaned as I held tightly to the handlebar. This two-lane highway had no shoulder. The pavement ended inches beyond the white line. The strongest gusts threatened to push me off the road, and sometimes I leaned to the left to combat it. This could have been a dangerous move, but there were so few cars. Then the thought hit me: if had a flat tire in this wild territory, the wind gusts could mar my chances of fixing it. This was far from relaxing.

The conditions were hostile for cycling, but the scenery was peaceful. Miles out was a group of cattle, about twenty-five of them near an old-fashioned windmill. There were also two ranch entrances that led way out to someone's home with a windmill and water tank. There were more miles of riding with no shoulder. One car passed, a novelty.

Then large dips developed on the road—annoying ups and downs that had more ascent than descent. The climbing was draining my energy as I strove to maintain my pace, while fighting that unnerving wind that howled like a wicked witch laughing. My skin felt numb. Windburn, the effect of wind and cold, stung against my face. I passed a sign that read it was eight more miles to Datil, and soon I was out of the plains. I hoped the forest would provide some abatement from the wind, but it found a way through the trees—slamming me, taunting me. I wanted to go crazy. *Will this ride ever end?*

Finally, it did.

Datil, New Mexico.

A gas station, cafe, restaurant and motel were at the junction of Highways 12 and 60, which seemed like the heart of town. There was a small post office, an auto garage that housed a feed store and some rundown commercial buildings with no businesses inside. Next to the motel was a newly-built elementary school. Some driveways to houses and ranches sprouted off the road. Datil wasn't much, but to me, it felt like a world-class city after today's long ride. And, I was so overjoyed to be out of that punishing wind.

Now it was time to celebrate.

The restaurant seemed like a fitting place to begin. Its ambiance included fireplaces and hunting trophies on the walls, and tin mugs and antiques on shelves. The menu offered a variety of enticing choices, and yet I ended up ordering the usual—a green chile cheeseburger with french fries. And this time, I had it with a beer. No wimpy iced tea or soda for me. My run-in with those crosswinds was over and now was the time to revel in my accomplishment. I ate my dinner with passion, enjoying every bite, and I finished with a hunk of German chocolate cake for dessert. Never had food tasted this good.

Dave arrived just as the sun was setting. I arose and shouted his name when I saw him, giving him a hug. The first thing out of my mouth was about how he had helped me during the flat tire meltdown.

"See? I made it. I'm still going," I joked.

"You're a long way from Phoenix. Good job!" said Dave.

Dave, a cycling friend with whom I ride about once per year, drove from Farmington (266 miles away) to visit me. Dave is in his forties, is of Spanish descent, and has short black hair. Everyone likes Dave. His tender voice matches well with his warm personality. He's always kind, always gentle.

"Do you still want to go to Pietown?" he asked. Dave and I had talked about visiting this nearby town, named so because of a well-known bakery that makes and ships pies throughout the world. We wanted to check it out.

"Let's go!" I said, and off we went, in search of pie and adventure.

Dave's pickup truck cruised at seventy-five miles per hour on another empty two-lane highway. All the roads were like this out here.

"I can't believe how fast you're going!"

"Sorry, I can slow down if you like," said Dave.

"No, no, no. You don't understand. You're just driving a normal speed, but this is stunning to me. Are you aware my average pace on the bike is twelve miles an hour? That's right, twelve!"

I marveled at how the truck ate up the road, with no effort on our part other than to sit comfortably with the heat vents providing warmth.

We crossed over the Continental Divide and arrived in Pietown. If anything had been open, we would have bought pies and taken pictures, but every store was closed. We pulled into a parking spot in front of one shop, and Dave got out to investigate. I followed slowly. Then suddenly, I became sluggish. This was more than the usual tired and achy feelings after a day's ride. I was trashed. My body gave all the warning signals that I ought to lie down soon. If I had to exert much more energy, I might have fallen over.

I explained the situation to Dave. "With this bike trip, my body determines what I do. There's no way I can just be a normal person and hang out all evening. When my body says it's time to rest, I obey. Period. I'll be back on the bike in twelve hours, and I can feel the clock ticking."

Dave was understanding. "Hey, I'm a cyclist too. I remember the annual Buena Vista to Leadville ride, which is 103 miles. I was so out of it by the end, and I can only describe it as extreme fatigue. My stamina was zero. I couldn't believe I could still pedal."

"Ah yes, you do understand," I said, with a snicker.

"I'll never forget: I was so sore and walking funny afterward," said Dave, "Anyway, we're too late to do anything. Nothing is open."

We returned to Datil and relaxed in my motel room. Dave was staying the night since he'd come so far. He brought his stuff in including his road bike, while I lay on my bed like a zombie. The windburn effect had taken a major toll on me. My face was reddened and irritated, and I had a lingering headache.

"I want to take pictures of you riding tomorrow and maybe bike with you a little," said Dave.

"That would be an honor. You'll be the first person to bike with me on this journey."

Dave turned on the TV and surfed the channels, but nothing interested him. Meanwhile, I was sprawled on my bed facing the ceiling, not talking, expressionless. Then Dave had questions for me.

"So is it what you expected?" he asked.

"Other than the crazy stuff that happened in Blythe and Arizona, the trip has felt ordinary. I've had some good rides, and some rides that kicked my butt."

"This is like a full-time job for you."

"Yep. All I do is bike on lonely roads, for the most part. And the funny thing is, I'm experiencing America through convenience stores, motels and restaurants. All the cashiers, clerks and waitresses I encounter are starting the look the same. And most rides are tedious. Don't get me wrong, I'm loving this, but I'm also the type of guy where once I start my ride in the morning, I get fixated on reaching the end.

Am I enjoying each present moment? Do I enjoy the pedaling motion on a bike for hours? I honestly don't know."

And with that, I gave a nervous laugh.

"I betcha most people who do this trip feel the same way," said Dave.

"It does feel great to make this dream happen."

"You are. I remember when you were talking about this years ago."

Then the thought occurred to me. *Why are we talking about me?*

"What about you? You're the one that should be biking across America."

"I'd like to someday. I'd have to get myself in better shape. Right now I've got school and other things going on."

"You're a more experienced biker than I am. You've biked more miles than me. Can you estimate your lifetime mileage?"

Dave did some calculating in his head. "Over 10,000 miles."

"There you have it."

I wanted to affirm Dave. If I could make this trip, there was no doubt that he could as well.

"And you worked as a mechanic in a bicycle shop," I added, "I know you can handle things like flat tires better than I can."

We talked more, but soon it became harder for me to stay awake. We turned off the overhead light and gradually I dozed off. I had no idea what Dave did in the meantime. My body was in bliss to be horizontal, falling into a deep sleep.

***

I awoke early, itching to ride as usual.

Dave suggested I wait until the temperature warmed, but that would mean fewer hours to rest in the afternoon or evening. Besides, I had too much energy—I'll call it "cyclist anxiety"—to sit around. For better or worse, this journey had me on my own clock and rhythm. I didn't expect anyone to understand. We agreed I would start my sixty-mile ride, and Dave would pack his things, check out of the motel and meet me on the road in his truck.

Within the first mile, I was out of Datil and onto the plains in a gentle descent. With the Continental Divide behind me and a town split by the Rio Grande ahead of me, I liked the prospect of an easier ride to Socorro, my destination.

The road was breathtakingly empty as it met the horizon, with the bright blue southwestern sky meeting the land in the middle. Countless acres of golden-shaded grass surrounded the highway, with only a barbed wire fence running beside it. Buttes, some covered with snow, stood far in the distance. It looked like something you'd see in an imaginative oil painting.

At one point, I stopped, turned back and snapped a picture of the barren road I had been traveling on. Faintly, I could see Dave's truck approaching from miles away. Eventually, he caught up and stopped with the truck running on the east-bound lane of the two-lane road. There were no cars anywhere.

"You better not cause a traffic jam!" I shouted.

"You're telling me. This might be the loneliest road in America."

Dave got out of the truck with his camera and its massive lens strapped around his neck. He held his elbows tightly and shivered.

"It's too cold! How the heck are you doing this? I guess you have the benefit of being warmed up," he said.

I grinned. Dave had been coddled by the warmth of his truck and was now paying the price. Right on the highway, we had a photo op. I felt like a model as he snapped pictures of me with all the spacious scenery. I've wondered why I'm so obsessed with photography—it's partly to tell a story, to prompt memories and to post them online so I can share my experiences with others. And now, I had the benefit of a skilled photographer in Dave doing it. I did have some digital images of myself, but without a tripod, it required a lot of effort to get a self-portrait, either by asking a stranger or using the timer on my camera.

I rode a few miles with Dave's truck moving beside me, as I chatted with him from the passenger side. For a minute, I grabbed the truck and let him pull me.

"This is nice! You want to take me to Texas?" I asked.

"Let's go!"

"Oh no," I said with a laugh, "This is cheating! I can't have that."

I let go and stayed with his pace.

There was something to notice in this massive, barren valley. Ahead was the Very Large Array, an astronomy observatory with a group of circular dishes with antennae. A sign said that these large structures, strung out in the shape of a "Y," can be seen from satellites in space. It was another opportunity to stop and take pictures.

Then Dave drove ahead. Because I was riding in one direction, if he wanted to bike with me, he had to go miles in the distance and then bike in the opposite direction until we met. Then we'd ride together.

My gradual descent continued and had me in the sixteen to eighteen miles per hour range. I was savoring the ride. This was better than a steep hill that brings me down fast and furiously in only minutes.

When Dave joined me, we biked side by side at a relaxed pace.

"I feel bad that you've had more uphill to reach me," I said.

"Yeah, but this is a good workout. I'm just glad to be out. It's my first real ride since the accident."

Dave was referring to a fateful event that changed his life two years ago. On Christmas Day, he was riding his bike to his parents' home in town. A few cars passed in routine fashion. Then, he heard the sound of a vehicle unusually close behind, and a car plowed into him. The impact destroyed his bike and threw him to the ground. Semi-conscious, he knew something had happened, but he was disoriented and badly injured. Dave was lucky in one respect. I've heard of many incidents where cyclists have been hit by cars, and then it became a "hit and run" scene when the driver didn't stop or report the collision. In this case, the teen driver did the right thing by calling for emergency help.

The physical damage to Dave was serious with his left side bearing the worst injuries. He had a clean break in his fibula (knee cap), and there was other bone damage to his left leg. His clavicle (shoulder) was broken, he had a bruised kidney, and he suffered a moderate concussion. His left ankle was badly hurt too. Thankfully, the driver's insurance covered nearly all of the medical bills. After the accident, Dave and the motorist connected in person at the hospital. It turned out that he was a teen who obtained his license weeks earlier, and he admitted that he was hitting the controls on his radio when he struck him. He expressed his sorrow and asked for forgiveness, and Dave gave it to him. He's that kind of guy. Since then, Dave has been on a two-year journey of physical recovery. He used crutches for eighteen months and had begun to walk on his own only recently, albeit with a significant limp. All that suffering, and I had never witnessed Dave complain. Not once.

As we went together, it felt like an ordinary ride, but that was only from my perspective.

"This is my first road bike ride on a real highway," Dave said, "I'll admit I'm a little nervous."

A car passed us at a swift speed. The driver moved far to the middle of the road, and we were on a wide shoulder. There was plenty of space between us and the car, but it was still a challenge for Dave.

"When that one passed I said, 'Ooooooooh,' but I'm okay now," he said.

Some might have given up on cycling after such a traumatic experience, but Dave didn't want to renounce the sport. Also, he could bike more easily than he could walk, and doctors said riding would quicken his recovery.

Thankfully this road was safe by cycling standards, but there are no guarantees. The troubling reality is that a major crash on a bike can be deadly. It can be a simple mistake a driver makes—not paying attention to the road and swerving into the shoulder while doing something distracting like eating or talking on a cell phone. Or, it can be something innocent like being swiped by a side view mirror as a car passes too closely. Of course, bicyclists can make errors that cause their own accidents. Either way, when a vehicle and bike make contact, regardless of whose fault, it is usually disasterous for the bicyclist.

I have never been hit by a car. And only once have I had an ugly crash, coincidentally with Dave by my side as we rode in Colorado Springs. I hit a patch of sand beyond a traffic intersection while traveling at about eight miles per hour. The lack of speed made my front wheel skid and when I pedaled I lost balance. The fall on my left side caused only minor scrapes to my left arm. By now, I had made peace with the inherent vulnerability of cycling. I figured when it was my time to go, it was my time. Not that I'm foolish enough to deny that it could happen to me. For years, I have read news articles about tragic crashes in which a cyclist had little chance of surviving after being hit. If something like that happened, I figured I would be with God anyway—it's all in his hands.

Dave started to feel better and moved into the empty driving lane. "This is a monumental advance for me," he said, as he stood up on the pedals and increased his speed. "I can put more pressure into my pedal strokes. No pain."

"Nice!"

"Last month I extended my left leg on the pedal for the first time. Now I can put pressure into my stroke without any discomfort."

I was so happy for him. Dave is a living example of perseverance, of taking what life had to offer and pushing on. He could have quit, declared he'd had enough from life, and never challenged himself again. Instead, he was riding with me as a testament to heart and hope. If I had only one person to bike with me on this trip, I couldn't have chosen a more worthy companion.

Dave returned to the shoulder and we cruised together.

"Aside from the stolen bike, have you had any problems?"

I recounted the mean truck driver and the guy who yelled at me, both in eastern Arizona, but that was it.

"It's funny how people can be so rude and cowardly. And they do it from the confines of their car knowing they'll never look you in the face," he said.

"I hear ya, but I'm over it now."

"I do worry about you being by yourself. You could get hurt and maybe nobody would be around to help."

"Well, I've got my cell phone."

"I'm thinking of stupid stuff. A while back, there was a guy who was throwing stuff at bicyclists from his car. It was happening to a few people in the cycling community in Farmington."

"That's just wrong."

Dave nodded and said, "One day I was riding outside of town by myself, and a car came up and a guy in the passenger seat tossed an empty plastic bottle at me. The thing was, he did it near a sharp turn, and his car slowed down enough that I caught the license plate and reported it. Police couldn't do anything, but the driver was warned. They said, 'We're onto you. We know what you're doing.' And after that, there were no more problems."

We reached Dave's truck in Magdalena, and at a gas station Dave snapped more photos. Again, I was the model, and he was the photographer. I stood by the bike in various poses—some serious, some silly—and we were laughing hard. One older man pumping fuel in his truck saw us. He merely gazed our way, seemingly unsure of what to think, and that made us laugh more.

With us rested and Dave's camera back in his case, we did the routine again. He drove ahead ten miles, biked back the way he'd come, and we met in the middle. An hour later, we ended our ride in Socorro at sixty-one miles for the day.

For lunch, we ate at a Mexican place, and I had chicken enchiladas with heaps of red chili and gooey cheese. Also, my shredded beef taco with spicy salsa hit the spot. Dave worked on a massive burrito with beans and rice, and he told me about something he's involved in.

"His name is Tim. He's a renowned big foot researcher."

"How did you meet him?"

"A friend of mine reported weird bigfoot activity to him. Soon after, Tim invited my friend to Paris, Texas and I tagged along. It's bizarre, but there are groups of people who go on searches."

I snickered and put my head down. "Do you really think there's a bigfoot?"

"No, but he was interesting to hang out with. There's supposedly some DNA evidence. I'm skeptical of all of it. I know, it sounds crazy."

Amidst our eating, Dave said, "The way you're going, you could bike home to Colorado if you wanted."

"I definitely feel like I could."

From the beginning, Socorro had been a meaningful spot on my route. If there was ever a time to quit, this town would be the ideal place. My home in Buena Vista, Colorado is a straight six-hour drive from here, and local friends were clear that they'd help if I needed assistance or a ride back home. However, quitting was nowhere on the radar. My confidence was high. After all I had been through, how could I stop now?

Dave needed to return home by the day's end and before leaving me at a motel, he helped with a favor. With his vehicle, I wanted to scout routes outside of Socorro. Tomorrow's itinerary called for me to bike to Mountainair via Interstate 25 north and then U.S. Highway 60 east. As I examined my map, however, I noticed a road marked with a gray line that went northeast. If I could find it, this would be a short cut from Socorro and I could avoid riding on the interstate. We searched all over but couldn't find it, and upon returning to town, we stopped at the New Mexico State Police headquarters to inquire about this mysterious road. With me in the lobby and a police officer behind bullet-proof glass, she explained that no road existed and that my map must have been outdated.

Now, if I had thanked her for the information and exited, I would have been fine, but I had the not-so-bright idea of confirming that it was lawful to ride a bicycle on this section of Interstate 25.

"It's okay to ride by bike on the interstate, right?"

It was a simple question, but she wouldn't give me a straight answer. She warned me that bicyclists had been stopped by state troopers when there were strong crosswinds, but she also acknowledged that cyclists bike the route all the time.

"So is it lawful to bike on the interstate or not?"

She rambled more with no clear answer.

When I continued to press her, she said, "Use your discretion."

What did that mean? Either it was legal and she wouldn't admit it, or it was illegal but she wouldn't admit that they don't enforce the law. Whatever her reason, her unwillingness to answer was lame. Back home, I have two friends who are police officers who love to talk about their work, including what is legal and illegal, the laws they enforce the most, their greatest joys and challenges while on duty, etc., but this officer was useless.

I stewed inside, knowing I shouldn't have bothered asking, because I got my answer from doing Internet research months earlier that it was legal. But this was one of those instances where I wanted one-hundred percent psychological certainty that I'd be okay. "It's better to apologize than to ask for permission" goes the saying, but the possibility, however slight, that I'd be stopped by state police and forced to return to Socorro was not something I wanted to face.

I tried one last time.

"If I ride on the Interstate and a police officer sees me, will I be pulled—"

Just then the outer station door banged open. Dave entered the lobby, speaking loudly on his cell phone. "Do either of you have a pen?" he asked. He fumbled through papers on a desk and found one. "Four, one two, two, six . . ." he recited, as he wrote down the numbers.

With that distraction, I gave up. I didn't know what caused Dave's interruption, but it was probably for the best. I forced a fake smile, thanked the officer for her time and walked out.

Back in the truck, Dave tried to return the phone call but couldn't.

"I must have written down a number wrong," he said, rereading the paper. "Tim doesn't call unless something's going on."

Dave had received a call from his bigfoot expedition leader, and his cheap cell phone didn't have a caller ID function. He couldn't return his call.

"Tim is the kind of guy who wants you to jump immediately if he calls or has news to share. He's very commanding," he said.

As we cruised, Dave was exasperated and I was over-thinking my situation. Though the possibility of a conflict with a state trooper on the interstate was miniscule, peace of mind was paramount. One option for me was to take an alternative route by traveling seven miles south to San Antonio, where U.S. Highway 380 would take me east into Texas.

The new route didn't seem to have any disadvantages, but it was not my original plan and I didn't want change. As conflicted as I was, I let go and accepted the new route. Highway 380 traveled hundreds of miles into eastern Texas; I'd reconnect with my planned route somewhere out there.

Dave agreed to drive me down the frontage road from Socorro to San Antonio to evaluate the route, which was an ugly, winding frontage road with no shoulder. As it would do sometimes, seeing what was ahead was a mistake. As a cyclist, roads look scarier from inside a car.

"If there's a motel in San Antonio," I said, "Why don't you drop me off there?"

I knew this seven miles would be cheating. My conscience had me feeling uneasy, but not for long.

"The heck with it!" I shouted, "This one's on the New Mexico State Police!"

Suddenly, I started laughing at the absurdity of it all.

In San Antonio, Dave noticed a bed-and-breakfast sign. "That would probably be more expensive than a motel," he said. We checked it out anyway. When the hostess quoted me a rate that was just slightly more than an average motel room, I took it.

It was meant to be that I'd stay in this small town of 165 people. The ambiance of the Casa Blanca Bed & Breakfast was homey and delightful. Rocking chairs were on the front porch. My room had a large oval rug in stylish pastel colors with a thick comforter blanket over the bed. There were two bookcases full of intriguing titles, many of them travel books.

It seemed awkward to bring my bike into such a cozy place.

"There's a shed out back for that," said the hostess.

Inside the shed, we found her husband doing woodwork. Sawdust blanketed the floor. I leaned my bike against a wall, thanked them both, and returned to Dave who was on his cell phone out front. He had managed to reach his friend.

"Was bigfoot found? Inquiring minds want to know."

Dave laughed. "No, but it was an interesting talk."

Then we said our good-byes and he departed.

I wandered around San Antonio, which didn't seem to have much open other than a convenience store and deli. Inside I met a friendly woman who was the owner and her teen son. I told them about my mission.

"We get a lot of bikers doing that. A lot of them come through and we let them camp out back. Where are you staying?"

"At the B&B."

"That's a nice place. Now, with all your riding, you need nourishment. What can I get you?"

"First of all, can you brew more coffee?"

"Sure," she said.

As I waited, I lusted at their wide selection of hard-pack ice cream flavors, and I got a chocolate chip cookie dough ice cream in a waffle cone. I guess you could call that "nourishment" ... for my taste buds, at least.

With my coffee and ice cream, I checked out their merchandise. There was a rack of t-shirts, many in tie-dye designs, and there was a shirt that was most plentiful in stock. With the state's shape of New Mexico, it read, "San Antonio, New Mexico: Not really new and not really Mexico." I would have immediately bought the shirt out of love for the funny slogan, but I had to refrain because of the limited carrying space on my bike.

As I returned to the B&B, I had a frightening thought. *Is the shed that's housing my bike secure and locked?* I started to worry about my bike being stolen. The man was still there when I got back.

"Does this get locked at night?" I asked.

He said no, but he assured me I had nothing to worry about. His strong, calm demeanor should have been enough to take his word. After all, this was a small town that probably had little crime, but I couldn't stay silent about this.

"I had my bike stolen in Phoenix. This is a new one. So I'm more nervous about theft than the average person. Is there any way this could be locked?"

"Really? I'm so sorry about your loss," he said. "I can lock the shed for you."

That helped me breathe easier.

Back in my room, I spoke with and texted many friends. There was a reply from an old buddy named Sharon, the younger sister of my best childhood friend. Sharon's always been a dreamer, an artist and a traveler, and I failed to tell her about my bicycle journey until now. In one text she wrote, "I ask that somewhere along the way you look at a passing landscape and dedicate that act to me. See you sometime, somewhere in America." That message gave me the warmest and fuzziest feeling of happiness; I knew Sharon was proud of me.

In the evening, I enjoyed my amenities. I kept the TV off and browsed the books in my room. There were large picture books—they're usually called "coffee table books"—of the works of traveling photographers. There was one for Kaua'i, an island of Hawaii. Another had images of beaches throughout South America. As I leafed through the pages, I thought about the dusty, windy, barren landscapes of New Mexico and smiled. Oh yes, I was joyful to be a traveler in the Land of Enchantment.

CHAPTER X

MOTELS AND MILEAGE

I travel not to go anywhere, but to go.
I travel for travel's sake.
The great affair is to move.

Robert Louis Stevenson

*M*any things changed day by day. The scenery. The weather. The wind. The cycling-friendliness of the roads. The route was ever-changing too, as I went through cities and towns, and a whole lot of open space. I was experiencing this trip to the fullest by traveling slowly, mile by deliberate mile, on my bike. The days were blending together with the same routines of waking up, riding, resting, eating and sleeping. And there was one other constant— tiredness. There was always an element of exhaustion no matter what, where, when or with whom.

Out of San Antonio, I crossed the Rio Grande. I biked through a high desert plain named Jordana Del Muerto, which means the "The

Journey of the Dead" in Spanish. Among many hills and mountains afar, Carrizozo Peak (elevation 9,090 feet) stood as the most prominent. I had a gradual climb throughout the morning, and then at the end, I finally enjoyed some speed from a descent. Along the way, I passed the Valley of Fires State Park, with charcoal and black-shaded rocks that are considered the youngest lava flow from nearby extinct volcanoes.

At sixty-four miles, I arrived in Carrizozo and was finished for the day. There was a motel on each side of the road and at random, I chose the left one. The design of its sign made it obvious that this lodge was built in the 1960s. The typography of the door numbers and awning style also screamed of the same era, like they were hung and not touched since. The parking lot was empty, but it was only one o'clock and a weekday, so that wasn't a clear indication of anything.

I entered the lobby and heard the commotion of a baby wailing in the back room. A young woman came out wearing a tank top, gray stone-washed jeans and an unsightly belly button piercing. Her aloofness and lack of eye contact with me matched her unprofessional clothing for even this type of low-end motel, but I told myself this was small town New Mexico and to go with the flow. I gave her my debit card to pay for the room. She slid it through the machine, and we waited for verification. We both stood silently for a few minutes, and then she hit cancel and tried again.

"Sometimes the machine has problems," she said, with a tone that implied this had happened before.

More minutes went by. She hit cancel again and hit a few more buttons.

"It has to do with the phone connection," she explained.

Then she swiped my card again.

Tired and just needing to rest, I said, "How about if I get settled in my room, and I'll come back later to sign the receipt?"

She agreed and gave my card back with my room key.

The room was terrible from a fashion standpoint. An ugly brown lamp sat gracelessly on the utilitarian dresser. The bedspread had a checkered pattern with brown, orange and white squares. The walls were painted an awful aqua blue. At every turn, my senses were staggered by the garish and outdated fixtures. None of this mattered however, because all I needed were the basics.

I turned on the shower, but there was no hot water. I tinkered with the knob and let the water run for a while. No luck.

I called the front desk, and the same woman answered.

"You need to let it run for about five minutes," she said.

I had already done that, but I let it run longer once more. Still cold. I called back.

"There's still no hot water."

The woman acted surprised and asked if I gave it time.

"Of course, I did."

"I'll have a repairman look at it," she said. I got no apology. No offer of a different room. This was turning into an adventure at the Slumlord Motel. After two and a half weeks of staying in motels, I had become savvy enough to know when I was being scammed. I knew better than to expect a repairman to show up, and obviously she should have put me in a different room. This woman was lying to me. She probably knew there was no hot water in the first place.

I packed my belongings, returned to the front desk, and told her I was leaving. She didn't argue or try to change my mind. She said my debit card hadn't been charged, because (big surprise…) the credit card machine still wasn't working either.

I checked into the other motel and at the counter, I asked the clerk with embarrassment, "So, you really do have hot water in your showers, right?"

"Of course."

"The place across the street didn't."

"Are they still selling rooms?" she exclaimed, "They haven't had hot water for a couple of months!"

My new motel room was nothing fancy but still an upgrade. White walls. A few framed pictures of western scenery. A mauve bedspread. I was becoming quite the critic of motels. With so many experiences on this journey, I could compare beds, bathrooms, showers, furniture, TVs and their remote controls, the heating and air systems, the locks on the door, the flooring, the cleanliness of the parking lot and even the grass and shrubbery on the grounds, if any. The thickness of the walls was another factor: could I hear my next door neighbors? When I checked in, was I greeted with a welcoming attitude? Or was I merely a "name and a number" to them—someone to get money from as quickly as possible?

Many images come to mind when I think of lodging and traveling. Growing up, my experiences of hotels and motels were during family vacations with my parents and brothers. In those days, staying at such places was a treat with strange new beds and typically a swimming pool where we could expend all our energy. If there was an elevator, my brothers and I would play in it. We'd race the elevator by running down the stairs. Sometimes we'd cheat—we'd be on the fifth floor and click the fourth, third, and second floor buttons and then race down to the ground level. We'd stand at the bottom with glee as people exited in frustration that some button-pushing idiot slowed them.

Then, as I got older, I developed an uneasy feeling that bad things could happen in out-of-the-way motels. Affairs. Prostitutes. Drug use. Making methamphetamine. Anything covert. But on this trip, these motels had become my refuge—a place to take cover from the elements. They were portable homes with hot water and a clean bed. Rent a tiny haven for a night, safe from the world's threats and troubles. The common opinion I've heard about lower-end motels is that they tend to be dirty, but never did I see unwashed bed sheets, bugs or anything too disturbing. In fact, every motel room was cleaner and less cluttered than my messy bachelor pad back home.

That afternoon, I went out in search of a place to eat lunch. It felt good to walk around Carrizozo, looking at neighborhoods and enjoying the sunny day. Eventually I came upon two appealing choices: a cozy bar and grill and an unpretentious burger joint. Either would have been acceptable, but unfortunately neither of them accepted credit or debit cards. I had depleted the last of the check I had cashed in California, and I didn't want to use an ATM. I am stubborn about this: I don't like ATM fees and forget my PIN anyway. From here on out, all of my purchases would be through a VISA card, whether debit or credit.

Then I entered a third restaurant that accepted plastic, a traditional "sit down" restaurant with waitstaff. The place seemed busy, but no one greeted me. I stood awkwardly, with several patrons noticing me and some employees working the tables. Was there a special code or action necessary to get a table? I considered just sitting down somewhere. Then I debated whether I should eat there in the first place. Would the food be as poor as the service? The restaurant seemed so quiet. There was no background music, and the only noise was the occasional clanging of someone's silverware hitting a plate. It was unsettling and spooky, like something out of a movie, and I bolted. In lieu of formal dining, I bought a personal-sized pizza at a convenience store near the motel. The pizza was dry, probably from being under overhead heated lights for too long, but it satisfied my needs. Pizza is always good, even when it's bad. Later in the evening, I had a modest dinner at the same convenience store: a chicken sandwich with a bundle of wedge fries. I cracked up as I sat by myself at a spare table in the store, for I was experiencing America, one greasy meal at a time.

***

By the way, I really did eat better in the mornings. A banana and grapes was my breakfast before I biked out of Carrizozo on Highway 380. Today I anticipated it would be a red-letter day with Roswell, eighty-eight miles away, as my destination.

At twenty miles, I had conquered a tough climb in Lincoln National Forest and arrived in Capitan, a mountain village with ski slopes, cabin rentals, fishing holes and vacation appeal. I could have rested in front of the supermarket all day, but I had to keep moving.

At thirty-three miles, I made it to Lincoln, an even smaller hamlet with homes built at the turn of the twentieth century. A sign told of its flavorful settlement history, including shootouts, run-ins with Billy The Kid (who once escaped from the local jail), and the regional Civil War of 1876-1879. Many western towns have their own versions of a "Civil War"—usually people feuding over water, land or mining claims before a stable police force and court system could be established.

At forty-three miles, I approached Hondo. By then I had eaten two energy bars, and I was down to my last bottle of water with no food. A rest break and stocking up was in order. As I biked through the village, I saw a general store on the right, but I didn't feel comfortable about the bars covering the windows and there were no good places to lock my bike. On the left was a Mexican restaurant without sufficient front windows; that wouldn't work either. I kept riding, figuring I'd find a place around the next bend, but before I knew it, I had gone five miles out and there were no other services. I was furious—with myself! I pulled out my map and noticed there were no other towns between here and Roswell, and that made me nervous. I considered turning back, but that would mean adding ten miles to an already long day. Sure, I had one remaining bottle of water and I could survive a few more hours without food, but I was now out of my comfort zone. Usually I liked to have more than enough supplies on me. I told myself to suck it up and ride. Just conserve. One water bottle is enough.

It was a great pep talk, but it didn't stop panic from setting in.

You moron! Why didn't you stop at that store?

Somehow, I fought the head games and continued.

Miles ahead, the valley narrowed. There were fewer trees with rocky, rugged hills. A creek flowed beside the road in my direction. Then, at fifty-seven miles, I approached a sign that read "Riverside." No such place was on my map, and I could see why. There were no homes and only some dilapidated cabins and barns in sight, but after a turn in the road, I saw a general store ahead. A sign with changeable plastic letters read, "God bless this place!"

Was this a mirage? A figment of my imagination? No, it wasn't! I pulled into the gravel parking lot, hopped off the bike and let out a joyous sigh of relief. The store was filled with packaged foods that you'd see at any convenience store, but there were also greeting cards, mugs, bumper stickers with amusing slogans and unique artwork. I purchased a blueberry muffin, granola bar and a drink, and then sat at one of two tables near the front window. Only one woman was running the shop.

She had long, flowing gray hair and wore mountain boots and jeans. She came to my table and introduced herself as Bella, the owner.

"It is so good to be here," I said with enthusiasm.

"That's a serious bike you've got there," she said, "The wheels are big."

"It's an average road bike," I said with a laugh.

"You're right. I guess I'm thinking of those bikes that have the huge front wheel and the small back wheel. You see them in pictures from the turn of the century. They look really dangerous, but apparently people rode them."

"Oh! You're talking about penny-farthing bicycles," I said, "Yeah, those are crazy."

"So where are you headed?"

"Roswell."

"That's where I grew up," she said, and she suggested places I should visit.

Bella sat down across from me as if she had all the time in the world. She shared about how God had led her to sell her home in California, move back to New Mexico and start this business which serves as a truck stop, general store and RV park. She also had plans to open a restaurant in the building next door.

"I've trusted God with every aspect of my business," she said, "It hasn't been easy, but it's been worth it. I want this place to touch people's lives, to make a difference."

I nodded with a huge grin, thinking that on my account alone, she had succeeded. What a cool lady. She seemed ethereal and reminded me of Jae and other women who are strong, proud and successful. Maybe it was because she had done something similar to me—she followed an instinct that told her to get out of her rut and do something profound.

"By the way, did you see the bighorn sheep?" she asked.

"No, I didn't."

"They're all over the hills. You'll see them if you start looking."

"All right," I said.

"You probably have a lot of time to think, don't ya?" she asked,

"No distractions to keep you from thinking about life."

I smiled at that common misconception. "No, it's not like that," I said, "Usually I'm too tired to think. I'm too exhausted for most things. Like this phone … I'm too drained to call people back and if I do, I'm way too tired to have a normal conversation."

"That sounds intense," she said, sounding like a concerned mother, "I want you to relax right now. You're here. This is my little piece of heaven, I call it."

I laughed. "Sounds good to me."

I sat for another fifteen minutes as Bella tended to other things, then she came back and gave me a tour of the grounds. We strolled to the creek behind the store and she told me about the history of the abandoned farming structures across the highway. The property seemed like a modest parcel, and everything about it was peaceful. Then, a semi pulled up. The driver waved to Bella and entered the store. Needing to let her attend to business, I said good-bye.

With food in my belly and extra drinks and snacks packed on the bike, I was reinvigorated when I left Bella's store. I had one last climb before I cruised on the plains for the final thirty-two miles to Roswell. When I arrived, the elevation had dropped to 3,573 feet and my cycling workouts in the Rocky Mountains were over. There would be no more brutal climbs and no more blissful descents either.

The first motel I spotted was on the west side of the city in an older neighborhood. It had a worn neon sign in front, a relic of the past. If I was traveling by car, I may have searched longer for other options, but I was too tired for that. I had hauled myself eighty-eight miles and my muscles were groaning to get off this bike. I checked in. The motel was shaped like a horseshoe with the parking lot in the middle. Upon entering my room, a glance at the furniture, overhead light and walls suggested that the place hadn't been renovated in decades, but everything appeared clean. More disconcerting was the clamor of a screaming baby that came through wall from next door.

I got into my routine. A shower. I put on my set of extra clothing. I charged my cell phone and camera batteries. And then, I was ready to search for a place to eat. As I started to leave, something sinister hit me hard, and it was becoming a problem. I got hit with jitters about my bike being stolen. Although this room was probably the safest place for my bike, I just didn't feel good about leaving it in here. What if someone broke into my room and stole it? Would a housekeeper find a reason to do it? I checked the lock on the room. It seemed sturdy, but I couldn't shake off the fear. Then I decided to lock my bike to a chair in the room. If someone tried to steal it and they couldn't cut the lock, at least they'd have another barrier in taking apart the chair, or they'd look foolish hefting both the chair and bike.

Eventually, I dined at a Sonic restaurant across the street and sat on an outdoor table with a view of my motel room door. Only a busy four-lane road separated us, but I kept checking the door. Fear was driving me, and I couldn't let it go. Looking back, I handled the stolen bike incident in Phoenix well, but now I was struggling with a lingering uneasiness that it could happen again. Truth be told, I was the victim of a crime. The psychological effects on crime victims are numerous. One might experience shock, flashbacks or anxiety. Victims might overcompensate by adopting behaviors that help them feel more in control, but it may not guide them toward wellness in the long run. Feelings of despair, helplessness and shame are common. And in some cases, victims might blame themselves for the crime happening in the first place. Whatever the situation, crime victims are wise to go easy on themselves and to be deliberate in caring for their wellness.

After returning to my motel room, my mind remained on overdrive about danger. It was probably all in my head, but I thought I was in a drug-infested motel. Surely, only bad characters would stay here. Again the baby next door began to cry, which contributed to my anxiety. I turned the air on high; the hum blocked much of the noise. I dead-bolted the lock and had the television on for a while, but eventually I turned it off and lay on my bed in darkness. Eventually I fell asleep.

I didn't see much in Roswell. I didn't take even one picture of the city—nothing about the supposed UFO sightings and reports of extraterrestrial life that have made the place famous. Later, I learned there is a UFO museum and some of the street light covers are designed like aliens' faces, but I didn't see any on my straight-line route across town.

***

The next morning, about twenty-five miles into my ride, the land east of Roswell was stunning. Never have I seen so much unanticipated nothing. Yellow grassy plains, a blue sky and so few signs of humanity. It was like being on another planet. With no cars around, I stopped in the middle of the road and took pictures of where I had come and where I would ride. My images were eerily the same, with a two-lane road disappearing into the horizon. The flat land was pretty in an understated way; you could walk out there in a straight line and who knows what you'd encounter, if anything. That prospect seemed enticing, but the desolation was unnerving. Surely you could perish out there. If you hurt yourself or were stranded without cell service, you could die and no one would ever know. Your body would lie unrecovered, and vultures would devour your flesh.

This wasn't my first time in this terrain. I've driven many times across the flat plains of western Kansas, eastern Colorado, the Oklahoma panhandle and west Texas. When you're driving through it, the scenery becomes monotonous and it becomes a place that you want to get through quickly. However, when you're biking in it, you just can't get through that fast. You have to submit to the land's desolation. Complaining won't do any good and you're forced to face the reality that happiness comes from the inside.

A gentle crosswind was pushing tumbleweeds across the road. Other than the few vehicles that passed, it was just me and the tumbleweeds out here. One got swept by a gust of wind and nearly met me at a ninety-degree angle. While in a car, I can attest that they're fun to smash into and initially I was about to do the same with my bike. But my sensible side took over and I maneuvered around it. All the brittle thorns on the ends of tumbleweeds would be a death wish for my tires. I smiled and felt a kinship with rolling plants. They were fellow travelers—their destination determined by the whim of the winds.

At seventy-three miles, I arrived at Tatum (population 683) and called it a day. My motel room had brown paneling on the walls with decorations and a bedspread in shades of maize. The color scheme was awful, but at least the room felt cozier than the one in Roswell, and it was clear that management had made an effort. The Waldorf-Astoria it wasn't, but neither was the price.

I spent time in the library to catch up on communications through the Internet. Then, at a restaurant on the main avenue, I had a chicken burrito with red chile and a side of chips and salsa. I rested and watched TV in my room, and in the evening, I went for another walk as it was getting dark. At the edge of a cattle ranch, I had a perfect seat to watch the sunset. Two large oak trees stood nearby, the wind rustling the leaves gently on this warm night. As I gazed at the shades of violet surrounding the fiery orange sun, I reflected on how far I had come. What a wonderful groove I had enjoyed since riding out of Phoenix. I did a calculation of the distance I'd traveled in the past five days—354 miles, which was the best five-day total in my life. Now *this* was what I had envisioned when I planned my trip. I was tearing it up. It was there that I had a comforting thought: I knew I would finish. I wasn't naïve to the probability that I'd have more troubles—no, not at all—but based on my abilities and determination, I would be okay. I knew I would see the Atlantic Ocean. Joy filled my soul.

I returned to the motel and attempted to settle for the night. Next door, in the parking lot, two men were standing by a truck, drinking a beer, with Mexican music blasting—the kind of traditional music with energetic brass instruments and folksy lyrics that one might hear in a Mexican restaurant. I sighed, dreading a night of listening to that.

The men didn't seem mean or terribly drunk, but in the past, it has rarely worked well when I've asked a neighbor to tone down their noise. I was hesitant to say anything, and as I lay on the bed and stared at the ceiling, the music kept booming. The more I tried to not let the noise bother me, the more it did. Part of me thought it was funny: it had been one lousy motel experience after another in southeast New Mexico. The scene outside had to be dealt with, but I knew it couldn't be me who did it. So I did the expedient thing—I complained to the front desk clerk by phone.

"Oh, those are construction workers," the woman said. "They stay here now and then. I'll let them know they need to quiet down." From her tone of voice, it sounded like she didn't look forward to confronting them either.

I decided to go for one last walk to buy supplies. It was also a good time to call Glenda; her family intended to host me in thirty-six hours.

"I was worried about you when I heard your bike was stolen," said Glenda.

"Yeah, that was a while back."

"And what else happened? Something about you had flat tires and your bicycle chain got tangled?"

"Yes, yes, yes," I said, with a chuckle. "I'll fill you in later. All I have is sixty-one miles to get to Brownfield tomorrow."

"Only sixty-one miles?" she said with a laugh, "Steve …"

"That's an average day for me. You're picking me up, right?"

"Oh yes. You're staying at our place. We'll see you Tuesday."

When I returned to the motel, the parking lot was quiet, but I could hear my neighbors in the room next to me. I turned the ventilation fan on high, which by now, I had learned was the best thing to drown out noisy people. Maybe noise was becoming a pet peeve.

The next morning was cold as I rode out of Tatum. I could see my breath and I was bundled in all layers of clothing. On the east side, a school bus lumbered toward me from the opposite direction. Kids peered at me through the window, and I'm sure they thought that I was crazy.

It would be another ride on the plains. The land seemed even flatter than before, as if that were possible. A few oil pump jacks and windmills dotted the land. At fifteen miles, there was a green sign reading "Welcome to Texas" at the site of Bronco, Texas. There were a few homes nearby—some appearing abandoned—with a general store. I leaned my bike against the sign and stretched my legs. Besides the occasional car or truck passing by, I was all alone. Those few drivers probably noticed me with curiosity. My presence on the shoulder was a break from the banal scenery.

West Texas marked a new phase of this trip, as I crossed into Central time zone and lost an hour. Actual clock time, however, didn't matter much. My cycling was based on sunlight. I usually awoke at dawn and was ready to ride as the early morning sun warmed the day.

Another ride, it was. Sixty-three miles to Brownfield. I checked into a motel that seemed nicer than recent ones. With my key in hand, I walked to my room with the bike beside me, feeling like a finely-tuned cardiovascular machine with 417 miles under my belt in the past six days.

I entered my room and placed the bike gently against a wall. I used the bathroom and settled in for about five minutes. Then I gathered my most important items.

Camera, check.

Cell phone, check.

Wallet ...

I couldn't find my wallet. I searched the bike's saddlebags, my pockets, the counters, the bed. It was nowhere to be found. Sometimes I toss things without thinking, and so I searched the trashcan and the floor. I even yanked away the bedspread. No luck.

I took a deep breath. When I paid for this room, I had my wallet.

I rushed outside, hoping the motel owner still had it. He didn't.

A surge of panic hit me. If my wallet was lost or stolen, forget about the remainder of the trip. I'd need to file a report with the police and probably go home to make sure I was not a victim of identity theft. After all the obstacles I'd overcome, what an awful way this journey might end. My frantic search continued.

Suddenly, I found it. My wallet was lying on the sidewalk near the front entrance of the motel lobby. Often after riding, I would take off my helmet and use it like a basket to carry things. Somehow it had fallen out. It must have been on the ground for about ten minutes.

Overjoyed and relieved, I told the motel owner. He didn't seem as surprised as I was. "You don't have to worry about things being stolen in this town," he said with pride. He recounted a time when he had left hundreds of dollars on the counter overnight, and when morning guests spotted it, they called him immediately.

I returned to my room shaking my head. I was so happy, and yet my nerves were shot. Having a bike stolen early and continuing with a new one would make for an amazing story, but what if another horrible thing happened like losing my wallet? Or what if my bike got stolen again? How embarrassing would that be? I couldn't slay those fears. All I could do was acknowledge them and keep moving.

CHAPTER XI

THROUGH WEST TEXAS

Texas is the finest portion
of the globe
that has ever blessed my vision.

Sam Houston

"Make yourself at home," said Glenda in her living room, "As you can see, we have many options. Sit anywhere. Lie down if you want."

I opted for the leather couch. My sore muscles had me groaning as I got horizontal, but then my body was in bliss—stationary and on something soft. Today was a leave of absence from my cycling duties, and the west Texas home of my friends Sean and Glenda would be my resting headquarters. Their living room invited you to get comfortable. Artwork by their ten-year-old daughter hung beside family pictures on the wall. There was a large-screen television, and above it was a landscape painting of Glenda's great-grandfather's homestead. During my stay, I did nothing that required much energy. I had a refreshing homemade mint iced tea, took a nap and used the family laptop to surf the Internet. All seemed right. Earlier in the morning, these friends drove to Brownfield and shuttled me forty miles to their home in Whiteface, and tomorrow they'd do it again to take me back. Aside from me loafing around, we did do some leisure activities. We had Mexican for lunch, attended a high school basketball game and took a tour of the oil pump jacks surrounding their town.

That night, Sean grilled dinner. "We've got it down to a science," he explained, "Some of it's done in the oven, and we cook more outside. When I grill, I usually make a lot of stuff. What's the point of grilling if it only lasts for a meal? This will last us a whole week!"

We sat down to a cornucopia of food. Grilled chicken, bratwurst, salmon, spicy sausage, potatoes, corn, salad and chocolate chip cookies. I ate and ate. I asked for permission to have a second helping. Then a third. I think my appetite grew from the chance to eat something home-cooked.

"Have you ever considered opening a restaurant?" I joked, "I'd be a regular customer."

Originally I met this family when they, like many others, took interest in my photography and discussion forums on www. ColoradoGuy.com. In the previous year, we got together when they vacationed in Colorado and we immediately hit it off. It made me pause to consider how the Internet has changed the world. What is possible in this day and age—the opportunities for networking and connecting with those who are long distance—was not possible even twenty years ago. As I enjoyed being face-to-face with these friends, feeling at home and having a good time, I was so grateful for this fact.

Sean and Glenda are lifelong Texans. Sean has a talkative personality that makes him the "life of the party." He always has something to say or an amusing story to tell over any topic. While Glenda is by no means timid in comparison, she's softer spoken and more grounded. Both work at a nearby high school. He's a teacher and coach; she's a secretary. Their daughter, Leyna, seemed like a happy child, but her predominant look toward me was one of suspicion. Why was this strange, long-haired man with a bike in her home?

We were nearing the end of dinner when Sean said, "Your entire trip boggles me. I don't know how you're doing it."

"I take it one day at a time," I said, shrugging my shoulders. "Look at it like this: Imagine riding your bike around your neighborhood for exercise. Now, do that everyday but instead go in a straight line."

"Your analogy is lost on me. You're riding how many miles a day?"

"Fifty or sixty. Sometimes more."

Sean laughed. "If I rode my bike ten miles, that would be a lot for me."

"Okay, maybe it's more than that, but you treat it like your full-time job. Your duty is to go for a few hours, and you just keep going in one direction." Then I started laughing and added, "Whatever you do, don't turn back."

"But the country's so big!"

"It is," I said, "But it's faster than some other modes of transportation. I betcha if you search online, you'll find people who've walked across America, or rode a horse or even skateboarded across the country."

Glenda said, "Before I knew you, I had no idea people bike like this, and I'm sure I'm not alone. Anyway, we're so glad you're here, and you get to see west Texas too." Then she smiled with sarcasm. "I'm sure you're overwhelmed with all the wonderful scenery."

"Why do you say that?" I asked.

She just kept smiling, refusing to dignify my question.

"I really like west Texas," I added, "I could see myself living here."

"But you're too active," said Sean, "What would you do? Instead of hiking, I guess you could wander and photograph the oil pump jacks.

"But what were you telling me earlier?" I interjected, "You said there's a lower cost of living in these small Texas towns. Homes are cheap. Schools are good. And you never lock your doors in this neighborhood."

"All that's true," Glenda said, "But like many people, sometimes we have that feeling that the grass is greener somewhere else. Remember, everything's brown and ugly this way. We don't have any hiking trails, and you just can't go on a power walk on someone's farm. The closest park is a hundred fifty miles away in Amarillo. Don't get me wrong, I love Texas. It's in our blood. But there's something called 'quality of life' that Colorado has over Texas and most states. And here, the dirt storms are the worst."

"Dirt storms?" I asked.

"It's when the wind blows so hard that it flings dirt everywhere. It's awful—you can't go outside. What you saw today was nothing. When I was studying at Texas Tech, sometimes I had to cover my face just to breathe. You get to class and sit down and there's dirt all over your hair. It sticks to your nose and face . . . and your lipstick. On hot days, if you wear sunscreen, the dirt really sticks to you."

"That sounds bad."

"I worry about you," she said, "I hope you don't encounter a nasty dirt storm on your bike."

"I've had some windy days, but not like what you're describing. I'd just have to deal with it, I guess."

"And there's the threat of wildfires too."

"In late February?"

"We had some last year that were a real problem around this time, and already they're raising the warnings for fires. This region tends to be very dry. Lightning strikes have started fires, but sometimes it begins with an idiot throwing a cigarette out the window. If it's windy, a fire can spread like crazy over hillsides. It'll cross highways and head right into a town."

"Look, I'm not disputing what you're saying," I contended, "but I've got enough to worry about. Cars hitting me, dealing with flats and sometimes I'm so tired and achy that getting out of bed in the morning is a big deal. I must keep going, no matter what."

Glenda understood, but she wanted to make her point.

"If there's a wildfire nearby, you better be careful," she said,

"This wind is not to be messed with. I've lived here long enough to know."

A joke was in order to break up the seriousness. "Then at least you can fly kites here," I said, "This would be a kid's haven for that. Maybe your town could host an annual kite-flying competition and people could fly kites shaped like cowboy hats, longhorns or pick-up trucks. That would be so Texas!"

"And blue bonnets!" added Sean, "A kite shaped like a clump of blue bonnets."

That had me laughing hard.

Then Sean stood, saying mysteriously, "You said you want lots of pictures of everything on your trip, right? I've got something to show you."

He returned holding an enormous snake, its head in front of him, the latter half hung around his neck and shoulder.

"Don't worry, he's non-poisonous and very tame," he said, "He doesn't bite. His name is Reston. Right now he's happy; I can tell by the way he's wrapping himself around me."

I stood back. I'm all about adventure and learning new things, but not in this case. I froze. "Don't come close to me, okay?" I asked, as I snapped pictures.

The next morning, after a phenomenal night of sleep, Glenda drove me back to Brownfield in her minivan. Mostly everything was covered in the brown dirt of farmland; the only natural vegetation was the yellow grass on the roadside. Oil drills and an occasional windmill dotted the otherwise empty landscape. As we cruised, the wind gently swept a thin layer of sand across the road.

My back ached as I sat in the passenger seat. All I wanted was to take a nap. "I think you spoiled me too much," I said. "I'm so lazy right now. I don't feel like riding."

"You could stay with us another day. You're very welcome to," said Glenda.

Another day of lounging around was tempting, but I knew I had to get back to my trip. In Arizona, I had taken my time. Now something compelled me to pack on the miles.

When we arrived in Brownfield, I got out and braced myself

against the blustery wind, and it made me edgy. It took longer than usual to get my things ready. I struggled to put my thicker wool gloves over my cycling gloves. I put on my helmet and sunglasses, but then took them off in frustration because I realized I hadn't yet applied sunscreen. Glenda was helpful; she rubbed in sunscreen on parts of my face that normally I couldn't see. I was tired and grumpy, and I started to whine. Then I felt embarrassed that Glenda was seeing me this way. Shouldn't I look tougher to her? As though I could handle this without a problem?

Glenda had me pose for pictures, and as I stood with my bike, I felt a rush of pride. Yes, I was not yet in the mood to pedal, but I realized something greater was happening in the moment. It was obvious Glenda was delighting in my journey, and she gave me the gift of support and admiration as she snapped photos.

"Put on your helmet on. Take off your sunglasses. Get in front of your bike," she ordered.

Then I held out my arms and looked down at my bright yellow pullover. "Did you know I bought this for only six dollars at Kmart in Phoenix?" I asked.

"Very nice."

I smiled more. My early morning grumpiness was subsiding. I told myself that there was no point in being uptight. If I have to bike today, I might as well be loose and enjoy this much as I can. After all, not many people get to do a life-changing feat like this. Also, I was including Glenda in my adventure. Seneca, an ancient Roman philosopher once said, "There is no delight in owning anything unshared." How true. All who had helped and everyone I had met were part of this journey, and of course, they wanted me to succeed. Making it to the end was not just for me; it also was for them.

Glenda and I talked more, but soon, it was time to leave. As I rode off, I turned back and waved as she took more pictures. Then within a few hundred yards, I passed the town's final trees and exited city limits, returning to the plains.

Quickly, I got into a rhythm. I held the handlebar tightly on the wide and clear shoulder, the only obstructions being pieces of cotton leftover from nearby fields from last year's harvest. Creases across the shoulder every thirty feet made the ride bumpy with each jolt, the vibration felt in my posterior, arms, and hands.

The wind picked up. At first, it seemed like an average breeze, but that was only because I was going with it. The gusts howled with intensity. The grass beside the road bobbed harshly to the east, pointing the way. And the riding came easy—really easy. Were these the infamous west Texas winds that Glenda had warned me about? She called them "dirt storms," but I didn't see any soil blowing, and if there was, it was only slamming into my back. All I knew was that I was enjoying the conditions tremendously, as my cruising speed increased to twenty-five miles per hour. If only every cycling day could be this effortless. I felt like I had wings. Or that angels were pushing me.

The counties in much of west Texas are shaped like squares, each thirty-two miles in length and width. Riding through each felt like a miniature state, and today I sensed I could speed through many if the wind kept up. At twenty miles, I stopped at the Lynn County line to take off my pullover, when for the first time I grasped the wind's power in a stationary position. For fun, I pulled up some grass from the ground, and immediately after letting go, the blades were gone. I laughed at how this massive westerly current was aiding me. Thank heaven I was not riding against it!

At thirty miles, I arrived ahead of schedule in Tahoka. A few garbage pails were tipped over in front of homes. Along the main avenue trees shook with misery from the bullying wind. Broken branches began to tell me more about the force of the wind. Ordinarily I may have rested, but I was riding so quickly that it seemed pointless. Within minutes, I was through the town and back on the plains.

I noticed that in west Texas the drivers seemed friendlier. Sometimes oncoming trucks drove on their shoulder, as a measure of courtesy and safety. Although I had a wide shoulder that day, occasionally a driver coming from behind would lean to the left and hit a rumble strip in the middle. That sound usually startled me. Sometimes such a maneuver caused conflict if there was oncoming traffic with a car hitting their horn in angst. As far as I was concerned, since I occupied a shoulder wide enough for a car, I was okay with vehicles staying in their lane next to me.

The tail winds continued into Garza County, and upon my arrival in Post, I had cycled the easiest fifty-four miles in my life. At a convenience store and fueling station, my presence elicited some conversation with locals.

"This wind is no good at all," said one man.

"Oh no. I'm heading east, so it's all at my back."

He looked at me like I was crazy.

The store blocked me from the wind, but beyond the edge of the building, the gusts rushed by. Whatever was loose tumbled with reckless abandon—litter, extra leaves, and stray strands of cotton. Post was my intended destination for today, a mere fifty-four miles, but the next town with lodging on Highway 380 was seventy miles farther. I debated over whether to continue, and the adventurous and practical sides of me duked it out.

Come on, it's only noon; you can't possibly stop here.

But another seventy miles is a long way, even with a tailwind.

I wasn't sure what to do, so I took a break and went inside the store to buy a few things. Back outside, the wind continued its assault. It was loud. If I wasn't on a bike, I'm sure it would have been an irritation, but being the beneficiary of it, I knew I had to continue. I doubted I'd have such strong tail winds like this ever again. Off I went.

I biked through downtown Post, with charming buildings on each sides of the main avenue and beautiful old trees in the center median. Storefronts looked interesting as did some restaurants, and a bed-and-breakfast with Victorian-style architecture caught my eye. I didn't like the idea of riding so quickly past an appealing place, but today I was biking across the country in earnest. With these winds, it was a day to move.

Beyond town limits, the road led me into terrain with hills. There were fewer farms, ranches and signs of people. Mesquite and other bushes clung to the arid land. Eventually the wind reduced to an average breeze, still helping, but not as generously as before.

This was lonely country. The term "flyover country" came to mind, and it's often used pejoratively. The idea is that the population majorities on the coasts only see this kind of land from way up in an aircraft. This region probably doesn't get much respect. If you're traveling by car, it's merely a place to pass through. And while I hated the feeling, I adopted that mentality as I began to long to reach my destination of Aspermont. Then again, the scenery was pretty in its own way. If only I had more time, money and perhaps help from a vehicle, maybe I would have explored what this region had to offer. But I had to bare this land, mile for mile. By now, I was so used to cycling that I scoffed at what I viewed as the cushy life of driving cars. A motorist can stop anywhere, step outside and then get back in their car once they want to take cover. For me, that wasn't an option; I had to endure the outer elements. Sometimes deep down I longed for someone to follow in a vehicle so I *could* get a reprieve whenever I desired.

The riding continued into the mid-afternoon. At 102 miles, I stopped near Jayton in Kent County. I would have stayed the night here, but there was no lodging in this town of 534 people. I leaned the bike against a road sign, stretched my back and legs, and paced along the road.

A pickup truck stopped across from me. "Do you need help?" the driver shouted.

I waved. "I'm fine. Thanks, though!"

"Is there anything you need? I have water."

"No, I've got some."

"You sure? I have bottles and bottles of it."

Have you ever met someone who tried too hard to be helpful and it got to the point that it became a nuisance to say "no" over and over again? Truly, it's not bad in the grand scheme of things.

"I'm totally okay. Thanks again!" I shouted.

I giggled to myself. Someday, if there's a second bicycle trip and I can afford it, I'll contract this affable man as the driver of my full-time support vehicle.

The man drove away, and I got back on the bike to take on the final twenty-five miles to Aspermont. Then, as if Mother Nature was giving an encore from the morning festivities, the westerly winds came back in a torrent. I was moving fast on the shoulder. In the driver's lane, there were wheel ruts where the pavement was especially smooth, and when no cars were around, I moved over and biked on the right rut to enjoy even more speed. I grinned like only a speeding cyclist can grin. It was yet another advantage; it had been too easy today. I crossed into one more county, Stonewall County, and the wind was blowing so hard at the county line, that the sign was shaking violently like something out of a horror movie.

Long at last, I made it to Aspermont, and my body had had it. A shower in my motel room restored some sense of normalcy. It's amazing the dirt and grime that you accumulate after a long ride. Standing in the water that drummed down on my head and body, I could feel every corpuscle within me being renewed, rejuvenated and replenished. Sweet life-giving hydration. I couldn't have been happier idling in a tropical waterfall. Afterward, I collapsed on the bed and mulled over the accomplishment. My cyclometer read 127.9 miles. This was a big deal—the longest distance I'd ever biked in a day. Not only had the wind driven me, a drop in elevation had assisted as well. I had begun in Brownfield at 3,320 feet, had blown past Post at 2,605 feet and landed in Aspermont at 1,775 feet.

I wandered outside in the late afternoon, in search of dinner. The main drag through Aspermont is a north-south road, and the howling, westerly winds clobbered me from the side. This was no leisure walk. In fact, I saw others who dared to be outside darting from one place to the next. I couldn't find any restaurants that were open and I ended up in front of a fast-food grill at a convenience store. I bought three chicken strips, a bean burrito, and a large Pepsi.

With my meal in a brown bag, I headed to the main square in Aspermont. The buildings looked old and tired. Most of the storefronts were either boarded or showed no extant business. A concrete bench was my dining table, and the wind that had been my friend all day became a pest. Anything loose was swept by the wind. The cellophane wrapper of the burrito almost flew out of my hand. I wedged a napkin underneath my leg, but when I tried to grab it, it blew away so fast that there was no chance of chasing it down. The wind made for a chaotic meal. I tried to enjoy myself, but the raucous rustling of nearby tree branches had me uneasy. It sounded like a hurricane might be coming through. It was obvious that I couldn't sit there in peace. The winds were sending me home and teaching me a lesson: nobody can fight these west Texas winds.

As I walked back, I called my friend Charles in Memphis to give him an update. I recalled with joy how we talked by phone the day before this colossal journey began, and now I was anticipating seeing him in two weeks.

"I'm in Texas!" I screamed into the phone, trying to overcome the noise of the wind, "I'm about 700 miles away from you. I'm getting closer!"

"What's that? A truck?" he asked.

"No, it's the wind."

Charles began to tell me about his day, but I could barely hear him. It had been silly for me to call him in these blazing winds. I told him I'd call him later to discuss how and when we'd meet.

After a nap and watching television, another meal was in order. This time, I went to a Dairy Queen where oddly, there were no customers. On the menu was a combo meal named the "belt buster"—a double cheeseburger with fries and a soda. Earlier that day, I had noticed in the bathroom mirror that I was losing weight (especially in the stomach), and I thought the name of the order was appropriate. Maybe it was because of the dearth of other patrons in the restaurant, but I began to tell the worker about my journey. She welcomed my attempt to be sociable.

"Really!" she exclaimed.

Then she went back to tell her co-worker, a teen who was preparing my order, and then they both came out and sat by me when my dinner was ready. After all, there were only three of us in the joint.

"What are you doing riding your bike in the middle of winter?"

the young man asked, a note of judgment in his tone.

"Should I ride across Texas in the summer when it's a hundred degrees?" I countered.

He laughed and conceded my point.

They introduced themselves. Their names were Sandy and Josh.

"So do you ride at night? Do you have headlights on your bike?" she asked.

"No, only during the day. That'd be crazy to bike in the dark."

As I worked on my meal, Josh talked about six-man football, a common sport in small towns where they can't field eleven high school students for a team. He also told me about what it's like living there.

"Aspermont is dead. Most kids move away the first chance they get," he said.

Sandy appeared to be in her thirties and shared a recollection. "I remember my first bike. It was pink and white with tassels that hung from the handlebars."

That put a smile on my face. "I had a yellow bike made by Ross. It had a banana seat," I said.

"And mine had those reflectors in the wheels," she added.

"Mine too. How I wish I still had that bike!"

"It'd be worth a lot of money today," she said.

"Your bike was probably a one-speed. To stop, you had to back the pedal in the opposite direction. You could make great skids."

Josh had a question. "Why were bikes designed differently for men and women? The man's bike shouldn't have the bar, considering their anatomy. Fall on that thing and it's going to hurt a man's crotch badly."

I laughed and said, "From what I understand, in the old days it was made that way for women to accommodate their dresses or skirts. Also, women wouldn't have to make unladylike maneuvers to get over the crossbar."

"This is good that you're here," said Sandy, "You're the biking expert if you've made it from California."

"That's right. You should be in the newspaper!" added Josh.

I smiled and shook my head.

"Come on," I said modestly.

"He's right," Sandy said, "This is Aspermont. All we need to do is call the paper and tell them we have something worthy and they'll come out. It can be anything. My daughter and a friend chose to pick up road trash with big bags. I thought it was so great—I was so proud of them—that I got the girls featured in the newspaper. Then they received a card from the school superintendent, thanking them for representing students in such a wonderful light."

"That's a nice story," I said with a laugh, "I'm open to whatever, but I leave tomorrow morning."

Sandy thought for a moment, "That might be too soon."

Josh blurted, "Stay awhile. Take a day off and hang out with us!"

That sounded flattering. The youth in these towns tend to be good kids and culturally-deprived, and they are refreshingly innocent in a way that I hope never goes away. Sandy and Josh welcomed me into their world and treated me as if they didn't see a lot of excitement. That's not to judge them—not all excitement is good. But maybe my journey was a gift to them, and I was on the receiving end too. So often, I biked through the main street of towns, and I wondered about the residents and what it was like to live there. These two gave me a glimpse into their lives, and made me realize how broad my own world had become. We talked more about things outside cycling. How life can be cruel and disappointing. But also about getting through hard times, and being a better person on the other side. There's always hope. Near the end, Josh shared about his family background which had its difficulties, and I mainly listened. Sandy seemed to know Josh well and she encouraged him. She probably knew him since he was born. It felt like we were all becoming friends.

Before I left, I ordered a chocolate chip cookie dough ice cream. As I devoured my dessert, a customer came in and they had to return to work behind the counter. It was sad to leave. I said "good-bye" and they both stopped to acknowledge me one last time. What a memorable day.

As I returned to my motel, I savored the last spoonful of ice cream as that wind—God bless that powerful wind—swept through from the west.

***

The next morning, I was tired. My legs felt cranky. My lower back was bothering me again. And my tight neck muscles craved a massage. As I biked out of Aspermont, I hoped for more tail winds, but there was only a gentle breeze coming from the north. Yesterday's exhilarating ride spoiled me. *You mean I have to ride without the scandalous assistance from Mother Nature?* Even with the day promising to be warm with bright blue skies, my morale was low. My body never got going. I biked through two hamlets that broke up the plains—Old Glory and Rule—and arrived in Haskell with thirty-two miles under my belt.

As I entered a convenience store, a customer approached me. "I passed you and saw you looking at a map," he said, "Are you searching for something?"

"Yeah, Seymour. It's up this road, right?"

"It sure is. But why are you going there?"

"I'm biking across America."

"No kidding," he said, "When I saw how you signaled with your arm, and you were in the middle of the lane at the traffic light, it was obvious you weren't from here. The saddlebags on your bike. You holding a map. Just everything."

I told him about yesterday's tail winds. Oh I longed for more of it.

"Well, you know what they say about Texas," he said, "If you don't like the weather, wait a minute and it'll change."

"They say that where I'm from too."

The young man behind the counter had overheard us.

"That's great about what you're doing," he said, "Not much happens in this town."

I laughed to myself, thinking about what I heard yesterday in Aspermont.

He said, "This is farming and ranching country with family operations that have been running for generations. You know what they say? Haskell's greatest export is young people. My parents say its a great place to raise kids, and I don't argue with them, but a lot of high school graduates move on. There's just not much going on here."

"And what are your plans?" I asked.

"I graduate this spring and I'm headed to college in Oklahoma," he said proudly.

The customer beside me said, "No, Haskell isn't anyone's dream vacation destination. There's no glitz or flash, unless you love the sights and smells of a rancher herding hundreds of cattle from one pasture to another. This community is filled with hard-working people. And it's very conservative. Be polite—most Texans carry. And Haskell County is dry. You want to buy beer or go to a bar? You'll have to go to another county. That's just the way it is," he said, with a smile.

I'm not much of a drinker, but I'll admit that once I know there's a law disallowing me to buy booze, my mouth waters for an ice cold beer. But then I realized a benefit of banning alcohol sales.

"As I think about it," I said, "I haven't seen much litter and roadside glass from beer bottles recently."

"That's right," he said, "Less trash on the road. Less drunk driving. Less domestic violence. Not that we don't have societal problems like everyone else. As for drinking, here's the running joke. The Baptists drink like fish, but they hide it. The Methodists do too, only they throw parties out in the open."

"So which one are you?" I asked.

He laughed to himself, but wouldn't answer.

I was enjoying the conversation, happening as it did in an ordinary convenience store. So many places are too busy and see too many people to elicit friendly talks like this, but not here. I was starting to like Haskell.

As I rested outside the store, I had a decision to make. From this town, one option was to head northeast for forty-four miles to Seymour, the next place with lodging. This would bring me to Highway 82, my originally planned route. However, if I rode straight east on Highway 380, I would ride closer to my friend Cheyenne in Denton. I noticed that northerly breeze had grown stronger, and on the first option, I'd be biking into a headwind. I knew I could do it, but morale was low and truth be told, I felt lazy. My researcher Jill hadn't found any motels in Haskell, but I wondered if she might have missed something. This town had a courthouse, as it was the seat of government for Haskell County, so it probably had some lodging for those who had to stay for court cases and so on. I went back in the store and asked the guy behind the counter.

"There are two," he said, "One is south of the traffic light and there's a newer one on First Street."

Problem solved. Today, I would stay in Haskell.

Cycling is an outstanding sport, but it had become my full-time job. I needed a break. It was Sunday, and with the sunny weather, it seemed like a perfect day to go for a walk, have a picnic in a park, or just sit around outside. Also, something inside me knew that I couldn't leave Highway 380 just yet. This modest two-lane highway had been so good to me and had saved me from the confusion about routes in Socorro. Locals who drive this road probably regard it as an ordinary highway on the plains, but this was my special route. It is well-maintained with ample shoulder throughout isolated areas, and it had guided me 446 miles in the past six days. This road ends beyond the Dallas metropolitan area, and I guess all roads, like living things, must come to an end, but for now I couldn't leave. I wouldn't. Call it a fake love affair or a sentimental allegiance, but I planted my flag in the asphalt and claimed it as my own.

I got a room, and after showering and getting settled, I set out to explore Haskell. I wandered around the town square, with its courthouse in the middle surrounded by storefronts. The pavement was made of brick, not as elegant as cobblestone, but pretty nonetheless. I went for an afternoon walk and caught up with friends by cell phone. The town was small enough that I made it to the north and east edges of the village in an hour. In the evening, the only open restaurant that I could find was a Dairy Queen near the motel. Booths lined the outside with tables in the middle. Texas themes adorned the walls—photos of cattle ranches and black-and-white framed pictures of the town's old days. A bulletin board overflowed with announcements, business cards, and advertisements for upcoming events. A Texas flag inside a wooden frame hung prominently on the back wall.

With chicken fingers, french fries and a soda on the way, I overheard a conversation of a teen girl explaining to her grandparents that she had no interest in living in Haskell when she got older. Four people sat on the other side of the restaurant, wearing immaculate church attire and laughing loudly. Two elderly couples, the men wearing cowboy hats, sat at another table and spoke quietly with each other. And then there was me—my insecurities making me feel like I stuck out like a sore thumb—as I wore my sandals, red Arizona Cardinals shirt and khaki shorts in spite of the evening temperature dropping to forty-eight degrees.

After dinner, I returned to the counter to order ice cream and coffee.

"Are you an Arizona Cardinal?" asked a woman behind me in the line. She pointed out that I didn't look like a local at all.

I laughed. "No, I'm from Colorado."

"Me too."

She invited me to sit with her and her companion. They introduced themselves as Carol and Maggie. Carol had short gray hair and wore glasses. Maggie's hair was whiter and she spoke with a deep Texas accent.

Carol leaned in, "You know, I could tell you're not from here," she said, "Your hair. You're too laid-back. Just kind of different."

I smiled with embarrassment. This was the second time I heard something like this in Haskell.

Then she exclaimed, "And I don't mean that as a bad thing!"

I laughed. "No worries. I'm actually biking through," I said, and I told them about my bike tour.

They told me they had attended a horse show in central Texas and were on their way back home to Colorado. They were also staying in Haskell for the night. Carol shared about her expertise in horses. For years, she wrote a column for a popular equine magazine. The more she talked about different kinds of horses, the more I didn't understand. I just nodded and caught bits and pieces of what she was saying.

Maggie asked, "Now what about your Cardinals shirt. Why do you have that?"

"I've been there a few times and like the area."

"I ask because I lived in Phoenix," she said.

It was then that I recounted how my bike had been stolen there.

"That sounds just horrible," she said, "I know the exact spot where your bike was stolen. I've been to that pharmacy."

The conversation came easy. I felt like one of the popular kids in high school who had made new friends. I joked about how the town's name reminded me of Eddie Haskell of the "Leave It To Beaver" television series in the 1950s. "They played reruns in the eighties on cable TV. I remember that," I said.

We also talked about cycling. Carol said, "When I see someone riding, I look at them with respect and admiration. They must be in great shape. But I also get scared. I don't want to hit them."

I nodded. "Me too."

"Is there a way that we should pass?"

"Not really," I said, "Just be courteous and don't pass too close. But you don't have to go far out of your way either."

Then Maggie had a question and she snickered as she let it out. "I've done some biking, but to be frank, I don't like how sore my butt gets after riding. This is embarrassing to ask, but how does yours survive?"

I laughed aloud at that. It was a valid question.

"After a day or two of biking, your butt gets used to the seat," I said, "Yes, it hurts at first, especially if you haven't done much riding lately. Right now, I don't even think about my bottom. It doesn't hurt. But the key is you must ride consistently. Otherwise, there is that two-day period or so where your behind will be sore."

She wasn't persuaded by my answer. "I'll probably stick to raising horses," she said, "And I do walk a lot, too."

Before leaving, I got a picture with these two women. All of us smiled. For the second consecutive night, I made new friends in a Dairy

Queen. These are the in-person social networks in these Texas towns.

"Remember us when you get to the end," said Carol, an encouragement as we we parted.

As I continued biking east the next morning, the conditions changed. For the first time, I felt humidity in the air, and with it reaching eighty degrees it was enjoyable to wear only my shorts and short-sleeve jersey much of the time. The scenery was changing too. There were more trees, which blocked my ability to see far ahead. As I biked through Throckmorton and Newcastle, there were many signs for lakes and fishing spots. Lake Graham seemed like a grand body of water as I crossed it over a long bridge. Eventually I made it to Graham, seventy-three miles total, and called it a day.

On the south side, I entered an Italian restaurant named Vitoni's, and at 2:30 p.m. I was the only customer. Their prices were higher than what I was used to, but I felt like celebrating. Eat something robust. A large Italian meal.

My waiter was also the owner, and in a strong accent, he introduced himself as Viktor. He had to have been the most hospitable man in Graham. He walked me to a table, handed me a menu, and made me feel like the most important person he'd seen all day. He was energetic, with dark curly hair and bright hazel eyes that danced with joy and humor. Granted, the place was empty, and he probably did this with most patrons, but it put a smile on my face anyway.

I asked for his recommendation. "What should I have? Is the chicken parmigiana good?"

"Oh yes," he said.

"I'm pretty hungry. Is it enough for a guy like me?"

"Yes sir," he insisted.

I debated whether to tell him about my journey. At times, I loved telling people because it usually meant that I'd get some attention and a conversation. Other times, I withheld because I wanted people to treat me like they would anyone else. This time, though, Viktor seemed like a neat guy. I had to tell him about my mission.

"Are you with people?" he asked.

"Nope."

He put his ordering pad down and looked at me incredulously. "You are riding all alone? What happens if you get stuck?"

"I have my cell phone and a couple of friends in Texas I could call."

"But you don't have anyone with you each day," he said, "You have no one to talk to."

"Well, I'm talking to you, aren't I?" I said, with a big grin. "Sometimes you've got to do things whether you have partners or not."

"Can I ask you, why are you doing this?"

My mind went blank. I was asked this question in Arizona, and again I struggled to give an answer. I wanted to say something profound, maybe a touch philosophical, but I had nothing. Finally, I spit something out about always wanting to do it. He nodded with a big smile, so I guess I answered the question well.

"I've lost a lot of weight since I started," I said, "so I'm ready to eat a lot."

"Now, I understand." he said, "The chicken parmigiana is delicious. You'll love it!"

When he delivered bread to my table, I asked him if he was Italian. His accent was strong enough that he could have been.

"Yes. We came here many years ago. My wife is American and we have a child," he said, as he pointed to a young boy in the back with coloring books on the floor.

"That's what I thought," I said. "My grandparents and great-grandparents came over about a hundred years ago from Italy."

I told him my last name, "Garufi," and he pronounced it with ease: Ga-ROOF-ee.

His accent warmed my heart. He was one of those special business owners that acted like he had all the time in the world to listen. And he was genuine.

The chicken parmigiana with spaghetti was delectable, as were the soft, warm bread rolls. I should have ordered wine, but instead settled for refills of Pepsi.

Viktor thanked me as I paid my bill. By now, it felt like I had made another friend. He looked me in the eye and said, "Please. Be safe."

He said it three times as I was leaving.

I laughed nervously, partly embarrassed that he showed how much he cared.

"I promise. I will."

***

The next morning was windy and perhaps the coldest it had been on this trip.

I placed my key on the motel's front desk and checked out, when the clerk asked, "Are you biking in the cold?"

I shrugged. *Of course I'm riding.*

Then again, I hadn't looked at the forecast. I couldn't find the Weather Channel on television and never got around to watching the news. Yesterday I enjoyed a high temperature in the eighties, and I couldn't imagine it being so cold today. Based on past experiences, I figured it would warm later on. By now, I had become accustomed to non-bicyclists expressing their uneasiness with some proffering reasons as to why I shouldn't go. "It's too cold," "You're all alone," or "You should rest more," they'd contend. All excuses. Nobody bikes across America if they're prone to believe every worrisome thought that comes to mind.

Such was my thinking before I got on my bike and headed north on the main avenue toward downtown Graham. The wind bristled against me, a direct and ruthless headwind, and it was as cold and as a harsh as a winter day. Outside of town, I'd be biking east, which would make this a more tolerable crosswind. Still, my instincts told me it would be unwise to keep riding. (I guess that motel clerk had some wisdom after all!) Pulling over at a gas station, I called Jill to get information about the weather forecast.

"What is going on out here?" I asked.

I heard her typing on the computer. "It's twenty-six in Graham and expected to reach fifty today," she said, "There's a massive system going through the middle of the country. It's cold pretty much everywhere."

Fifty degrees wasn't too bad for cycling, but those winds would make it feel harsher. "I think I'll hang around for an hour or two, then decide," I said.

"Okay, let me know if you need anything," she said.

Jill was so helpful on this journey. She's a full-time attorney and single mother of two children. Often she's busy but usually she answered her phone whenever I called. And, if she couldn't answer, she'd send me a text message. Many times I knew where lodging was. If a town's population was big enough, there would be motels and hotels of all kinds. Usually I had a daily destination, but with many small towns on the route, it was generally helpful to know where there was other lodging should I choose to have a shorter or longer ride.

In the meantime, I explored the town square in Graham, a more bustling place compared to others I'd seen. The wind whipped mercilessly at the flags above the courthouse. After two hours, it had warmed only to thirty-five degrees. I wrestled with whether to go. If the wind would have been at my back, I may have gone. Ruefully I resigned myself to stay in Graham. Returning to the motel, I hoped the woman I shrugged off earlier wasn't there to see my surrender. She wasn't.

Even though days off helped my muscles recover, being in an unfamiliar town with little to do was difficult. This would be my fifth full rest day. When it was planned to see friends, such as Phil in Arizona and Sean and Glenda in Texas, they were enjoyable. But when it was forced because of weather (Reserve, NM; Graham, TX) or bicycle problems (Blythe, CA), they were tough on me. On days like this, I wandered by foot, anchored to a motel.

I looked for distractions. I spent an hour at the library. I strolled the main avenue, asking all the while, "Who in their right mind would be roaming outside on a blustery, freezing-cold day like this?" Based on the design of the roads, there wasn't much pedestrian traffic near the motel. Vehicles whipped past me as I trudged on broken, weed-laden concrete with no sidewalk. It occurred to me that with rare exceptions, not having a car in America is a strong indicator that you're in a lower class. For lunch, I ate tacos at a fast food restaurant and lingered over a coffee. Then I called Jason, a friend I'd talked to by phone one other time during this trip.

"Where are you?" he asked.

"Graham, Texas."

"It's good to hear your voice."

"By the way, I loved your voice mail a while back."

Weeks earlier, Jason left a humorous message: "Steve, I have two pieces of advice: pedal hard and keep riding east." That's all he said.

"You liked that, didn't you?" said Jason, "I'll drop more nuggets of wisdom at some opportune time."

"Like when you need a break at work?"

"That's right," he said, with a laugh.

Jason is a fellow therapist. We had met while we were both employed at a counseling agency that specialized in court-ordered outpatient drug and alcohol treatment.

"So how's your trip going? Tell me what you're experiencing," he said.

"No doubt it feels good to be doing this," I said, "but honestly, the day-to-day has a lot of humdrum. I've seen more road shoulders, motels, gas stations, convenience stores and restaurants than ever."

"But you have to enjoy this," said Jason, "Trust me, you're doing a once-in-a-lifetime thing."

"I hear ya, and I guess I'm joking. I don't want to sound like I'm complaining—I'm not—but I think I'm ready to be finished."

"I get it. Just have the time of your life. And I'd love to hear what you're learning about yourself."

I wasn't sure.

"I feel like the same guy," I said, "It's only been twenty-six days."

"You might be learning that you have what it takes. You had your bike stolen, yet you're still going! What an example of perseverance," said Jason.

True, this nomadic lifestyle on a bicycle had become my new normal. Staying in the same home every night and heading to the same workplace day after day was becoming hard to fathom.

"All I know is I ride my bike long distances and I'm tired all the time," I said, "My legs feel as strong as tree trunks. What can you gather from that?"

"Steve …"

"Maybe I don't need to learn anything."

"Are you still planning to write a book?" he asked.

I raised my voice. "What does that have to do with this?"

"I'm just asking."

Yes, the plan was to write a book all along, but so what if my story didn't come out with insightful lessons? I can't stand most stories where the main character has a transformation with an unrealistic, happily-ever-after ending. Real life isn't like that. Life is messy. And sometimes stories have sad endings. A lot of travel books play the tired plot of a middle-aged person seeking change in their life. He's sick of his job, or he realized he's been a jerk to his spouse and kids all these years, and if he doesn't change, he might lose it all. Maybe he's overweight and realizes that if he biked like a maniac and ate healthier foods, then he'd lose weight. Some stories are cloaked with the overdone theme of being in search of something that's missing in their souls, or they project it by declaring they're "in search of America." Why not be honest and say, "I don't know what I'm searching for. I just want to do this and I finally mustered the courage to do it."?

Jason wasn't persuaded.

"Come on, Steve, you're riding a bicycle across the country," he said, "How can that not change you? I know you well. You have a lot of depth. My question to you is: have you had any moments of clarity where you recognized a single truth, no matter how slight? There's got to be something. You will have so much to offer others."

That sounded good. "Okay, I promise to think about it," I said.

I heard someone speaking to Jason in the background.

"I've got to go. Work is calling. Remember, have the time of your life!" he said.

It was great to hear Jason's voice, and I realized I was more crotchety with him that I should have been. It was a dreary day. Cold and depressing. Even the steely gray sky gnawed at me. I struggle like this when I have nothing to do.

In the afternoon, I watched TV in my room, and in the evening, the chill in the air became even colder. I thought about returning to Vitoni's, but I didn't want to walk such a long distance. Instead I found a restaurant near the motel, a cozy sit-down type of place. I stood near the host's platform in the foyer as other patrons came and left. Standing there awkwardly for about a minute, and passively insisting that I be acknowledged, I grabbed and read a menu. Maybe it was my edginess and impatience over the day that contributed to it, but bad vibes about the establishment were setting in.

Finally, the man behind the host desk turned to the woman at the register. Nodding at me, he said what sounded like, "I'll help her next."

The place was kind of noisy, but it sure sounded like he called me *her*.

I looked down at the menu and pretended to read, all the while I was fuming. Had he insulted me because of my long hair? Should I confront him? I was tired and not in the sharpest frame of mind—maybe I hadn't heard him correctly. On rare occasions, someone with poor eyesight has said something that indicated they thought I was a female, and in those cases, it always made me laugh hard. But in this instance, my gut told me this was an insult. Still, I didn't understand why I was so upset. I rarely let people get to me like this, especially over my appearance or something shallow like my hair, but this time it did. I walked out, refusing to eat there.

Back outside, I went a few blocks toward other restaurants, but I couldn't find anything appealing that was open.

Then I heard someone holler, "You fag!"

It was a young guy in a pickup driving past.

Did I just hear what I heard? This time, I was certain. I have not experienced much bigotry in my life, but it had me thinking. And hurting. I am a straight man, and he had no way of knowing my sexual preference. Labeling of any kind strips people of their humanity. The slur reduces them to a level of inferiority. It is always wrong.

Maddening idleness. Gloomy cold weather. And now two insults. This was turning into a bad day all around. There was one new conviction that I was certain about: my adventure had reached a turning point. Graham was near the halfway mark between the oceans. No longer did I think of my ride in terms of where I had started; now I was focused on how I would finish.

Ahead, almost as if I hadn't seen it before, the lights of a Dairy Queen sign stood brightly on the main drag, and I made that my destination. When a teen girl employee began to converse with me, the magic began like past evenings in Aspermont and Haskell. Then, a family with three playful and hyper kids overheard us and joined our conversation. For at least an hour, I enjoyed pleasant, symbiotic discussion with locals. And with that, my heart was encouraged. The evening was salvaged.

I thought about all the people I had encountered in Texas. It started with warm friends in Sean and Glenda, and then it had been one stranger after another. How neat it was to bike from place to place and drop into others' lives, however briefly. Meeting them felt as random as a ball bouncing in a roulette wheel until it settled. Will the people I meet remember me? Did I make an impact on them? And turning things around, how have they changed me? There is a notion that there's a God, some higher power beyond our five senses, who is somehow working through every scene of our lives. That every encounter with another is a divine appointment. Whatever your views, we should probably act like that anyway. Treat people more important than yourself. Bless them. Get to know them. Find a way to encourage them. And whatever we do, don't cause any harm. We're fellow travelers on this journey.

Like Jason had challenged me earlier, this trip might make positive changes in me so I could benefit others. I was okay with that. On the other hand, even if nothing new came out of this experience, that was okay too. Simply going was enough. The key for me was to be happy and enjoy as many moments as I could in the Lone Star State. And speaking of which, there was still a whole lot of Texas in front of me.

CHAPTER XII

EAST TEXAS, OUT YONDER

Bicycling is a big part of the future.
It has to be.
There's something wrong with a society
that drives a car
to workout in a gym.

Bill Nye, the Science Guy

As I rode out of Graham the next day, everything seemed different. The cold front had passed, and the morning sun shone with the promise of a warmer day. My pace was swift too. The rest had helped my muscles recover, even if my psyche was knocked a little sideways. Yesterday there was a lot of gloom, like there was a dark cloud hovering over my head, but now I was pedaling on a bright sunny morning with energy and confidence.

In a better mood all around, I found myself laughing over yesterday's two slights. I still wasn't sure whether they happened as I perceived them, but it didn't matter now. Interestingly, I couldn't find my ponytail holder and so I biked with my hair flying wildly beneath my helmet. Oh yes, I am proud to be a long-haired man. People say it's part of my personality, my brand. The critics can sit in the corner and cry; they're the ones with the problem.

Onward the wheels of my journey continued into the countryside of eastern Texas. On a ranch near Bryson, an elderly man drove a tractor with a wagon in tow. He stared out, as if he'd driven it many times before. When he noticed me, I waved. He raised his hand slowly for a return greeting. Ahead. a Buick came to a stop on a dirt road intersecting with my side of the highway. The driver was an older woman with a man in the passenger seat. I had the right of way, but as usual, I made sure I made eye contact with her. I waved and shouted, "Thank you!" for added measure, and she cracked a shy smile. Farther along was a home with a tall white fence that neatly bordered what appeared to be a junkyard. With the exception of the driveway, every part of the lawn was covered with old boats, tractors, trucks and cars, many rusted and gutted out for parts. I cracked up—maybe the scenery on this side of Texas wouldn't offer any majestic mountains, but where else could I see places like this?

Near Jacksboro, a group of cattle grazing in a field noticed me riding through. At first, the closest ones raised their heads, and then like falling dominoes one by one they all turned toward me quizzically. I'm sure they were well-acquainted with cars and trucks speeding by, but who or what was I? Some of the steers ambled toward me, and then much of the herd followed. When they reached the barbed-wire fence between us, they ran adjacent to me as if it was some kind of rodeo. A parade of steers galloped noisily at my side and I shouted "Yee-haw!" to my fellow travelers. After a half mile, the cattle bunched into a crowd in the corner of the ranch's edge and watched me a little more. Then, as I was long gone, they lost interest and wandered in their field like nothing had happened.

It was another lengthy ride. More humidity. More bodies of water. The land was thick with mesquite and cedar trees. In Runaway Bay, the road crossed the sizable Lake Bridgeport, a popular spot for fishing and boating. As I rested at a convenience store, I noticed that I wasn't feeling well. I kept sneezing. My nose was horribly runny. And my sinuses were clogged. It felt like I could take a nap in broad daylight. Was I getting sick?

As I approached Decatur, the highway widened to four lanes. Businesses of many kinds lined the road with cars entering and exiting. According to my map, I was getting closer to the Dallas-Fort Worth Metroplex, and Highway 287 seemed like a buzzing thoroughfare when I crossed it. At long last, I arrived in Decatur at sixty-six miles and called it a day. With Highway 380 bypassing town and becoming a roaring highway of its own, I turned off onto a local road, passed a few businesses, and then realized some of the older motels I'd be interested in were stationed on that very bypass. I worked my way back and checked into a room. Showered and relaxed on my bed, that was when I noticed how itchy my eyes were. My nose was still running too. It felt like a piece of metal was behind the front of my face.

Lying there and suffering, I called Jill to give her an update.

"You sound congested," she said.

"Yeah, I don't know what it is."

"It's the grasses," she said, "In Oklahoma, they're giving off pollen and it's probably the same down there. Are you taking anything?"

"No, I just have napkins that I have here and there."

Jill laughed hard at me. "You're blowing your nose with napkins while you're biking? Why not buy something when you get a chance? Why suffer like that?"

"You're right. Sometimes I don't do things for myself when I know I should, especially when it comes to health."

"You're a typical male, that's why."

"Yeah, I know," I said. My nose was so stuffy that I didn't feel like arguing.

"By the way, I did some research for the rest of Texas. You're set. There's lodging in Gainesville, Sherman, Paris, New Boston and Texarkana."

What a great helper Jill was.

Lunch called. Across the busy, four-lane bypass was an intriguing placed named "Eat at Yesterday's Texas." Crossing the highway seemed like a real-life game of Frogger. With so many cars speeding through, I tightened my sandals because this would require some running. I darted across one side, gracefully leaped over a concrete median, and then when there was another gap in traffic, I sprinted to the restaurant. Whew. Lunch required courage and a workout! Inside, the décor had a 1950s theme with period posters and mementos and an old-style lunch counter with stools. I grabbed a booth by a window and put my feet up on the seat across from me. I hadn't noticed the waitress because I was going through my camera's pictures so intently.

"Sorry," I said, "I'm traveling and I'm obsessed with my photos."

"Yeah? Where are you going? And where are you from?" she asked. She was young and perky. Maybe twenty-years-old at most with blonde hair and pimples on her face. Her inquiry was my opening to tell her about my trip.

"You biked close to my hometown!" she exclaimed, "I grew up in Lovington, New Mexico. When you went through Tatum, you were about twenty miles north of it. I can't believe you biked here. I drive back to see my family and it's far enough by car."

I laughed. "It was long enough by bike too," I said.

"So how many miles have you gone?"

"About 1,500."

"What do you do when you're tired?"

"What I'm doing right now. My feet are up," I said.

She took my order, a chicken sandwich with a side of fruit. The sandwich was enormous. My cup of fruit had mostly cantaloupe and honeydew melon with some strawberries and grapes. As was becoming common, I was eating between lunch and dinnertime and the place was empty. When the waitress delivered my check, she sat down across from me and introduced herself as Alison. This girl was clearly the type who didn't have difficulty making friends. I've noticed that young people tend to be less inhibited and more curious. They're more willing to engage with others. I certainly remember being more gregarious when

I was younger—for better or worse. Then, as we get older, it's a bigger deal to smile, make an effort or connect with a new person, but none of that was the case with Alison.

"I couldn't imagine biking for ten miles, let alone across the country," she said, "And I haven't been on a bike in years. When I was a kid, I wanted a ten-speed bike, but my Mom worried that it would hurt my back. She said I'd be hunched over for the rest of my life. So my parents bought me a John Deere bike—the same color as the tractors and it had a bar across for men. It was the first gift that I ever hated, but I rode it for years."

She started laughing.

"It was a good bike though," she added, "I can't complain."

"What's neat is almost everyone has a bike story," I said.

"For sure," she said.

That got my creative juices were flowing. "A book full of stories about bicycles—funny stories, extraordinary stories, romantic stories. Maybe even sad stories or how they've played a role in world events. Wouldn't that be entertaining?"

Then again, I told her that maybe I should focus on this book first.

"I could be included in your story?" she asked.

"Maybe."

She grinned. Then she wrote down her social media addresses and gave them to me before returning to her work duties.

Today, if there was any loneliness, it was brief, for in the evening my friend Cheyenne from Denton came to see me. Before she could even get out of the car, I was already by her door, ready to give her a hug. Cheyenne had driven for an hour to see me, and my appreciation was emphatic.

"It's no big deal to drive here," she said, "Right now I'm in college, and I'm doing the housewife thing. I do a lot of driving as it is. We had to meet."

Cheyenne is in her thirties with long and straight black hair and dark eyes. She wore blue jeans and a denim jacket and had a big smile. She'd lost a lot of weight from the last time I saw her, but I didn't say anything right there.

"Where do you want to go?" she asked, "I'm paying."

I gestured in the negative. "You don't have to do that."

"I know, but I've got money. I want to treat you. You want steak?"

"That does sound good," I said.

Together, we explored Decatur by car and found a place named Sweetie Pie's Ribeyes. After parking, we noticed nearby was the courthouse for Wise County. Its beautiful architecture made it look like an old Scottish castle. I was in awe. I had biked through many Texas towns that had charming squares with a courthouse—undoubtedly the architectural pride of the community—but this was the best I'd seen. Inside the restaurant, we were seated at a table below a gigantic framed scene of longhorns in a prairie. Right there, I thought about the many ranches I'd passed in Texas and knew a steak dinner was right. Cheyenne and I began to catch up in earnest.

"How long have you been doing this?" she asked.

"Today's day twenty-six," I said.

"Wow," she said, "All that riding. California must seem so far away by now."

"It does."

I paused for a moment, and reveled in far how I'd come. And now, seeing Cheyenne would be the highlight of my time in east Texas. She was a familiar face. And someone who cared. That's what I needed. She and I were acquaintances for many years from online communication. It was always platonic between us. Then, a few years ago, I had traveled to Dallas to meet a woman from an online dating website, and it didn't work out at all. In fact, I ended up leaving feeling humiliated and angry that I had my wasted time. But the trip was redeemed when I met Cheyenne and her family who were hosting a Halloween Party at their home. I had fun with many of her friends and slept on their couch. It was a fun night. At the time, she was in the tail end of a tumultuous marriage with a husband who used drugs. She had tried to reconcile and salvage some kind of normal relationship, but things got so bad that he ended up in prison. After her divorce, she had other dating and relationship problems as I did, but that was years ago. What struck me this evening was how much happier she seemed and I told her just that.

"Oh yes, things are better—way better. We got married last year, and we're doing well," she said, her eyes beaming. "He's a good, caring man who's stable. He also has a great-paying job, and he's supportive of me going to college. Nothing is ever perfect in life, but it's a night-and-day difference when you have a loving spouse by your side who helps you be the best in your pursuits. Would you believe it? Right now I'm in a band as a back-up singer and we perform all over. It's fun."

"That's so great," I said.

"There's no more toxic, depressing stuff of the past. That's all done," she said.

I grimaced, thinking about my own experiences. "By the way, I want to apologize for the last time we met. I drove twelve hours to visit that girl and everything blew up and then I crashed at your house. I remember—I was on the verge of breakdown in your kitchen."

"Don't worry about it," she said warmly, "We've both made mistakes."

"We've probably both grown up a lot."

Then Cheyenne raised herself up in her seat. "And have you noticed? I've lost a lot of weight."

"I was going to say something," I said, with a massive smile, "Yes, you look great."

We felt like two kids having fun in a restaurant without a care in the world. Truly, I want to be overjoyed when my friends have success, and conversely, I need to be somber when they're suffering. That's the way it should be.

The waitress approached and began her spiel about the specials and all the unique steaks they offer. Once she was finished, Cheyenne had to brag about me.

"My friend is biking across America …" she said with a grin.

"Naaaah. Don't go there," I said.

"No, let me talk," insisted Cheyenne, "He's modest, but it took him twenty-six days to bike here ... from where?"

"Del Mar, California."

The waitress turned to me.

"I used to live in southern California," she said, "I know where you started." Then she asked in a suspicious tone, "How many flat tires have you had?"

"Three," I said without hesitation.

Her eyes locked with mine and she smiled. Then our waitress left to give us more time to decide on our orders. When she came back, she spoke to me much of the time and ignored Cheyenne. She told me about the different types of steaks, and pointed on my menu while elaborating about the side items. After we ordered and the waitress left, Cheyenne shook her head in amusement.

"I think she likes you," she said.

"I don't know about that," I said with laughter.

"She was very flirtatious with you. She gave you lots of eye contact. I saw it!"

Then it happened again with the waitress. This time, it was before our steaks came out, and she wanted to confirm the way we wanted our baked potatoes done. Again, she described all the different ways I could have my baked potato—with cream, chives, butter or whatever else. I asked a follow-up question and then she elaborated more. Cheyenne was giggling quietly to herself.

"Stop it," I blurted, when the waitress was gone. "You're embarrassing me!"

"It's a compliment that she's hitting on you," she said.

I put my face down and laughed with her.

Our steaks were tender and tasty. Everything we had was delectable. And the conversation flowed.

"I still can't believe you've made it to Texas," she said.

"On *this* side of Texas too."

"How has my state treated you? It's okay—be honest."

I didn't know what to say.

"As with any region," said Cheyenne, "people have stereotypes about it, whether real or not. Texas is known for its size."

I would spend the most time on this journey in Texas—ten days—and state lines didn't matter. Had Texas been divided into little states as they are in New England, I could have biked through twenty to thirty states. Or, if I had gone through El Paso, that would have been more days in Texas and less in New Mexico.

"Texas should be big," I said, "Everyone I've ever met from Texas are proud. Sure, they complain about the heat and tornadoes and things like that, but they're still proud."

"That's right," she said, "We were, after all, our own republic. And that's a big deal to natives. More than probably anywhere else, Texans don't care what others think of them."

Right there at the dinner table, I grew tired and my allergies began to bother me more. My nose was terribly runny, and I had used much of the toilet paper I brought with me to blow my nose. Because we only had cloth napkins at the table, I went into the bathroom, rolled down some brown paper towels and came back to the table.

"I'm sorry I look disgusting," I said, "I have these allergies."

"Do you have medicine?"

"No."

"Let's go to Wal-Mart and get that taken care of," she said.

Soon after, we were again driving around Decatur. I sat contently in the passenger seat, enjoying the music playing and thinking how nice this was. She was another friend to share this experience with.

Inside the Wal-Mart, I was shocked at their low prices. After four weeks I had grown accustomed to convenience store rates. I bought pills that reduce allergy symptoms and stocked up on drinks and food. Back at the motel, Cheyenne was curious about my bike and wanted to see it. It was leaning against the wall near the television.

"I'm in the presence of the bike," she said, pushing down on the seat, "It's like we're on holy ground."

"In this old motel? Um no," I said with laughter.

"Oh yes, we are," she insisted, "You're doing something special."

***

Riding out of Decatur, I left Highway 380 and was uncertain over how to feel about it. Should I be somber? For eleven days and 600 miles, this road had become my trusted thoroughfare as I biked over mountain passes, enjoyed some tail winds and got a beguiling tour of towns on the plains. Back on that day in Socorro when I was confused about route options, I took a chance on this highway and I can vouch to other long-distance cyclists that this road did me well. It's true that I could have continued on this route for another eighty-seven miles before it merged with Interstate 30 in Greenville, but I wanted to avoid higher traffic levels in Denton and McKinney. And so, in lieu of having a good-bye ceremony, I snapped a photo of a sign with the highway's number and continued on.

Riding northeast through prairie with ranches, at thirty miles I reached Gainesville. Here I reconnected with my original and planned route, and U.S. Highway 82 would take me all the way to the Atlantic Ocean. I still had a long way to go, but my destination was closer than my starting point. Once inside the town, I crossed under the bridges carrying Interstate 35. This crossing carried additional significance. North-to-south interstate highways are given odd numbers. On the west coast, these numbers are low, increasing in an easterly direction. I crossed I-5 and I-15 in California, I-17 in Arizona, and I-25 in New Mexico. And here was I-35, which travels north from Laredo, Texas to Duluth, Minnesota. The goal was to cross under I-95, which runs along the east coast from Maine to Florida. Then I'd know that the finish line would be oh so near.

That afternoon, I finished at seventy-two miles in Sherman. With shopping malls, big box stores and many chain restaurants in the area, I figured lodging would be easy to spot, but I couldn't find motels. I biked all over in my search. I probably should have asked someone for help, but when I finally spotted a higher-end hotel chain, I gave in. I was so tired and had to get off the bike. If there were many more nights like this, I'd be out of money, but for one night I just didn't care. I enjoyed the pool and hot tub. My cushy bed had lots of pillows in different sizes—

some specifically marked "foam," "feather" and "cotton." I couldn't hear noise from my neighbors, and the full breakfast in the lobby was lavish.

The next morning, I had logged only a few miles when I pulled in at a truck stop because I felt so tired. Getting warmed up always took time, but this morning I felt especially drained. The place had the usual fuel pumps with a convenience store and an area for tractor-trailer parking. I locked my bike in front. Inside, I hobbled around and browsed the merchandise. Not that I needed anything; I just wanted to procrastinate. Can't a man do that on a bicycle journey across America? A rack of items with sports logos caught my fancy—gloves, hats, shirts, mugs, shot glasses and even baby bibs. The most plentiful were the ones with the Dallas Cowboys star; others had emblems of the Oklahoma Sooners and Texas Longhorns. Eventually I bought a coffee and sat outside on the concrete near the entrance with my bike beside me.

As people entered and exited, sometimes I said "hi" like a greeter.

One man took interest in my bike.

"I gotta get my bike worked on," he said, "I haven't ridden in a year."

"You want to ride this one?" I joked, "It's all yours."

An older woman asked, "Where you headed?"

"Out yonder," I said, pointing east.

She giggled and went inside.

Oh yes, laziness was my bosom buddy this morning. It was early and I couldn't get myself in the mood to ride just yet. I could have sat there all day, relaxing and being social to strangers, but after another fifteen minutes, the adventure began to call. I hopped on my bike and entered the two-lane road, and pedaled my way out of Sherman. The shoulder was wide. Slowly, I got into a groove. Then one of hundreds of vehicles that would pass that day caught my attention.

"Heeeeeey!" a young man shouted from the passenger window. He was in a pickup truck with others inside. I stared ahead. It's hard to read people's motives, but the encounter didn't seem friendly. His yell was more like a "let's see if we can scare him" kind of thing. Maybe they were drunk.

The incident didn't faze me. Soon, I was riding well. Those morning aches were gone. The day was warming too. Although it seemed like a major east-west corridor according to my map, the road wasn't too busy. More people live on the east side of America, and now when I'm between towns, while it might be considered rural and the boonies, it was nothing like the stunning absence of humanity in the Southwest. I cycled through bursts of forests. There were gigantic ranches and manufactured homes on small plots of land—all intermingled to comprise the east Texas countryside.

At eighteen miles, I rested under a bridge and paced in a sandy area to use different muscles. To my surprise, sections of the sand were more like mud and my feet sank in deeply. I scampered back to the pavement, but not before my shoes were brown and caked with mud. The muck even got on my socks. I kicked against a guard rail and got some of it off. I didn't feel like removing my shoes to get all off it, and soon I got back to riding. It was tougher to clip my shoes into the pedals, but with extra wiggles, I got them in. I was riding easy again.

At twenty-eight miles, I stopped in Bonham. A sign noted that this was the hometown of Sam Rayburn, the long-time Speaker of the U.S. House of Representatives. I approached a convenience store and as I slowed near a fence, I pulled out my right shoe from the pedal ... but I couldn't get my left foot out. It was stuck because of the mud! Suddenly my body and bike began a tilt to the left. I panicked in that split second, but there was nothing I could do. My shoulder hit the fence. Finally, I unclipped my left shoe. I looked around—nobody saw what happened—and I laughed. No, I didn't count that as a fall, but admittedly it was close. The lesson was learned: respect the mud.

I entered the store, bought some things and used the restroom. Then I stood outside. Soon after, two of the store employees came out for a smoke. We got to talking about my trip.

"Were you the one on TV recently?" she asked, "They did a story about a guy on a bike."

"No, I'm just a boring person doing this," I said. Immediately I realized I should have said 'yes' to see where the conversation went.

"There was a guy with a torch hoisted on his bike," she said, "It looked like the Statue of Liberty or something. He was riding to Washington D.C. for a cause."

The other woman had a raspy voice and started coughing in front of us.

"My brother rides bikes like you," she said, "He's been telling me I should ride with him, but I don't know how far I'd get. I gotta stop smoking first."

It was a long day of cycling, sixty-five miles in all, and when I entered the town limits of Paris, I knew I'd be off the bike soon. On the west side, I passed the chamber of commerce and thought I'd stop in to ask questions. Inside, the friendly woman informed me most of the motels were on the north and east sides of Paris, but there was one named the Kings Inn that I'd pass if I continued on the Highway 82 business route. She felt honored I was going through Paris on a bike-across-America ride, and she told me about a museum and a park with a sixty-five-foot-tall Eiffel Tower replica that has a red cowboy hat adorning the top. She gave me a paper map that showed the tower was on the south side. It all sounded great, but I couldn't bear to tell her that I was done riding today. If that place wasn't within walking distance, I wouldn't see it.

I continued to the Paris square and stopped at a red light. As I gazed at the people and activity happening around me, I heard another shout directed toward me from a vehicle. It was a woman's voice and sounded like, "Whooooo!" No, this wasn't a form of antagonism; that's the scream a woman makes when she thinks a guy is hot. I waved with embarrassment. Certainly this was better than the yahoo who tried to scare me earlier.

I continued through the heart of Paris on a congested street with no shoulder. I remembered what the chamber representative told me about a motel on this road, but I figured something would go wrong—that I wouldn't find it. Oh how I wanted to get off the bike and be done

… now. Feeling exasperated, I said a modest prayer and asked God to help me find lodging soon. "And if it's not too much trouble," I added, "how about a Chinese buffet restaurant near the motel?" A mile later, I saw the sign for the Kings Inn. And this is the kicker—there were two! A Chinese buffet was across the street and there was another adjacent to the motel. I was howling and carrying on, stunned over what happened. From my motel room door, I estimated the distance between my motel room and the entrance of the closer restaurant was only one-hundred feet.

Dining at the buffet across the street, I thought about this amazing turn of events as I ate plates full of egg rolls, beef-and-broccoli and sesame chicken, with cups and cups of wonton soup. To be honest, I think I had ignored God all day—no prayer, no communication. I didn't even think much about him. It was one of those times when once I needed something, I turned to him as if he's a magic genie or a person who can give me whatever I want. And the hard truth is, often my prayers are *not* answered the way I'd like. Sometimes it feels like they aren't answered at all.

As I was eating, I texted Cheyenne to give her an update after two days.

"I'm in Paris, Texas," I wrote.

"Already? That's where my husband was born!"

"At the hospital?" I asked, "I passed that a few blocks back."

"Just asked him. He said yes!"

I smiled. With texting, you're never far away from friends.

My last full day in Texas bore the usual routine. I struggled until my body warmed up. Then, near Avery, something exciting happened. A tall and lanky dog on a front porch went on alert when he saw me ride by. He dashed across the highway in pursuit of me in spite of many speeding cars. When I was well beyond him, I looked back just in time to see a car slam its breaks to avoid the dog. Last I saw, he was wandering in the road, seemingly clueless about the danger.

In De Kalb, I encountered the first fellow bicyclist since riding with Dave in New Mexico. He was an older man with a bushy beard and disheveled clothes. I was riding quickly through an intersection when he asked, "Where ya headed?" I didn't have time to answer other than shout, "East!"

At sixty-nine miles, I had arrived at my destination of New Boston in the northeast corner of Texas. For the third consecutive day, I had difficulty finding lodging. This time, I had the phone number of the motel where I planned to stay, but the person who answered had a hard-to-understand accent. I asked a second time for directions and still couldn't understand her, and then I didn't want to ask a third or fourth time for fear of offending her. I asked two women at a discount store, but neither of them knew of any motels. I asked a man in the center of town, but he didn't know either. Then I stopped in a park, frustrated at these locals and yet mad at myself that I stubbornly wouldn't call back the motel.

Then I remembered one extra piece of information that Jill gave me: a McDonald's was near the motel. I recalled a popular book and movie that recently shook things up about fast food and our culture— *Fast Food Nation*, a best-seller by Eric Schlosser and *Super Size Me*, the movie—and I knew I'd find this motel soon. I biked into a neighborhood, and the next people I saw were sitting on couches on a front porch.

"Do you know where the McDonald's is?" I shouted.

They sure did and gave me directions. My lodging was a short distance away.

CHAPTER XIII

ARKANSAS IN THE COUNTRY

There are no foreign lands.
It is the traveler only who is foreign.

Robert Louis Stevenson

Often I've considered myself an ambassador for cyclists. I try to be courteous and obey road rules. If I make a traffic mistake around other vehicles, I usually acknowledge the oversight with friendliness in my gestures and body language. Most days I made an effort to wave at drivers. In Hooks, I shouted "hello" at a man pumping fuel into his car as I went by. He seemed surprised at my goodwill, then gave me a nod. A mile ahead, a dump truck with a loud engine passed in the opposite direction. I waved and the operator reciprocated. Then, three more cars were recipients of a smile and wave. Two waved back; the other didn't. I had made a game of it.

On this final morning in Texas, the riding was easy with no major aches and pains. I was moving and happy. Travelers are a special breed. They have this bug inside them. The key is to move. Kayak down the river. Walk beside the railroad tracks. Drive to the next town. Ride the snowmobile in the canyon. Fly. Explore. Have a new experience. Just go. If you don't do it, you're missing out. To some, it might seem like the devout traveler is never content with where they are. But traveling is about wonder and the mystique of seeing and learning what else is out there.

As a kid growing up in New Jersey, often my family would visit New York City to see my grandparents. During the short twenty-mile ride, I'd stare at the guardrails from the back seat as we sped by. It'd move back and forth with the contours of the road. Much of the time, we'd be on Interstate 80, and I'd daydream about taking it all the way to its western end in San Francisco, California. As I biked that morning far into the northeast corner of Texas, I had a similar child-like enthusiasm, because I was approaching the Arkansas state line. Hanging around borders between states, provinces and countries is another novelty for the traveler, isn't it?

To the north was the faint sound of Interstate 30, which heads toward Texarkana like my route. A thick array of trees—sweet gum cypress, bald cypress and elm—lined the road. My route was relaxed with few cars and plenty of shoulder. I biked through the city streets of Texarkana, and beyond an ordinary intersection, I rode up to the "Welcome To Arkansas" sign. I pulled over and chuckled as I took pictures. Although state borders may appear neat and tidy on road atlases, they can seem random like this one. Behind the welcome sign was a grassy embankment and the parking lot to a hospital. On one corner was an auto repair shop. On the other side was an empty storefront with a laundromat beside it. A few cars casually pulled to the light.

And to add to the oddity, I had crossed into a different Texarkana. On each side of the border are the two respective cities of Texarkana, Texas and Texarkana, Arkansas. They share one city, cut in the middle by this cross street named State Line Road. By now, I had crossed four states: California, Arizona, New Mexico and Texas. The four remaining states—Arkansas, Mississippi, Alabama and

Georgia—were much smaller. Obviously I was past the halfway mark of the journey, and I couldn't help but smile at this feat as some drivers glanced curiously my way.

I took more minutes to rest and paced on the sidewalk. I drank more grape-flavored Powerade. By now, I was growing tired of the sports drinks—Powerade, Gatorade, or whatever the brand that replenishes electrolytes for exercisers like me. They had tasted pretty good for weeks, but my overuse had me weary. I vowed that next time I'd buy something I'd never had before.

Upon inspecting my bike, it was clear that more than 1,000 miles of pavement in three weeks had worn my tires. The back tire was especially smooth. A common road bike tire usually lasts 1,000 to 1,500 miles, and because of the extra friction from the weight of a person sitting on the seat, back tires tend to wear quicker. I suppose I could have rotated the tires, but my intuition said not to touch anything. "If it ain't broke, don't fix it," they say. Everything was riding well with no flats since Arizona. Why risk screwing up something?

Still I wondered. Jill had informed me that there was a bicycle shop in Texarkana, but it was not open on Sundays and Mondays. It was my unfortunate timing that it was Sunday morning and I didn't want to wait until Tuesday for the shop to open. There was another bike shop on my route in Greenville, Mississippi, only two or three riding days away. It was settled, then: I'd get a new tire replacement there.

Off I went through the east side of Texarkana, and soon I was beyond city limits. I looked down at the pavement and noticed I was riding intermittently over layers of pine needles on the shoulder. Mailboxes beside the road had Arkansas Razorbacks decals and designs. Little purple flowers—weeds, I would guess—graced a couple of lawns. I passed larger residences and horse ranches that were intermixed with trailers and modular homes. And then things became entirely rural. It was just me, the road and the forest. The country.

By the afternoon, it became a drawn-out ride. The sky grew overcast, and layers of clouds gave different textures of gray to the horizon. And then the wind blew with an intensity that indicated a storm was near. Tree branches were swaying. Pine needles were sweeping across the road. I knew from weather reports that it wasn't due to rain until the evening, but nature was flexing its muscles. The forest gave way into an open field and the winds blew stronger, slamming against me from right to left. It stung, and the noise was so loud that I couldn't hear if a car was coming behind me. I had biked forty-five miles at that point, and I was nervous to be in the middle-of-nowhere with another thirty-one miles to go. There was nowhere to rest or take cover from the wind. I turned off my brain ... and just rode.

Ahead were cattle ranches on both sides. On the right, a group of steers noticed me. One by one they turned their heads toward me. I hoped for some excitement like the herd had given me in north Texas.

"C'mon, run with me!" I shouted.

Maybe the wind drowned my voice. They seemed unenthused by my presence and reverted to grazing.

Then, as if the cycling demons were testing me, I faced another challenge. The road turned south by ninety degrees, and suddenly those gusts became a demoralizing head wind. My speed slowed. It was like driving a car in first or second gear: it requires a lot of RPMs to accelerate, but the moment you let go of the gas, the engine slows you. I lowered my head and shoulders and stared at the pavement moving by. The wind blasted against me without mercy for three long miles. Then with relief I saw a turn ahead. I was approaching a bridge over the Red River, a waterway so massive that bridges are few in the region.

I've seen the Red River way upstream, where it borders Oklahoma and Texas. In some places, it's a modest desert river. In others, it's a massive lake thanks to humanity's creation of dams. On my map it wiggled and looped (sometimes back on itself) as it flowed southward. Here, it was large and sluggish. The banks were swampy with water in shades of gray and brown. On the other side of the bridge, Highway 82 continued east and soon I was back into forestland. Its tall trees provided enough cover from the wind.

Eventually I entered Lewisville, which looked like a tiny hamlet and dying place. The highway crossed the village's south side, where

I stopped at a convenience store that was closed. Another gas station was out of business next door—an older-style filling station. The building had been neglected and tires were piled beside the gas pumps. Abandoned cars rusted. Thick weeds grew in the cracks of the concrete. The site looked like a piece of automotive history: imagine stopping here in a 1964 Dodge Dart while an attendant checked your fluids and wiped your windshield. It seemed so nostalgic.

I biked through Stamps and Buckner and continued past a sign reading I was only eleven miles from Magnolia. Over sixty miles down and on my way. Then suddenly I was riding slower. Something was wrong. As usual my first reaction was denial, hoping that whatever was happening would go away, but there was no denying that the back wheel had given in. By the time I stopped, it was completely flat.

This was my fourth flat tire on this expedition. As much as I hoped that I'd never get another, I figured this would happen eventually. In one respect, I couldn't complain. I had traveled through eastern Arizona and across New Mexico and Texas on these tires. My, how Landis Cyclery seemed far and removed from here.

As I leaned down to assess the situation, I laughed over how much I had dreaded this next flat tire, whenever it would come. After the mechanical troubles in Arizona, my uneasiness over the past three weeks came down to this question: would I have more problems with fixing a flat? I knew the issue wasn't really about the tire—it was about feeling confident that I could handle anything that arose. There was always a specter of fear that I might have another ordeal—some kind of crisis where I'm stranded on the road like I was outside of Phoenix. Gazing at the wheel, I felt like a kid who wanted to sit back and let a grown-up take care of the job. Then there was that moment of knowing that I was the adult here and I was alone. I had to deal with it.

As for fixing the flat, I did just fine. All it took was five minutes of work, and my confidence was restored. No longer did I have to fear. Was this a microcosm of what I do in life? How much time have I wasted being captive to fear, when freedom is usually one bold action away?

As I resumed pedaling with the back tire rock hard, I had a

huge smile as cars passed in oncoming traffic. I hope those drivers saw me. Even though much of my body was hurting, my energy level was renewed. When I finished that day's ride of seventy-six miles, the five-day total of 348 miles elated me. By now, I felt like the epitome of fitness.

Magnolia seemed like a quaint southern town. Numerous homes had front porches with rocking chairs. Being home to Southern Arkansas University, there were college students milling around the streets. I checked into a motel and went for a walk. The square seemed quiet even with a courthouse in the middle. In the 1950s, the square was everything. Thanks in part to the growth and domination of the automobile, two generations later suburban sprawl has made these places less important. Shopping malls and big box stores surrounded by huge parking lots is the norm. I did like the slower-pace of Magnolia; it was my kind of place. I think it's sad when a town grows past a critical mass in population and people lose their sense of community. They stop saying "hi" to each other and conclude it's too hard to get to know their neighbors. It's a shame for everybody.

Eventually, I sat on a bench and watched the cars go by. I felt lonely and wanted to talk to someone. Then I realized I could update Veronica, a friend in Atlanta who wanted to meet me in south Georgia.

"I'm in the South—I crossed into Arkansas today," I said, "I'm getting closer to you!"

"Oh no, I must correct you," she said with a scoff, "That not the South."

"Really?"

"You're closer and headed in the right direction, but you're not in the South just yet."

I was surprised. I stumbled over what to say and then recovered.

"How can you say that?" I contended, "In a McDonald's in Texarkana, they served sweet tea. And this town is named *Magnolia*. That's as southern a name as you can get."

"True, but you've got to get over to Alabama. That's where I'm from originally, and that's the real South," she insisted.

"What about the accents?" I said, "People here sound a lot like you."

Veronica laughed. "Actually you're the one with the accent," she said.

It was one of those conversations where I knew we were joking, and yet I sensed she was also serious. I know I've been guilty of this type of thing. Still, I had more to say.

"I'm pretty sure most people would say Arkansas is in the South," I contended, "It was part of the old Confederacy. I've seen porches with rocking chairs, redneck types driving old pick-up trucks, and there are churches everywhere. This is the Bible belt, after all. And I've seen a lot of trailer homes in the country—that kind of thing."

"We just call them trailers," she said.

We both laughed.

"I'm glad you called," she said. "My friend recently signed up for a thirty-two mile bike ride that's a fundraiser for a cancer charity. She's worried because she's not in shape and has never biked far. I should tell her about you."

"She'll be fine," I said, "Those events have staff who help. They'll probably have water stations and support vehicles that handle problems as they arise. Plus, you're riding with other people. Tell her to have fun."

***

When I returned to my motel it began to drizzle, and overnight it started to rain hard. This was a abundant and cold rainfall that pounded on the roof. Here, it seemed to downpour without much hope of change. The next morning, the rain was still coming down and it was obvious that I wouldn't be cycling anywhere. The forecast called for more precipitation throughout the day, and the news reported small tornadoes had touched down near DeKalb and Hooks. Both of these are northeast Texas towns that I had biked through just two days ago.

And so I paid for my room for another day, and lay in bed all morning. The rest was blissful for my legs, back and pretty much all of my muscles. I was probably due to rest anyway. I thought I'd give my faithful assistant Jill a call to say "hi" with no agenda but to see how she was doing. Quickly though, she went into research mode.

"You should probably think about buying an airline ticket soon," she said. "It looks like you'll be done in less than two weeks."

"You think?"

"I've been tracking you on a map, and at the pace you're going, yes, you'll be done soon."

Deep down, I knew she was right and liked her certainty. I felt good about handling yesterday's flat, and most days I was riding sixty to seven miles without a hitch. I'd gone 1,700 miles by now. I wouldn't allow myself to feel overconfident about the end, however. There had been too many snags and pitfalls beyond my control that had stopped me earlier.

"Look, I've got time," I said, "Let me get to Mississippi first. I know this is crazy, but I won't jinx myself with any talk about this right now. I gotta keep moving."

"Okay. Just know flying one way from Jacksonville to San Diego isn't too pricey if you buy the ticket ahead of time. And you do have time," she said. "By the way, you were right. Most airlines don't allow bicycles on planes."

"I didn't think so. Thanks for looking into that."

"But I followed your suggestion and found a bike shop in Jacksonville that will take apart your bike and box it up. Then you can Fedex it to your doorstep."

"Ahhhh. You're the greatest!"

"I try," Jill said modestly, "Lately, I've been stuck in my office and it's easy to research things. By the way, I'd visit you. You're not that far away, a day-long drive from Tulsa, but you picked the beginning of the work week to be there. And the kids. They like you, but would they want to travel all that way?"

"I understand. You'd be seeing me wince and hobble anyway. I'm so tired that I might fall asleep on you too. It's too bad that I didn't bike through your city."

"No problem. Maybe next time."

"Next time?" I said with a raised voice.

So today would be another rest day due to weather, and unlike previous periods of idleness, I didn't allow a day's worth of time to drive me crazy. In fact, I think I enjoyed myself.

The motel loaned me an umbrella, and I went about my day in Magnolia. I visited the library where I flipped through newspapers and surfed the Internet. I had lunch at a Chinese restaurant, and then I walked in the cold and sometimes intense rain. It didn't matter if I got wet; I just felt like being outside.

On the north side, I noticed a storefront that offered pedicures for cheap and believed this might be a sign to get one. I had only gotten my feet pampered once in my life, and I thoroughly enjoyed it. There's something about taking care of one's feet that tends to help the rest of one's mind, body and soul. Maybe I would get more pedicures if there wasn't a stigma against men getting an indulgence like this, but here nobody knew who I was. I had nothing to worry about.

So, I entered into the shop that was part of a strip mall. It was a spacious room with only one woman doing the nails of a teenage girl. There was no music and hardly any furniture. The place felt eerie. Upon asking, I learned that they didn't accept debit or credit cards. With no cash and still committed to putting everything on plastic, I left. A pedicure would have been nice, but I wouldn't allow myself to feel too disappointed.

Then only a block farther, I spotted a hair salon that advertised pedicures. I thought that maybe it was meant to be that I'd get one after all. Upon entering, I fell in love with a cute boxer that lay by the front window. The dog lifted her head when I entered, but then resumed her sleepy posture. This shop was busier with more hair stylists and customers in a typical noisy salon. A woman with shiny brown hair wearing a fuzzy purple sweater, a white belt and jeans greeted me. Here I felt comfortable and welcome.

"Can I get my hair shampooed and combed out?" I asked, as I pulled my hair out of my pony tail, "It's a little tangled right now."

"Sure," she said warmly.

"And can I get a pedicure too?"

Her reaction showed that she doesn't get that request often, at least from a man. Feeling self-conscious, I blurted, "Just so you know, I'm traveling through. I'm not some crazy person. I'm biking across the country and have the day off because of the rain."

"Really? You are? Sure, we can give you one," she said.

At that point, it seemed everyone had stopped what they were doing and were looking at us. I liked the vibes of this establishment, and maybe some of the ladies were impressed with my boldness and friendliness.

But then I added, "Oh! Do you take any credit cards? Any kind of plastic?"

"No, we don't."

I grew disappointed.

"There's an ATM at the bank two blocks up," she said.

"Okay, let me see what I can do."

As I walked out, my conscience pressed me to rethink the plastic vs. cash commitment I had made. Yes, I knew I was being stubborn to some extent, but I just didn't like carrying cash. Using my debit and credit cards was fine with me. Nearly every reputable business accepted plastic in this day and age. I knew I wouldn't go to the ATM up the road and rationalized that I shouldn't spend the money anyway. I laughed it off. My hopes were dashed, but there was no point in becoming upset.

The day continued to be uneventful. More rain. More eating. And more watching television at the motel. I really did have more peace without the drama of previous days off. I liked Magnolia too. It was busy enough to have things to do, but it was certainly on the small side. Magnolia felt like the kind of town where materialism wasn't so strong. There didn't seem to be much pressure to "keep up with the Joneses." It was a place where locals can live their lives as best as they can, and that's good enough.

For dinner I ordered barbeque ribs with sweet potato fries and green beans. Across the dining area and behind the bar was a metal sign for U.S. Highway 82. When I finished my meal, I asked the waitress to take a picture of me beside it, explaining that I had been biking on this road since Gainesville, Texas.

"Really? My hometown is Sherman," she said, "I drive back and forth on 82 when I go home."

I nodded with a smile.

"Ah yes, Sherman. That was four days ago," I said.

The next morning, the worst of the rainstorm was over but it was still drizzling at checkout time at the motel. Oh yes, I was going. I would not wait around another day.

The main road in Magnolia had busy traffic, with two lanes on each side and a fifth lane in the middle for making left turns. I rode fast through this corridor that was packed with businesses and shopping malls. The lack of any shoulder was troubling. I stayed right, sharing the lane with other vehicles. I pedaled as hard as I could. In times like this, my bright yellow pullover was helpful for increased visibility. And, while it may have been all in my head, I biked with confidence. I made eye contact with other drivers. Sometimes I waved. Always I "gave vibes" to motorists that I was important and present, and that I knew what I was doing—a telepathic declaration that motorists should notice me and be cautious.

Eventually I arrived in El Dorado, thirty-five miles to the east. The drizzling had stopped, but there was still enough dampness and chill in the air to make me cut the ride short. After checking in at a motel, I had lunch at what seemed like a popular joint, a family-owned place. An enormous Arkansas Razorback was matted on the wall with a Coca-Cola insignia. The cashier and waitress were friendly to most of the customers who seemed like locals. With me, the workers were cordial, but far from warm.

Then I walked the streets. El Dorado in Spanish means "the golden one," but I never learned why it was named such. Like Magnolia, El Dorado also had an appealing square and this one was busier. I spotted a pharmacy that also sold candies, ice cream and various items. Inside, I bought a coffee and rented time on a computer with views of the square. My wandering continued and eventually I found a hair salon with a sign on its front door proclaiming that they accepted plastic. Right then, I knew my afternoon would finish right.

The owner introduced herself as Billie, a woman with flowing blonde hair, sleek black leather boots and a deep twangy accent. Her salon didn't offer pedicures, but she deep conditioned and combed out my hair after putting a leotard cover over me. We talked about many things—the casinos in northern Louisiana, the difficulties of finding good workers for her salon and what her young adult children were doing with their lives. Eventually, I mentioned why I was in El Dorado.

"Traveling like that isn't good for your hair," she said, "I've gone all over the country on a bike with my husband. I know how bad it can be when your hair is flying in the wind. It knots up and the ends fray quicker."

My hunch was that she thought I was riding through on a motorcycle.

"No, I'm riding a bicycle," I said.

She grabbed my hair on the side and looked intently at me through the mirror.

"No kidding! And you made it to our south Arkansas town?!"

"That's right."

"Well bless your heart!" she shouted.

We both erupted in laughter.

***

The sun was fully out the next morning. As I rode out of El Dorado, I noticed changes in the land. Everything seemed greener with small muddy creeks meandering in the forest. And it was warm—birds were chirping as if spring's voice was calling. The cycling conditions were pleasant enough, and I was bursting with energy. After all, I'd only gone thirty-five miles in the past two days. Something daring inside was willing to ride all the way to Greenville, Mississippi, 108 miles away. With my concern about the worn back tire, I wanted to get to the bicycle shop sooner rather than later.

In the countryside, I passed a rickety house and heard the shuffling of footsteps on the porch. A middle-sized tan dog ran out from the yard, charging to my side. He was muscular, mean and barking furiously, no doubt protecting his territory. He was running hard along the grassy area next to the shoulder. It happened so fast. I shouted at him to settle down, and I didn't act scared. Soon I outpaced the dog, but my nerves were rattled. "What a nice way to start the morning!" I joked to myself.

About two miles ahead, it happened again. I heard a dog's high-pitched bark from a farmhouse. This time three dogs greeted me. The smallest one came out quickly, followed by two larger terriers with brown and white curly hair. One barked with vehemence and sped quickly to my side, running beside me. The other one must have been older and not interested in a serious chase. For a couple tenths of a mile, two of the dogs paced with me, barking to me about their territory. I was defenseless, and easily they could have lunged and taken a bite of my leg. Eventually they gave up and retreated.

It was then that I went through memories of previous dog incidents. There was an unleashed dog with an intimidating demeanor in Reserve, New Mexico, but that seemed like an isolated event at the time. There was also the hound in east Texas that ran across the street and nearly got hit by a car. But never in my years of cycling in Colorado had I experienced loose dogs like these.

At sixteen miles, I arrived in Gardner. It didn't seem like much—just a few clusters of homes—but there was a store. I bought some items and casually asked the cashier, "Can you tell me, what is up with these loose dogs around here?"

The young woman nodded and mumbled something quietly, as if she had asked the question herself. There was an awkward silence, and I didn't follow up with a request for an answer. It felt like I had asked a stupid question.

A few more miles brought me to Strong, and I rested in the parking lot of a pharmacy. With the temperatures rising, I removed layers of clothing. I drank more liquids and paced back and forth. Then a man from the pharmacy approached. He wore a brown dress shirt, jeans and mountain boots and walked up casually with his hands in his pocket. He was strong and fit, and somewhat older than me with a thick mustache. He was inspecting my bicycle with delight and curiosity.

"Where are you headed?" he asked.

"Greenville."

"My name's Jimmy and I'm a biker myself. I wish I could ride with you today, but I'm the pharmacist here."

"Yeah? This looks like a nice place," I said, revealing I was new here.

"It is. So Greenville is your destination? You'll be riding on Highway 82 then."

"That's right. I'm actually biking across the country. I started in California five weeks ago."

His eyes lit up and said, "Way to go, man. I've done a lot of riding and have entertained thoughts about doing it myself. Really, I have. But it's not in the cards right now with obligations toward my family and business. Plus, I'm the only pharmacist in town, and I couldn't be gone for too long."

"Could you get a replacement? Hire someone to work during that time?"

"No. That wouldn't work."

"Ahhhh okay." I knew to back off.

"So where are you from?"

"Colorado."

He smiled and I knew he was about to tell me about his experiences.

"I've been to your state many times. I've biked many of your passes. Wolf Creek Pass, Lizard Head Pass and all those passes by Leadville: Vail, Fremont, Independence and Cottonwood."

My grin grew bigger when he mentioned the last.

"If you biked Cottonwood Pass from the paved side, you went right past my house."

We were connecting like fellow cyclists. He leaned down and examined my bicycle. He was interested in the saddle bags and trunk box, and what I was bringing along. Then he looked up toward me.

"I get out a few times a week to ride. We don't have mountains and you have challenges here. The culture isn't too bike-friendly."

That reminded me of the two loose dog incidents and I had to ask about them.

"Yeah, that's a problem. Car crashes with dogs in the South is common. I've seen some nasty accidents." His face grew serious. "Be careful. Once my riding partner was taken down by a dog."

"Taken down?"

"Yep. It doesn't happen often, but it can get ugly. Some dogs will charge and make noise, threatening to bite. Others will run alongside and that's all there is to it. It's a crap shoot."

I sighed and nodded, knowing he was right.

"You'll be okay," he said, "You've gotten this far."

I thanked him. And with that, it was time to leave. But first I snapped a picture of him standing in front of his pharmacy. Maybe Jimmy would never bike across the country, but he had become part of my story, however small.

I resuming riding and about two miles out of town, it happened a third time. An enormous chocolate brown dog was sitting on a front lawn and chewing on something, when he noticed me. Immediately, he ran vigorously toward me, but this critter was fenced in. The canine barked and barked as it ran beside me for about a hundred yards until it reached the end of the fence.

"Is that the best you can do?" I shouted in laughter.

As I continued, the danger of loose dogs became a real concern. I felt vulnerable, like I could be attacked on a whim based on the negligence of a pet owner. And I didn't like the feeling that I couldn't do anything about it.[1]

I daydreamed about the next dog (if there was one) that might greet me by the road. If I was attacked, I'd want revenge. If the dog got hit by a car, surely I'd stop and take a photo of the dead critter, looking gruesome and bloody, that I'd display online for my friends. In a scenario where a dog chased me long enough, I thought I'd pull into the car's lane so it'd run out with me, then I'd swiftly return to the shoulder

---

[1]   After I finished this trip, I learned much about how to handle situations with dogs. Usually dousing a dog with water is enough to scare away most. Obviously, there are other measures of self-defense such as pepper spray, mace, dog tasers and firearms.

so a car could hit him. But this kind of thinking was madness. The truth was that I was scared. And on another level, I was angry. Anger and fear go hand in hand. I've seen it in myself. When we don't know what to do with our fears and let them fester within, eventually it'll come out as an expression of anger.

Somehow, I couldn't let these dogs get to me. Yes, I felt yucky feelings inside, but I forced myself to shake it off. Plus, it's not like I was attacked. I knew the chances of being assaulted were minimal. If a dog did tear into my flesh, it would likely mean it had attacked others, and there would be a good chance that the dog would have been investigated and/or "put down" already in the first place. I made myself experience the moment: the trees passing by, the birds chirping and the sound of the wheels and bike chain going, and I felt better. *Let go and let God, Steve.* It seemed to work.

For fifteen miles I traveled in the Lower Ouachita Swamp, a national wildlife area. Pine trees disappeared into its forest, their tall trunks standing as far away as the eye could see. Tranquil pockets of marshy olive green water nestled in the wilderness. The road elevated onto a bridge above the Ouachita River, which flows into Louisiana. And there were no homes anywhere. Nature was helping me relax.

At forty-five miles, I arrived in Crossett. Inside a convenience store, I paced among shelves of packaged items. I was hungry and unsure about what to buy and I took my time, for I needed a prolonged break anyway. Soon I found myself at the front with a young woman behind the counter, and being the only person there, I felt the need to say something.

"I don't know what I plan to get, but I know I need to rest," I said.

"That's all right." she said with a smile.

On the side was a tantalizing spread of foods behind a glass counter. Chicken tenders, corn dogs, burritos, taquitos, mozzarella sticks, potato wedges and other items were hot and ready for the willing.

I laughed and said, "I've noticed the different kinds of foods as I've gone along. Here in Arkansas, the foods are getting more elaborate ... more greasy ... more fatty."

She nodded.

"These chicken tenders are pretty good. They go quick."

I stared at them, agonizing whether to give in, then I turned to my bike leaning on the outside of the window.

"I just don't know. I'm biking through and going across the country," I said.

She leaned forward and pointed to my bike. "That's yours? It's obvious you're visiting. Am I right?"

I laughed and asked how she knew.

"You look like a city person."

We talked about my journey and I answered her questions. Many had become common by now. But she had one that I'd never heard before.

"What about bike lanes?" she asked, "Is there a route across the country with a bike lane?"

"Not really. Some cities that are progressive enough may have lanes."

"So where do you ride?"

"On the shoulder. Most roads have some kind of pavement on the side."

"You're going on Highway 82? You've got my respect!" she said.

"Awww ... it's that not that bad."

She smiled and said, "Crossett is mainly full of hicks."

"Well that's most of the South, isn't it?" I said jokingly.

"Yeah."

"Naaaw. I'm just teasing. That's a stereotype."

She looked at me matter-of-factly. "No, you're right. Most people don't do bike-riding or athletic things like that. They're into mud riding and getting drunk."

"Really?"

"Oh but its fun!" she said. Then she told me about adventures with her friends on ATVs. Eventually I bought some snacks and drinks, including one chicken strip. I stood by the door as she handled other customers. Then when there was a gap, she went back into her talk.

"Not much happens here," she said.

"Someone else told me that at a store. I think it was in west Texas. Maybe I could set you up with him."

"Funny," she said, "Really, most kids who grow up here leave. They move to Little Rock or Shreveport or even Dallas. Any place with plentiful jobs and enough population that people don't know your business."

Soon more customers had entered and were keeping her busy. I knew it was time to leave. As she was ringing up customers, I shouted, "Take care!" and she shouted good-bye back. I had made another friend, however briefly, and that was it. Back to work.

My riding continued through peaceful and wooded land. The cars and trucks became fewer—their whooshing sound as they passed grew more pronounced in the quiet. The humidity had grown thicker and I was sweatier than usual. My neck and shoulder muscles felt achy. Even with the break in Crossett, I felt especially tired. But that's the plight of a cyclist. My legs were on auto-pilot and I continued anyway, knowing it would be a long day.

At sixty-five miles, I crossed into Ashley County and was making progress. Ahead, I passed a man on the right who looked like an honest-to-goodness hillbilly. He was a portly gentleman who wore denim overalls and a straw hat. He was in his front yard and walking toward the road, perhaps to go to his mailbox. I was within fifteen feet of him and gave a friendly smile, but he didn't acknowledge me in any way. No eye contact—nothing. His face was expressionless. And as quick as a bike can ride past a house, he was out of sight.

One mile later, I was still thinking about him. I was disappointed because his appearance with those overalls was so interesting. And I would have loved to have talked or gotten a picture with him—any reason to stop and rest from this grueling ride. My imagination ran wild with questions: Why didn't he say "hi?" Was he scared of me? Was he sad? Maybe he didn't see me, or perhaps he had a lot on his mind. You just never know—maybe he was drunk. Or did race play any factor? For this man was black.

Most of the people I had encountered so far on this journey were white, with some Latinos, but beginning in northeast Texas, the racial makeup began to change. In southern Arkansas, about half of my interactions were with blacks. In most instances, I hadn't mentioned the races of people because as an author, I didn't think it was necessary in the telling of my narrative. But there is a common literary difficulty that writers grapple with, especially when describing people in scenes. If one leaves race out, will a majority of my readers assume the main characters are white? Will black readers picture those same characters with darker skin? It begs the question: do readers tend to assume a character's race as their own if race is left blank in a story? People's races had not mattered on this trip, and it wouldn't begin to matter now. I had enough to worry about as a bicyclist in an auto-dominated world.

I continued riding and thinking about that man. His face struck something in my heart. Maybe his likeness reminded me of my father, a man who usually kept most things inside. My thoughts about humanity's divisions, based on race and other characteristics, seemed to come to a head. The theme was about how we perish as a people when there is disconnect between neighbors, races and nations. Suddenly I burst into tears, sad at our human brokenness.[2]

Maybe my feelings were heightened because I felt so raw and tired. On a bike, I was so much closer to the land. It's different than driving in a car where motorists are in their own personal bubble and space. On a bicycle, within a second, I could stop and put my feet down on the ground, and I could interact with the people around me. I saw the land—its nuances, its moods, its textures, its aches.

The long ride continued. Near Montrose, the scenery opened with a break in the trees. Around me were acres of barren cotton fields. I returned to the forest, but soon the trees finally relinquished control. I was on the plains of the Arkansas Delta—the fertile and flat land west

---

2   Five years later, a resident in Hamburg read my online journal which included this experience. She informed me that the man's name is Robert. He likely didn't make eye contact with me because he has a mental disability. He lives with his grandmother and hitchhikes each morning into town. The locals care for him, making sure he is fed every day and that he finds his way home in the evening. It goes to show you: don't believe every thought that runs through your mind.

of the Mississippi River that is so good for growing. I crossed over creeks with names like Big Bayou, East Crooked Bayou, Bayou Macon and Little Lake Bayou. Each looked like a stagnant ditch. Beside the road were sizable man-made lakes that had something to do with farming.

Though the landscape piqued my curiosity, my body was having a rough time. I was exhausted, and my lower back muscles were nagging me. Then far in the distance, I noticed a cluster of trees with buildings. I focused as best as I could and saw a structure in the shape of a water tower. Granted, I was miles away, but that had to be Lake Village. Suddenly, I felt relieved and got a boost in morale—that community would be the last stop in Arkansas before crossing into Mississippi. And oh how I was ready for an extended rest!

I biked well for the remaining miles into Lake Village, and as I approached the first major road intersection, there was a rumbling in the back tire. I was slowing down; it was another flat in the back wheel. As I got off my the bike, I could see restaurants and services just blocks ahead, and my laziness kicked in. If this flat tire had happened in the country, I would have fixed it immediately, but with dinner, a hot shower and motel bed enticing me, I knew I was finished for the day. Although it was only four p.m. and only sixteen miles separated me from Greenville, this flat sucked the tenacity out of me. I felt bad that I wouldn't reach my goal, but then again, ninety-two miles of cycling was nothing to feel bad about.

I checked into a motor lodge with about eighty rooms. In one spot, two men sat outside a room, drinking beer. No big deal, I thought.

I checked in, obtained my key, and walked toward my room. As it turned out, my room was right next to these two men. One guy wore a brimmed hat sideways, with a sweatshirt and baggy pants. The other guy wore a white tank-top with sweatpants. I said "hi" as I passed, and one of them grunted softly in return.

Inside my room, the sound of their loud rap music blared through the wall. I turned on the air conditioner which partially drowned out the racket, but I could still hear the men talking outside. When there was a gap between songs, it sounded like someone was playing a video game with the volume way up, as if they wanted me to hear it. I did my best to cope and overlook the situation. However, after a refreshing shower, the music seemed louder and the walls were shaking too. It was obvious that I had to deal with the situation, and so I returned to the office.

"Can you please give me a different room? Maybe something over there?" I asked, while pointing toward the other side of the motel.

The woman behind the desk had her manager come out, and he nodded in frustration, as if he knew the instigators well. He explained that the rooms where I pointed were "doubles" (rooms having two queen beds). Although apologetic, he requested I pay ten dollars extra to move into one. It was tacky, but I agreed without arguing. I didn't have the energy to fight. I just needed to get away from the noisy people.

The second room was clean and much quieter. There was a short visit to a fast food restaurant across the street, and then I lay in bed and watched television throughout the evening. Little did I realize that Lake Village was a charming place that I would miss out on. Years later, I learned that the town sits on the edge of an oxbow of the Mississippi River. About five hundred years ago, the river looped on itself and left a narrow lake in the shape of a "C" on the village's east side. That evening, I saw none of Lake Village's spectacular scenery, because I was lying in bed like a slug with no energy to explore by foot.

Before falling sleep, I did fix the flat. The culprit: a metal wire lodged on the outside of the tire. By now, the back tire was showing more wear than I had ever seen. It looked like I could punch my finger through it. Fortunately, the bicycle shop was a short distance on the other side of the Mississippi River.

CHAPTER XIV

DOSE OF THE MISSISSIPPI BLUES

*The real glory
is being knocked to your knees
and then coming back.
That's real glory. That's the essence of it.*

Vince Lombardi

*T*he shoulder narrowed as I approached the Benjamin G. Humphreys Bridge. This bridge was far from anything to admire from a driving and cycling standpoint. Spanning three quarters of a mile over the Mississippi River, the architecture was a steel through-truss design—a non-aesthetic structure with only two lanes and no shoulder. Built in 1940, it soon became obsolete as the population grew and automotive traffic increased. Later I'd learn the Humphreys would soon be dismantled, piece by piece, and a world-class cable-stayed bridge would be constructed nearby. Critics have maintained this old bridge was located too close to a sharp bend in the river, which challenged the navigation skills of those piloting barges and other commercial boats.

Also, the narrow lanes squeezed its two-way traffic, making it a perilous trip for skittish drivers. As daunting as it would be for me to ride across the bridge, while planning my route I discovered that the Mississippi River had few bridges in this region. In fact, the nearest ones were north in Helena, Arkansas (110 miles) and south in Natchez, Mississippi (75 miles).

I could see ahead that the steel behemoth offered only inches of space between the white line and a guardrail. Both pedestrians and bicyclists had no alternative but to take the road. I biked as carefully as possible. Expansion joints spanned the pavement every twenty-five yards, jolting the bike as I crossed. They were like fingers put together with a small gap between them for drainage.

A few cars passed. I gave a wave with my left hand as I heard them close behind. Some mercifully moved to the middle of the two lanes to give me plenty of room. Some passed closer. The bridge's grade increased and my speed slowed. I didn't want to go at a snail's pace on such a narrow road while cars were passing, and so I pedaled harder. My leg muscles began to burn, but I didn't gain much speed. More cars went by. Then a large dump truck gently passed, its loud motor lumbering up the grade and giving me a nasty whiff of exhaust fumes. His speed wasn't much faster than mine. The whole experience was exhilarating. At least I wasn't bored. I coached myself: *ride hard and hope no one hits me!*

Another vehicle approached from behind and hovered at my pace of ten miles per hour, fearful it seemed, of passing me too close. Traffic in the oncoming lane was plentiful, making it impossible for the drivers behind to hit their accelerators and zoom by me. I didn't dare to look back to see if a long line of cars were crawling indignantly behind me, ready to vent their rage at the two-wheeled instigator of the bottleneck. Oh the intensity! I told myself to stay strong and confident. Act like you've done this before. Maybe then, people wouldn't view me as a nuisance when they finally move onward.

Once the oncoming traffic died down, a parade of cars began to pass this lone cyclist. No one was mean. No one honked or shouted. I smiled and kept pedaling, occasionally waving as I labored.

Soon I arrived at the middle of the bridge. The pavement had crested. And the cycling became easier. Although I hadn't noticed any signs prohibiting bicycles, it occurred to me it might not be wise to be here. Who knows? A police officer could give me a hard time. I was on that narrow bridge, with no way easy way out, surging forward to the eastern bank of the Mississippi River. Initially I didn't want to stop, but then a wiser voice counseled me, "Wait! You've got to stop! People will ask what you did at the Mississippi and you can't say you just biked over it fast." That wouldn't be acceptable.

When there was a break in traffic, I dismounted, stepped onto a metal ledge, lifted the bike and leaned it on the railing. This was not a pedestrian area, and there was barely enough space for a person to stand. The railing came up to my chest which made it safe to lean ahead. I looked down at the river, the water gently flowing south, and the distance scared me. It conjured morbid thoughts of suicide and what a great spot this would be to take a flying leap—with my beloved bike, of course. But that rumination drifted away as two tractor-trailers swooshed past me uncomfortably close, causing the bridge to convulse with their heavy loads. With me off the pavement, cars and trucks sped down the center of their lane, each giving me a burst of wind. The bridge shook with every vehicle, big and small.

As I became more at ease standing on that ledge, taking in all of the scenery, I was happy that I had stopped. This was one of those times that can take your breath away and I needed a moment to absorb it. This was the Mighty Mississippi, after all. She's the mother of all rivers in the middle of America, and the continent's largest drainage basin. Starting in Lake Itasca, a lake in Minnesota, she absorbs rivers from as far as the Rocky Mountains in Montana and Colorado. And from the east, waterways that begin in the Alleghany Mountains of Pennsylvania and West Virginia eventually flow to this massive river.

I had already biked over some major rivers like the Colorado, Rio Grande and Red River, but none compare to the legend of the Mississippi. The river runs deep in the psyche of American culture, and people's associations with it are many: Mark Twain's characters, Huckleberry Finn and Tom Sawyer with their high adventures on her, historic steamboats with their gamblers and traders, Lewis and Clark and their band of explorers, and Civil War battles for it including the 1863 Siege of Vicksburg.

I wondered what more practical associations some people today might have with the river. A friend in Minneapolis drives across it twice on her daily commute. It's a workplace for boatmen on tugboats and barges, and a playground for local fishermen. Magnificent and beautiful, nearly a mile wide in some sections, the river is the gateway to major cities like Minneapolis, St. Louis, Memphis and New Orleans. Its fame begins even in elementary school as its unique and memorable name forms the classic spelling challenge: M-I-S-S-I-S-S-I-P-P-I.

One of my writing mentors, Eddy Harris, is a man who grew up on the banks of the Mississippi in St. Louis. His first book, titled *Mississippi Solo*, is a memoir about his youthful canoe trip on the entire river from its headwaters in Minnesota to New Orleans. He began as a novice, not knowing how to paddle, and yet he learned as he went. He traveled alone and camped most nights. His encounters with people on the edges of the river and in other boats were mostly friendly, but a few not-so-friendly. He made it—it was his life dream—and as I clung to the railing on this bridge, I grinned and felt a kinship with Eddy. I was on my own long journey, and right here the routes of our respective adventures intersected.

As the sun bore down on the river, I squinted toward its water. In shades of gray and muddy brown, it flowed sluggishly without a care in the world. On one bank were grain silos with a line of trucks waiting patiently, engines idling. A wooden dock jutted out from the Arkansas side, a nice place to toss in a line and enjoy the river at its own pace. Under construction downriver, the new bridge already looked modern and elegant. It would soon have its own memories, and as much as it would be an improvement for drivers, pedestrians and bicyclists, I expect some will miss the Humphreys that must have been something "back in the day."

After about ten minutes, it was time to move on. I turned my body on the ledge and faced a number of moving cars and trucks. I smiled and gave a few waves to my fellow travelers. Some waved back. Then, when the last car of a procession of vehicles passed, I dropped the bike on the pavement and rode with urgency as if I was escaping from a bank robbery. I hoped I could reach the other end without more cars and trucks zipping past. My speed increased on the downhill, reaching twenty-five miles per hour. I thought I might be free and clear, but the bridge kept going and going on the east side.

Then the beastly sound of a tractor-trailer approached from behind. It downshifted thunderously, like it had come from a horror movie. With no shoulder, I had to stay balanced. Swerving left into traffic or crashing right into the guard rail would be catastrophic. And those pesky expansion joints seemed to be worse on this side, with each jolt feeling like I was hitting a pothole. I sensed this truck would pass any second. I gave a quick wave with my left hand. It was so intense. So horrifying, yet so enlivening.

The thought occurred to me, "I could die on this bridge. This could be it. When the ambulance picks up my dead body, they'll search my wallet, find my emergency card and call my brother!" Then the truck flew past with a roar. Immediately, a car passed, and then another massive semi was behind it. Thankfully they all gave me room to maneuver and breathe. I reached the end of the bridge's narrow segment and with much relief, I veered onto a sizable shoulder where there was a sign that read, "Welcome to Mississippi. It's Like Coming Home." My sentiments exactly.

I stopped, leaned the bike against the sign and turned back at the bridge. I bellowed out a hearty laugh. No river crossing had been as consuming as this one. I'd been tested by the mighty Mississippi … and I survived.

***

Kwik Keys & Bikes is in a busy section of Greenville and was easy to spot on Highway 82. It's in a shabby, concrete-faced building with two adjacent storefronts. A sign above the door read "Kwik Keys," with a drawing of a smiley-faced key riding a bicycle.

Inside, I shuffled to the back of the line of customers with my bike beside me. Kwik Keys had an entire wall with keys and an assortment of tools related to locksmith work. Only four used bicycles, all of them small enough for children, stood on the other side of the store. Keys and bicycles seemed like a peculiar business combination, but what did I care if they could help me? There were several customers in front of me, and nobody bought a bicycle. Everyone seemed to need copies of keys except me.

Eventually I got to the front and introduced myself.

"Oh, you're the guy that woman called about," said an employee, "You're going cross-country?"

"That's me," I said with a shy smile. I leaned the bike against the counter and showed him my worn back tire. Then I sat down and exhaled with much relief.

"I'm so proud," I said, "Those tires got me here from Arizona. But look at it now."

Two men stopped what they were doing to help. One of the older men, the mechanic who runs the bicycle side of the business, inspected my tires while the younger man shook my hand. They were interested in my trip, and I told them about how my first bike had been stolen, my total mileage so far, the weeks I'd been on the road … the usual.

"This is great that you're here. How did you find out about us?"

"Google. A friend does research while I'm riding."

"I remember that. She didn't know what day you'd get here, but my Dad runs the bicycle operation," he said, pointing to him, "He'll help you."

I was sweaty and red-faced. Eight miles from the bridge brought me to twenty-one for the day, and my riding had me on overdrive, similar to the adrenaline rush someone feels long after walking off a wild rollercoaster ride.

The bike mechanic spent a few minutes in the back, and then returned holding a standard road bike tire. "This isn't the same brand. Do you still want it?"

"As long as it fits," I blurted, before he finished asking his question. *Of course, I wanted it!* That back tire was beyond worn and I had to get a new one. Besides, I doubted that there were other bicycle shops around.

"All right," he said. He went back with my bike and raised it on a lift to do his work.

This man had asked a simple question, but something inside me snapped. The morning had me tired and short-tempered. To be honest, I was nervous that this key shop (which didn't look like a standard bike shop) might not be able to help. Whatever the case, I knew I'd been unnecessarily abrasive with my tone of voice. And so I stood up and apologized.

Then he stopped, stepped toward me and seemed confused. "I didn't take it like that at all," he said, "No offense taken. We're here for you and we'll do whatever we can to get you back on the road."

"Well, I felt like I was rude with you," I said, as I faced the floor. Then I nervously laughed and added, "I've been biking since eight o'clock. I made it over that crazy bridge. And I really should have had that tire replaced in Texarkana. I'm just a little frayed."

His eyes widened. "You biked on that bridge? That narrow thing with two lanes? Did you have trouble?"

"Not really," I said, and then I started laughing more, "After all, I made it. Right?"

He grinned and was impressed. "Not many people bike on that bridge. I'm glad you're okay," he said.

"Anyway, when you asked me the question about the tire, I felt I was rude. I definitely don't care what brand it is. If it fits, then it's certainly better than the old one."

"Gotcha," he said, warmly, "And let me say this to you: I ride myself. I love bikes, and it can be rough sometimes …"

"But it's so worth it," I said, finishing the sentence for him. We both nodded. "Anyway, I'll sit here quietly and let you work."

By now, the store had quieted. The younger man offered me coffee and I accepted. It was hot and bitter, the automatic kind, and dousing it with creamer didn't help. I didn't mind though. The hospitality felt good, like what I'd expect as a guest in a friend's living room. He approached me, leaning against the counter with his hands in his pocket. He told me about how hot and humid Mississippi can be in the summer, and when he learned I live in Colorado, he told me about his family vacations out west. Just small talk, really.

Then his voice grew curious. "Have you ever been to the Mississippi Delta?"

I hadn't. I'd only been in the southern part of the state in Hattiesburg and the coastal beaches.

"It's different here. Not in a good or bad way. There are no huge malls, no shopping scene. It's not very cosmopolitan. It's known as one of the poorest places in the country. And sometimes people have negative perceptions."

He didn't have to say it, but I knew what he was alluding to: the sad history of racism and the systematic oppression of non-whites. I couldn't deny that's the first thing that hits my mind when I think of Mississippi, but I'm open-minded too. Ultimately, what I care about is safety and having good roads for cycling. And no part of the country is perfect. No region, no group of people and no culture is without sin. And although it's foolish to believe humanity will ever live in perfect harmony, today the scene I saw when I walked in were three white men behind the counter and mostly black customers in line, and everyone was kind and neighborly. They almost seemed like family. The staff knew the names of many of their customers, and I heard one ask about the health of a family member.

I had a fun quip to share. "It's like coming home. That's the state motto. I like that a lot ... it's the best I've even seen on a welcome sign."

"That's right," he said, "I think it's a good place to live. I'm raising my family here. But like I said, the summers are brutal. If you don't have air conditioning, you're in trouble."

"Today I've got good weather. I'm sure Mississippi will be good to me. This is my sixth state, and after the eighth I'll be finished."

Then he added, "Hey, if you love the blues, we have the greatest blues music scene anywhere. Hunting is big here too. And catfish! I'm not the biggest fan, but people go wild over catfish, deep fried with a side of coleslaw and black eyed peas, or even deep fried hushpuppies."

I nodded, but I didn't tell him that I had no idea what deep fried hushpuppies were, and I was afraid to ask.

Within a short time, my bike was wheeled back to me. The new back tire looked great. Both tires were pumped rock hard. Their floor pump had aired them much firmer than my wimpy carry-on hand pump ever could, and he didn't charge me much money either.

Back on the road, I crossed the street and biked past a car wash with a crew of men standing with towels. I heard them carrying on about me, but I couldn't tell if they were making fun of me, shouting some encouragement, or just saying, "Hey, look at this guy!" I turned toward them and waved, but I was moving and well on my way.

Highway 82's business route through Greenville was packed with stores, shopping outlets, traffic lights and vehicles. I hoped I could avoid much of the ruckus while riding on a street one block over from the main drag. Right when I turned onto that residential road, I heard an odd, high-pitched whistling sound. Was it a bird? A noisy car? Then I noticed the sound was in synch with the rotation of my back tire. I looked down with fright; I'd gotten a flat tire in less than a half mile. I stopped and shook my head in disbelief. Sure, I could have fixed the flat right there, but I didn't want to use my carry-on pump ... and I was so close to Kwik Keys. I figured I'd have them fix this flat. Returning on the main drag, I walked with my bike alongside me. Across the street, the men at the car wash saw me once again, some pointing toward me. Were they laughing at me? I still couldn't tell.

Upon my arrival at Kwik Keys, the bike mechanic was out. He had gone on a house call and would be back in fifteen minutes. So I sat down once again, feeling embarrassed. *Wasn't I just here?* The two other men consoled me about the flat and stayed upbeat with me. After a long fifteen minutes, my trusted bike mechanic entered and when he saw me, he had a perplexed look on his face.

"Oh no, what happened?" he asked.

"A flat two blocks away."

He grew upset and apologized profusely. He sounded like a tourism representative who was disturbed that a visitor had a bad experience in their region. "I heard you talking to my son earlier," he said, "and I'm with him. I want you to have a good time here."

"Don't worry, flat tires happen," I said, "You know that."

He walked my bike to the back and found that a large piece of metal had created a hole in the tire. It was so substantial that he told me he would give me a new tire, free of charge.

"No, you're not doing that!" I said.

"Oh yes, I am."

It was one of those situations when a friend offers to pick up a restaurant tab and the two of you are arguing about it.

"You don't have to do that. You charged me so little in the first place!"

"No. No. No. I'm giving you a new tire."

His eyes locked with mine. He lowered his voice gently and authoritatively. "I'm insisting," he said.

And that was that. Ten minutes later, I had another new tire, rock hard with air.

"I'm sorry about what happened," he said, "Now you be careful." It sounded like parental advice.

"You have my word," I said warmly, "Thanks again, guys."

On this second attempt through Greenville, I stayed on the busy business road. Everyone would have to deal with me. I biked confidently and felt good about the extra care I received.

Mississippi. It's like coming home!

Outside city limits, I got into a groove. The sky was bright blue, and it was warm enough to ride with shorts and a short-sleeve jersey. I biked through Leland easily without taking a break.

Beyond, I rode into cotton and farming country—one of the regions where slavery was most prevalent in Mississippi. As I scanned the plantations today, I thought of days past when my fellow Americans were enslaved and oppressed by that peculiar institution. I've studied our nation's history and knew about the break up of families, the degradations and the cruelty. And it was impossible for me to pass by fields of crops and not envision the human suffering and pain inflicted on African-Americans in what was one of our nation's most tragic eras. In the early 1960s, this region was also where the toughest "freedom summers" transpired, when blacks dared to register to vote, usually unsuccessfully, with great risk of incurring police harassment, violence or death. Only after the federal government intervened were blacks granted the right to vote. Truly, I didn't want to think too much about this; every region has had its problems. And I always want to believe the best—to look a person in the eye, to spend time with them and to judge for yourself about their character. My problem was that I've studied too much history. I've read too many books. As I daydreamed about the old days, I sensed maybe there was something to learn, feel or see in the present.

From Leland, it was twelve miles to the Sunflower County line, and then my good cycling fortunes came to an end. The highway kept its four lanes with a wide, grassy median in the center. The pavement on my side practically disappeared, extending only two feet beyond the white line. To make it worse, a rumble strip encroached on this two-foot sliver, reducing my riding space to about eighteen inches. Sand and gravel covered the ground beyond the pavement, but I certainly couldn't ride on that.

My muscles tightened as I concentrated on staying balanced. Within a mile, I leaned too far to the left, and suddenly my arms and shoulders shook in contortions from the rumble strip. It was so abrupt that my carry-on pump fell to the ground. I stopped, retrieved the pump, and then took a deep breath. "Okay," I told myself, "Stay calm and definitely don't do that again."

I continued. My speed was slower and I pedaled timidly, worried about bearing a repeat. Most cars were giving me space when passing, but when both lanes were occupied, the right lane vehicles passed closely. There was one positive, at least: that rumble strip would alert a driver if they were about to hit me! Miles later, I managed to get myself in another fix by leaning too far to the right and into the gravel. I tried to maneuver back on to the pavement while feathering my brakes, but my momentum led me farther down the sloped edge and almost into tall, nasty weeds. Only when I hit my breaks hard, which had its own risks, was I able to regain control and get back on the pavement. It was a miserable situation.

Bicyclists know that they have a right to use the road, but we tend to be conservative in how much we grab—not just to be courteous, but for safety and to not irritate drivers who may already have a thing against us. With that in mind, I had the idea that I would only use the driver's lane if no cars were around, staying far to the right. I could lift my bike over the rumble strip, like a kid "popping a wheelie," and then enjoy the smooth pavement. But once a swarm of vehicles approached, quickly I returned back. There have been times where I've felt so much courage to assert my rights on the road, but in this case, I just didn't feel safe to share the lane.

The conditions got worse. My narrow shoulder started to have pockets of sand and litter. Also, small rock particles that I could normally avoid were sitting there, inevitably to be ridden over. There were flattened aluminum cans—some I dodged successfully, some not—and other hazards that compelled me to scan with intensity over anything that needed to be eluded.

I stared downward in distress. Remember my day off in Graham, Texas, when the seed of resolution to finish the trip had been planted? It proved to be relentless and would sprout again as I faced monotonous days in northeast Texas and agile loose dogs in Arkansas. Now with those cans, rumble strips and narrow pavement, my determination came to full bloom. I committed myself to pick up the pace and ride as quickly as possible to finish this trip.

Once more I moved onto the highway when no cars were behind. This time, I learned that if I cross the rumble strip at a sharp and nearly ninety-degree angle, the jolting was minimal. I rode harder and faster for about a mile, taking advantage of the extra space and cleaner pavement, but when vehicles approached I maneuvered back.

I did a modest wheelie over the rumble strip, thinking I was okay, but then I noticed a cluster of rocks a short distance ahead—two were the size of baseballs. It was too dangerous to maneuver around them, and I rode straight into the rocks with the front tire thumping hard against them. I screamed some expletives. I stopped and tapped my fingers against the tires to see if they were still holding air, and they were. Then I remembered the words of the bike mechanic at Kwik Keys: "You be careful out there." Over and over, his voice rang in my head like a broken record player. His stern voice grew louder and harsher, *"You be careful out there!"*

"I'm trying…" I uttered, "I'm trying."

At last, I arrived in Indianola, a town with ample services where I could rest and grab some lunch. As I approached the first traffic light, there was a black man on the sidewalk with sunglasses and short white hair surrounding the crown of his head. His t-shirt boldly read, "Got Jesus?" He also held a sign that read, "Church service at noon." He looked happy, maybe even joyful, as he tried to persuade passersby to attend his church's services. I stopped at the light and had to smile as I watched him perform. He was adamant and passionate, as he paced back and forth, pleading his case.

When he glanced over at me, I hollered at him, "Yes! I do have Jesus!"

It was obvious that most people were ignoring him. And I think my acknowledgment gave him a burst of energy, as he began to shout louder. He waved his hand at me and said, "That's why you're smiling! It don't matter what you're goin' through! You know it's gonna be okay with Jesus!"

I laughed with my hands on my hips and bike between my legs.

"Don't you know it!" I shouted back.

Scenes like this usually embarrass me, but I knew I had to loosen up after biking on that highway shoulder from hell. And the act of finally planting my feet on solid ground felt good, however short it would be.

"Where are you going?" he asked.

"Across the country," I said. By then, there was a line of cars idling next to me, so I doubt that he heard a word I said.

Seconds later, the light turned green and I rode off. Part of me wanted to get a picture of him (or with him), but then I felt funny about making too much of a scene. Past the intersection, I changed my mind. Immediately I pulled into a gas station and considered my options. *Should I photograph the man without him looking?* It didn't feel right to take his picture like he was a freak or zoo animal. *Should I park the bike and walk over there?* Maybe I could use my camera's timer to get a picture with him, I thought, but I felt too self-conscious. I didn't want to trivialize this man's zeal and effort. And so I stood in the gas station not knowing what to do, and the more I stood, the more my body appreciated the rest. Inertia kept me still.

At this point, it occurred to me that everyone at the gas station found something fascinating about this guy on his heavy-loaded bike. Three people beside their cars peered in my direction. Another man who was exiting the convenience store gave me a long stare as well. It felt like something out of a movie, where people were spying on me and reporting every detail. Then, one of the men at the gas pumps approached me from his SUV. He was a black man, sharp-dressed with a blue-collared shirt, red tie and dark elegant hat. His face was clean-shaven with eyes that revealed that he was more quizzical than menacing. He could have been a successful salesperson or one of my previous college professors.

"So what are you doing today?" he asked, his words friendly, his tone faintly suspicious.

"I'm riding to Greenwood, but I've been biking across America."

"No kidding!" he said, "With that bike?"

"That's right."

He introduced himself as Byron and shook my hand. His hands were large, his grip strong and tight. He asked some common questions about the journey and I answered them.

"You're riding on these roads? With all the time in the world?

That sounds nice. Man, you're blessed," he said, "You have the freedom to see the country. Now granted, you can't go too far in any given day."

It was obvious he had warmed up to me and vice versa. It was then that I saw his wife sitting in the passenger seat of his vehicle, watching us.

"So what do you think of Mississippi?" he asked.

"It's not bad," I said. I told him about Kwik Keys, and how brutal the highway was since I crossed into the county.

"We call this the Delta, the Mississippi Delta," he said, "My family has lived here since the 1800s, and I can tell you about the people. Usually they're cold or suspicious of visitors, but don't take it personally. Over time, once they get to know you, they'll warm up to ya," he said.

He added, "Are you doing this trip on purpose?"

"Oh yes," I said with a laugh, "It's not like I'm homeless."

"So why are you are you doing it?"

"Maybe I haven't grown up yet," I said.

Five weeks into this journey, I still didn't have a good answer. And I didn't like the words that just came out of my mouth. My insecurities, whether rooted in shame, unworthiness or who-knows-what, came out at an inopportune time. Maybe I blurted it because of how nicely dressed Byron was. He presented himself as a respectable adult, and I looked, well, like a well-worn cyclist.

My new friend said, "No! Don't say that. Don't grow up. The world needs people like you. Folks like you keep the world from being dull. We need some who take a different path, and you're the type who reminds us that life is more than work."

"You're right," I said, "I shouldn't have said it."

"I'm glad to hear that," he said, "You're setting a good example. You know how many people have aspirations who never end up doing it? Most don't even try. A lot of young people don't develop that part of themselves that cultivates dreams, and then they have kids and need to work and before they know it, they're too old to do anything."

"I hear ya."

"Have you ever thought about this? You're young. Well, at least you're younger than me and you're in good shape, but someday when you get old, you could be in a wheelchair. There will be a point when doing a bike ride like this won't be possible."

I liked this man's wisdom. I smiled with my arms folded, taking it all in.

"You want to know what I do for a living?" he asked, with a grin.

"Sure."

"My family runs a funeral home business. We work with dead people—well, more like for the families of the deceased who are grieving the loss of their loved ones."

"Wow," I said. "No wonder you're dressed so nice."

He smiled and appreciated the comment.

"Trust me when I say this. You're living, man. I had to approach you because it's rare to see people on bikes, especially on this road."

Eventually, he needed to get back.

"Be safe," he said, as he wrapped up our conversation, "I gotta say I'm nervous for you but you've made it this far. You must know what you're doing."

"Well ..." I said modestly.

He tilted his head and said matter-of-factly, "You're on your own and there are some people who don't mean well. That's the world we live in."

"I hear ya," I said, "But most people are fine, and most drivers are okay. And there are good people like you."

He seemed genuinely flattered by the compliment. Then he shook my hand again, "It's nice to talking to you. And welcome to Mississippi!"

It was such a pleasant encounter. Our chat was a well-needed pep talk for my heart and soul, and I hadn't realized I needed one until then. Once Byron drove away, my need to photograph the sidewalk preacher had passed, and I was happy enough that I got a photo of Byron.

After lunch, I rode feeling reinvigorated. As I surveyed those cotton fields, the timeless beauty and tranquility of the land began to romance me. A farmer driving a tractor came near the road and waved at me. I smiled, thankful for another friendly person. Outside of Indianola, the highway reverted to its previous layout that gave me just eighteen inches of shoulder, but having endured thirty miles already, I was growing accustomed it. In fact, I learned that biking faster made it easier to keep the tires on the pavement. Near the Leflore County line, I got another flat tire in the back wheel. Alone, I handled it well. All in a day's work.

My cyclometer read fifty-five miles by the afternoon, and a sign told me that Itta Bena and Mississippi Valley State University were ahead. I was still hoping that I could reach Winona, located at the junction of this road and Interstate 55. Mississippi is not very wide, and as a matter of pride, I wanted to brag that I biked halfway across the state in a day. Greenwood was my safe goal at seventy-two miles. Then, if I reached Winona, it would be gravy … but only if I got going.

It wasn't meant to be, however, because it happened again after only eight more miles of riding. A flat tire in the back wheel. Three in one day.

"What's going on?" I shouted in anger, as I laid the bike down.

Tall grass lined the roadside, and I didn't want to attempt to fix the flat in that. The shoulder for vehicles was sandy, and nowhere else was better to work on this. Ahead, I saw a gas station and traffic light faintly in the distance, and so I opted to fix the flat there. That's right—I rode the bike with the flat. Slowly my legs pedaled, and I got a huge workout with my bottom off the seat to keep my weight off the back wheel. My speed was only in the four-to-five miles per hour range, but at least it was better than walking.

A stream of agonizing questions ran through my mind. Was the new back tire of low quality? How else could one explain getting three flats so soon? The people at Kwik Keys were so kind and helpful, and I felt bad to even consider this could be their fault. The back tire seemed fine anyway. Or, was this some kind of concerted spiritual attack? I was convinced that the chaos and confusion I experienced outside of Phoenix was supernatural, but this time it seemed like a cop-out and excuse. Three flat tires in one day is a major pain-in-the-neck, but it's not the end of the world. Were my flat tire fixing skills to blame? I didn't think so. I'd handled the second flat well, and I'd just biked eight miles with a good tire.

The one other theory I had was maybe these Mississippi roads were as terrible as they seemed. I had dodged and biked through a constant deluge of gravel, sand, and debris—more than anywhere else in the country. Whatever the reason, it didn't matter. I just needed to continue riding and take care of things at the gas station. Getting there took much longer than I'd thought; it was like a mirage that kept moving farther away. The demanding pedaling was rough, even while shifted into the easiest gear. My thighs ached and my breathing was taxed. I knew I had to keep going or I'd come to a stop. Finally after about twenty minutes, I turned into the Shell station exhausted.

Again, it seemed like I was the center of attention as I walked with my bike in the parking lot. It turned out I was directly across from the campus of Mississippi Valley State University. I leaned my bike against a wall, locked it and entered the convenience store to get a drink first. It didn't take long to grab a soda and get in line.

"You've been riding hard?" asked the cashier.

"Sure have," I said with pride.

Then a guy interjected from behind. "I was driving a truck back and forth on the highway this morning, I saw you on the bridge!" he said.

I turned back. "You did?"

He was a burly man with short curly hair. "That's right. I just got off my shift, but I passed you a few times this morning. I first saw you crossing the river. You've gone a long distance. I kept seeing you and thought, 'Whatever this guy's doing, he's hardcore.'"

I grew a huge smile, incredulous. "Really? You saw me?" I didn't know what else to say or ask.

"That's right. What are you doing anyway?" he asked.

So I told him my story—the good, the bad and the ugly.

We talked more, and he became another guy who made my

day. To have my toilsome physical labor acknowledged by someone else felt so good. It was a great release from the stresses of today. It is so easy for me to get wrapped up in my own cycling world. When I'd wonder about what drivers might have thought about me, usually I dwelt on the negative—that some thought I was foolish or a danger to myself. But not here: it was nice to know some may have seen courage. I stood a little taller as I bought my drink.

Outside, I began working on the tire. Then the man exited the store and went toward his car at the gas pumps. This time, shyness didn't hold me back. I darted toward him and asked him to pose so I could get his picture.

"You made my day. I just want you to know that," I said.

Maybe today's frustrations were for a reason—so I could have this jubilant feeling from such a simple form of encouragement. There's a saying that you can't appreciate the beauty on the mountain top unless you spend time in the valley. Today, the flat tires and lack of shoulder had served as my valley. What a great story this will make for my life. Sure, I had some struggles, but it'll make reaching Greenwood all the more memorable. Energized, I fixed the flat quickly and rode off, recharged.

Only eight miles remained before I could call it a day in Greenwood. This would be a cakewalk. Back on the highway, I was pleased to see a paved shoulder that was as wide as a car. I made a fist pump. Eight miles should take no more than thirty minutes. I began to think about dinner, a hot shower and a soft bed that I'd surely enjoy soon. Within a half mile, the quality of the shoulder deteriorated. Broad creases spanned the pavement every ten yards; my bike made a big *ka-thunk* over each one. Gravel pockets lay on the shoulder, but I managed to maneuver around them well with so much more room to navigate. This, I thought, was still quite an improvement.

In another two miles, debris and sand appeared on the shoulder, and it only got worse with a plethora of flattened aluminum cans. It was around rush hour with increased traffic, and so it was out of the question to bike left of the white line to avoid this shoulder. Greatly concerned,

I gave myself a pep-talk: just take your time. Ride around as much of this junk as you can. Still, the conditions grew worse. It felt like a video game where the obstacles and hazards intensified the farther I went, testing me. More unavoidable spots came my way. Then I biked through an awful area with packed sand and rocks in wide cracks across the pavement. I winced, knowing how bad this could be.

Then, a short distance ahead, I felt a rumbling in my back tire. I was losing speed. The back tire was going flat. Again.

Four flats in one day!

Baffled, I hopped off the bike and shoved it in the grass. *Damn bike.*

I needed a way to release my anger. Beyond the highway embankment were trees and a swamp, and I walked down to it and left the bike by the road. A radical change in my environment was what I craved. I was done thinking about bikes and shoulders and the frustrations from the day, even if I could only escape for a few minutes. The motionless water, a bayou, covered the ground with trees standing in the water. Little motions were made by tadpoles, and it was therapeutic to watch them. I took in the peaceful nature scene as long as I could, even though I couldn't accept what had happened. Never in my cycling career had I had even two flat tires in a day, but now I had experienced the absurdity of four, a grand slam.

As I returned to the road, I decided not to change this tire. Why bother when there was a good chance I'd get another flat on this sandy, dirty shoulder? Greenwood was only a handful of miles away, and I decided to walk the remaining distance. I marched ahead with my bike, but realized this could take a while ... a long while.

And that's when I did something that I swore I wouldn't do again unless I was desperate: I stuck my thumb out to hitchhike. Numerous cars sped by, and no one stopped. I grew anxious and irritated with the sound of car after car whooshing by me, with none choosing to come to my aid. "Come on!" I grunted. It was obvious that I was a harmless, stranded bicyclist. My red jersey and bright red-and-white helmet made that obvious. How many criminals wear color-coordinated clothing? Also I had a bicycle beside me, for crying out loud.

I kept moving and called Charles. He had been planning to leave Memphis to drive to Mississippi, preferably Winona, to meet me after I would arrive, whether it would be this afternoon or tomorrow. I needed to tell him that I wouldn't make it there today. He answered his phone and I told him about what happened.

"Four flats? I think I'd go crazy. There's got to be something wrong with the tire. Where are you?" he asked.

"Outside of Greenwood. I don't think it's the tire. Long story made short, but these roads in Mississippi are in rough shape. They're horrible!"

"How far are you from Greenwood?"

"Maybe three miles."

"Three miles?!" he said, "That's a long way to walk. Are you sure you'll be okay?"

"Yeah, I'll be fine," I said, although I doubted I was convincing, "I'll stop at the first motel I find. Usually lodging is on the edge of town."

I felt a strange mix of feelings, somewhere between the agony of self-pity and the ecstasy of bravery, but I didn't like the focus on me. I hate when I catch myself or others dominating conversations by talking mostly about themselves, and so I asked Charles about his day. He told me about his work day—there was a long meeting in the afternoon and something that happened to his co-worker. I listened as best as I could, but it was hard with the highway noise beside me.

"Sorry, I always seem to talk to you when things are noisy," I said.

"Wait a minute. You're walking on the highway?!"

"Yeah, on the shoulder. Where else would I be? On some guy's cotton field?" I belted out some laughter with that one.

"Hold on, Steve. Walking three miles is far. Do you need help? I can come down there right now. I already talked to my wife and she's okay with it," he said.

"It would take you a couple of hours for you to drive here, right? That's too long. Let me just get to Greenwood and you can meet me tomorrow."

"I've got a road atlas. Let me look something up ..."

"Wait. Hold on!" I shouted.

Ahead was the dirtiest, most bicycle-unfriendly shoulder I had ever seen. Thick sand and gravel cover much of the pavement. A large pothole was on the left side with miniature piles of rocks and gravel from the broken pavement. There was only a small path where a cyclist could possibly avoid the massive mess with who-knows-what kind of litter.

"I gotta get a picture of this. I can't believe it. The shoulder on this road is awful. It's atrocious. It's beyond words. This is the worst piece of highway I've ever seen. Hold on ... I have my camera out," I said. I held the phone with my left hand and snapped pictures with my right. Then I put the phone back to my ear. "Are you still there? You gotta trust me on this. I'll show you a picture later."

Charles was adamant when he soberly said, "Steve, I'm really concerned about your situation."

I chuckled. "Yeah, I am too. I got a dose of the Mississippi blues today. Did you know the blues are popular down here? I just need to keep walking. Greenwood is somewhere ahead, and like I said, motels are usually on the edge of town. How about if I call you later?"

"Do that, please. Let me know you made it."

An hour later, I finally reached the outskirts of Greenwood, and fortunately motels were on the west side. It had taken me all day to travel seventy-two miles, and I surely counted those three walking miles as part of my mileage count. After all, I had the bike by my side. In the lobby of a Ramada Inn, my body was especially sore from the long walk. I hobbled the way an elderly man might. My upper left leg writhed in sharp muscle pain. In my room, I leaned the bike against a window sill and didn't bother to fix the flat for the remainder of the day. I figured if I did and something went wrong, I might lose what little sanity I had left. I'd take care of it tomorrow morning.

I plopped on my bed and tried to wind down. For about five minutes I stared at the ceiling and let my sweaty, achy body sink into the bed spread. Eventually, I showered. I told myself not to think about cycling and certainly not about the flat tires and that terrible road. Why ruin my night?

One thing I did know was that I needed food. Nearby was a Taco Bell, and within minutes I was inside and blankly staring at the overhead menu. I was too tired to even think about what I wanted. I stood a good distance from the counter, with nobody in front of me. The cashier waited. I pointed out how nice it was that no one was behind me, and she smiled and said that was fine. The worker appeared to be a teenager—an attractive black girl with soft brown skin that seemed to glow, with just a touch of makeup and not a wrinkle on her face. She stood there energetically, swaying forward and back, as if she was bored when she wasn't taking someone's order. Then I approached and a sign by the register said that their credit card machine was down. With no cash, this was not going to work, but with no one behind me in line, she and I began to talk.

"Sorry, I'm a little woozy right now," I said. Because I was wearing my spare clothing, I knew I wouldn't get any accolades as a cyclist unless I told her.

"I've been biking all day," I said.

"A bicycle that kids ride?" she asked.

"Yeah, a road bike. I've been going across the country for the past five weeks."

"For real?"

Then she stared me down, like boys her age who probably say something to flirt with her, only to realize they were full of it. She was suspicious of me.

"Yeah," I said, locking my eyes with hers.

"What states have you been through?" she asked pointedly.

I told her and added that Mississippi was my sixth state.

"So where's your bike?"

"It's in my motel room," and I pointed toward the Ramada Inn.

Something snapped and she knew I was for real. Then she shouted to the people working in the kitchen. "Hey, this dude is riding a bicycle across America. He started in California!"

A number of them stopped what they were doing and looked toward me; some were interested, while others didn't seem to care. Then she turned back to me with a grin and hurled questions at me.

"So what's the worst thing that's happened to you so far?"

"My bike was stolen in Arizona."

Her eyes grew sad. "Really? I think I'd cry if that happened to me. Did you cry?"

I laughed. "No, not that day."

"Did you get angry?"

"Not really."

"Why not?"

"I just had to deal with it, I guess."

"My brother had his bike stolen when he was younger," she said. "He locked it too, but someone had those big cutters."

"Yeah, I know."

I knew all too well.

She folded her arms, enjoying the interrogation. I knew she cared and was interested in my journey, but she seemed to be searching for something more out of the ordinary.

"What other bad things have happened to you?"

"A few rude drivers I've encountered, but nothing too bad."

"What else?"

"Today I had four flat tires," I said, while scratching one side of my scalp in frustration, "That was pretty rough. I'm having a great time in your state, but I may have to call your governor to request that he do something for cyclists on Highway 82. Do you have any connections?"

She laughed. "So what's been the most beautiful place you've seen?"

"Oh boy," I said, "Honestly, I'd say everywhere is nice."

"The only state I've visited is Alabama." she said, with a hint of disappointment.

"Well, you're young. You'll travel more when you're older. Are there any places you'd like to see?"

"Definitely New York City."

"I grew up outside of New York. I agree, you need to go."

Her eyes grew large. "You grew up there? I've got to go. It's the city that never sleeps. I want to go to plays and musicals, and see the skyscrapers. All the activity. All the noise. Nothing happens here in the Delta … nothing."

"But you do have a blues scene here. A guy told me about it today."

"We do. Don't get me wrong, Mississippi ain't bad …"

And I interjected, "… but it's where you grew up. You need to explore. I get it."

Then I added, "You need to go to New York and anywhere else you want. Can I lecture you? Trust me, I was in your position. I always wanted to live out west—in the desert where there's mountains and wide open spaces. When I was twenty-three, I once drove in a loop around the country, and it was one of the greatest experiences of my life. I encourage you to travel to other countries too. I spent a summer in Russia and learned so much."

She listened well, better than most teenagers when I dispense advice. And throughout this time, no one had gotten in line behind me.

"All right, Mr. Traveler, what would you like to order?" she said.

That's when I explained how I hate ATMs and that I was putting everything on my debit or credit card. Eating here wouldn't work.

She looked at me like I was a freak. "C'mon, what's wrong with you? Go get some cash for yourself."

"Well, I don't know. I mean, I—"

"You mean to tell me you've come all this way from California, and you haven't had any cash? You had your bike stolen …"

I began to crack up loudly. I can be very stubborn, and this young girl would not break me. It didn't matter what she said.

"You gave me advice about traveling, but I guess you don't take advice from others, do you?" she said.

"No, don't say that," I replied, while still laughing a bit.

"Go get some money so you can eat. There's a bank with an ATM across the street," she said. She was such a fun girl … and with an attitude. She spoke her mind, probably like the sister I never had whom I needed to get tough lectures from. I liked her.

Something about her challenge persuaded me. *Yeah. Why be so rigid about ATMs?* One of my excuses was that I didn't remember my

PIN, but it turned out I did and returned with $40 in my pocket. As I dined, this girl—I still didn't know her name—came out from behind the counter and sat with friends, apparently on a break. I overheard her telling them I was bicycling across America. The other girls looked at me with a critical eye, like teenagers sometimes do to adults. Sheepishly, I smiled and waved back. As I was about to leave, I wanted to bless her somehow, and I had a good idea. I pulled out my wallet, and dropped a ten-dollar bill on her table.

"It's only ten bucks, but here," I said.

"What's this?"

"Consider it a gift to your travel fund."

"So long, Mr. Biking Man!" she shouted with a big smile.

Connecting with the youth of Greenwood was a pleasant diversion, but once I returned to my motel room, my uneasiness about my cycling problems came back quickly. Sure, I could be phony with myself and act like everything would be okay, but a flurry of questions troubled me. Would the road conditions continue to be this bad all throughout the South? Would there be *any* shoulder for the remainder of this trip? And will I constantly have flat tires like today? I shuttered.

There was another troubling factor. Tomorrow's weather forecast was not looking good for biking. A mix of rain and snow was expected to sweep through, a rarity in Mississippi. With all of my concerns, the last thing I needed was a day off with nothing to do but think about this. I called Charles to let him know I was okay and to coordinate where we'd meet tomorrow. Maybe he could encourage me.

"First of all, I'm glad you're safe and sound," Charles said.

"I'm telling you," I said, as I raised my voice like I had to justify myself, "This is my thirty-fifth day and most days have been fine, but today was craziness."

"Well, my family intends to give you some warm hospitality soon."

Charles planned to take the day off work tomorrow and drive to Winona to meet me. His one-hundred mile distance from Memphis would take an hour and a half by car; my thirty miles would take about two hours by bike. We would try to synchronize our time of meeting.

However, in view of the possibility of inclement weather, Charles agreed to drive to either Greenwood or Winona, whichever worked best for me. I suppose the easy way out would have been to make Charles drive all the way here, but I knew that wouldn't work.

"I have to get back on the bike," I said. "Unless the conditions are truly dangerous, I'm riding. I'll meet you in Winona."

"Are you sure?"

"Yep."

Something of great importance was at stake. The only way I could get past this anxiety was to face it head on. "If you fall off a horse, get right back on," they say. A morning off in Greenwood, followed by a day and a half off in Memphis with Charles and his family would mess with my head too much. I would obsess about the four flat tires and wouldn't relax.

"All right. Make sure your cell phone is charged and handy. I want updates and I'll meet you wherever," said Charles.

"We're on!" I shouted.

I couldn't wait to see my friend.

As I lay in bed, lights out and the television off, so many thoughts were swirling in my mind. I closed my eyes and could picture the sights and sounds of my first day in Mississippi.

Crossing the river on that bridge.

The pathetic shoulder of Highway 82.

Four flat tires.

The long walk to Greenwood.

And the memorable people I encountered.

With my eyes closed and my mind beginning to dim, I could still feel the motions of my body on the bike, my hands gripping the handlebar, my legs pedaling. Many of my dreams had become related to cycling by now. Eventually I fell into a deep sleep, but my rest was not as peaceful as other nights. The problems of the day and the chance that more awaited me loomed. Late at night, I heard a roar of a semi slamming its horn as it came up beside me.

Hoooooooonk!

I woke up alarmed, my heart pumping fast. I turned on a lamp momentarily and stared at my bike against the wall. I was glad it was only a dream.

***

I've watched many movies and have read novels that have a plot with a main character who's living a mediocre life. They're often smart or gifted, but they're living far below their potential. Usually the plot thickens when the character is met with a force not of their making, challenging them to rise above themselves. They're forced to become heroic in some way, where they emerge stronger and better with a gain in self-realization. Maybe they slay a monster. Or win a battle to set the captives free. Or perhaps they rescue the beauty from the villain. Whatever the case, the stakes are high and the circumstances are against them, but they rise to the occasion.

Now, I realize a bicycle tour across a continent might not be as important as defeating the bad guys, but it felt like my journey had similarities to this theme. This expedition had become a tale, and I was keenly aware that every decision I made would affect the storyline.

This was my mindset as I got ready on the next morning in Greenwood. Outside it was only twenty-five degrees, but I was determined to go. I fixed the flat tire with ease and wore every layer of clothing I had. It was cold enough that I could see my breath. The sky was gloomy and gray, but there was no snowfall yet. Off, I rode. A mile ahead, I stopped at a traffic light and beside me were cars filled with people going to work or dropping kids off for school. They must have wondered who was the crazy guy riding a bike on one of the coldest days in Mississippi that year. I was defiant all right. I call this the "whatever it takes" mode. You do what you need to do. You quit worrying about what people think, what a responsible person might do or failure itself. I couldn't let the fear of flat tires or bad roads hold me captive. The only way out is through. Unless things became unmistakably dangerous, nothing besides an act of God would stop me from going for it.

On the east side, homes and businesses eventually became less and then lo' and behold, the highway blessed this determined bicyclist with a wide and paved shoulder. And, at least for the time being, there was hardly any debris, gravel or nasty potholes. I was overjoyed. And so grateful.

Despite the cold temperature, I told myself that I could suck it up for twenty-eight miles. An elevation gain of 300 feet led me into the forest and out of the Mississippi Delta. The clouds became darker and the winds picked up—an ominous warning that I better ride quickly to Winona. At twenty-one miles, I passed Carrollton and was almost there.

The temperature only warmed a little, topping off around thirty degrees. My hands and toes were stinging from the cold. I remember hearing that if you divert your attention away from where the pain is, then it won't feel so bad. I tried that, but it didn't work. I clinched my fingers into fists as I pressed the handlebar with my palms while rubbing my fingers. That helped somewhat. My ultimate relief was that this would be a short ride. Around a bend, I saw a water tower in the distance. That had to be my destination.

Today's ride was a moral victory. No flat tires. No narrow shoulders. And no snow or cold to stop me.

Winona didn't seem to have much besides the usual gas stations, convenience stores and fast food restaurants to serve traffic coming through. On the bridge over Interstate 55, I lifted my bike onto the sidewalk and watched cars and trucks speed by. I had arrived before Charles and called him.

"Where are you?" I asked.

"Near Oakland. I just saw a sign that said Winona is sixty-five miles away, so I should be there in about an hour. Sit tight, okay?"

"You'll definitely see me. I'm the only guy with a bike."

"Oh I believe that!"

"I'm so happy I could dance on this bridge!" I shouted.

On this chilly day in Mississippi, I was king of the hill and on top of my game. I stood on that bridge for another twenty minutes, talking on my cell phone with any friend who answered my call.

Nothing would upset me today. My cyclometer read twenty-eight miles, but I felt like I accomplished a lot more. If this experience really was some kind of legendary narrative work with me being the main character, I had reached the promised land—the small town of Winona, Mississippi.

That's "promised land" with no caps. Let's be real.

The Texas state line

Sean, Leyna and Glenda – my friends in west Texas

Me and an employee at the Dairy Queen in Graham

Dinner with Cheyenne in Decatur

U.S. Highway 82 in northeast Texas

The Arkansas state line

An abandoned gas station in Lewisville

At a hair salon in El Dorado

On the Benjamin G. Humphreys Bridge

Facing north, the Mississippi River

At a park in Memphis, Tennessee

BBQ at Corky's with the Smith family

U.S. Highway 82 in central Alabama

While lost in Montgomery, I approached this split for I-85 or I-65

My bicycle beside a sprinkler system near Shellman, Georgia. I fixed my final flat tire of the journey right here.

Arrival at the Atlantic Ocean

CHAPTER XV

MEMPHIS AND THE SMELL OF BARBEQUE

*In every personal encounter
there is no neutral exchange,
we either breathe life into people
or zap life out of them.*

Brennan Manning

C harles hugged me tightly when he finally arrived at the convenience store. Then he grabbed me by the shoulders and gave me an inspection. "Look at you," he said, "Your hair is wild and all over the place. And you're not shaving? My goodness, you look like someone who came straight out of a Bible story."

"You're right," I said, knowing I had to take his teasing, "It's too much work." Usually I'd go five or six days without shaving, long enough to have grubby facial hair. Then I'd grow tired of it and shave myself clean.

"To be honest, I'm the same way," he said with a grin.

This was the one and only Charles. Oh, how I longed to see

my good friend! When I first told Charles that my bike route included Mississippi, in relative proximity to him in Memphis, the prospect of meeting seemed far away. I estimated the time period would be sometime in March and left it at that.

Charles is a handsome black man and close to my age. He is bald, with hair stubbles on the sides of his shaven head, and he had his own thin, scruffy beard. He wore a casual sweatshirt and wrinkly jeans. Charles is a character—one of those talkative, gregarious types that you don't easily forget. He usually has something to say. If he wasn't a senior technical analyst with a corporation in Memphis, I'm convinced he could probably use that strong and deep voice to be a sports announcer. I had met so many neat people on these roads, but it was special to be with someone I already knew. I didn't have to introduce myself. Or explain myself. In fact, I could breathe a sigh of relief, for Charles was in charge now. He would drive me to his suburban home outside Memphis, and I wouldn't have to do much except be a slug in his passenger seat and then be a guest with his family for the next day and a half. Whatever I would do with them, it wouldn't include much physical exertion and definitely no cycling.

Charles surveyed my bike and admired it. He squeezed the brake levers back and forth. He pushed the buttons on my cyclometer. He wanted to see my total mileage, and I showed him.

He reminisced, "How many weeks has it been? You've been in one dimension to me. I wondered when I would hear from you by phone. And now this journey is coming alive … for me, at least. You're here!"

I smiled and said, "That's right. And let me tell you how thankful I am you've driven here. You're so generous."

Charles walked the bike to his car and deftly lifted it onto his bike rack. Then we got inside the car. As I leaned down to sit in the passenger seat, I let out an audible groan.

"Are you okay?" asked Charles, with concern.

"I'm fine. My legs didn't appreciate that strange motion of getting into a car."

"Sometimes mine don't either, and I don't even ride a bike,"

Charles quipped.

The speed was thrilling as we traveled north toward Memphis on Interstate 55. When I looked through the passenger side window, everything whooshed passed so quickly. Trees. Cracks in the shoulder. The land itself. I leaned over to check Charles' speedometer; we were cruising at seventy-two miles per hour. It was then that I distinctly noticed that we were passing mile markers minute-by-minute. How much longer it takes to pass them on a bicycle!

I turned to Charles, "You've got to realize, this is culture shock for me."

"What? Being with me? I have that effect on people I'm told," he said, with a laugh.

"No, I'm talking about moving this fast in a car. I haven't been in one since the outskirts of Dallas-Fort Worth. That was about 600 miles ago."

"I can't believe that," he said.

I faced Charles, who sat contently in the driver's seat, and said, "With a car, you can cruise at sixty-five miles an hour. You can sit comfortably, and you can turn on the heat or air conditioning if you want. And as you drive, you're not putting your body through stress."

Charles mischievously smiled and ran with my train of thought. "And you can turn on the radio and if you want someone to come along, they can sit beside you. Or you can talk on the phone. You obviously can't do any of that on your bike."

An epiphany hit me. "You could cross the country in three or four days in a car. Imagine that! It's taken me thirty-six days to get here from California! What a jackass I am. What was I thinking? I should have just driven across the USA."

"Look, Steve," he pointed to the coffee holder between us, "you could sip coffee as you travel and put it in a drink holder."

"I never thought of that. I suppose I could put coffee in my water bottles. Who says they have to hold water?"

"There you go," said Charles.

We passed Grenada, but we didn't see much. You rarely feel the character of a town from an interstate highway. The conversation about cars had me thinking, and I said, "When you're driving, it feels like you can go anywhere. Think about it. For a country to be a truly free society, there's got to be a healthy road system, where there's no undue road blocks or people controlling where you can and can't go. Driving stands for mobility. It's all about moving around geographically, and that translates psychologically too. I bet people have a greater ability to be creative and expansive with a generous road system. What do you think?"

"I see your point. That's kind of deep though. You probably have time to ponder the great mysteries of life while riding," he said.

At that moment, I began to love cars all the more for their speed.

"Mark my words," I said, "After this journey, I won't ever take for granted a leisure forty mile per hour drive in a car."

"Good point," said Charles.

"Then again, who am I kidding? The novelty will probably wear off once I'm back to a normal life."

"And what exactly is a normal life? I'd like to know," asked Charles rhetorically.

Our travel would require two hours by car to get to Charles' house, and I kept thinking about how the plan was for him to drive me back to Winona in a day and a half. How gracious a friend he was, and I kept telling him that.

"No worries. You gave me an excuse to take the day off. Araceli and I will be taking care of you. We've got the guest room all set, and we're taking you out for barbeque tomorrow. Tonight we're having lasagna. And as far as I'm concerned, I'll be happy to show you around Memphis or you can sleep most of the time. It's up to you."

"That sounds good. We'll play it by ear," I said.

When Charles said the word "sleep," I got more cozy in the passenger seat. Then I realized I could recline it and partially did. I asked after the fact, "Is it okay?"

Charles encouraged me. "Of course it is. That seat goes back farther. You can sleep horizontally too. Take a nap if you want," he said.

I didn't sleep, because I still felt funny that he was driving so much and thought it would be rude to nap in his presence. We continued catching up about what has happened in our lives since we had last talked.

Near Senatobia, Mississippi, it began to drizzle. Within minutes, the drizzle turned into snowflakes, but each flake melted when it hit the ground. We crossed into Memphis and then took another highway east. Soon, we were in his neighborhood in Collierville, Tennessee, a town that is probably considered the southeastern suburbs of Memphis. Their spacious suburban home is among hundreds of similar multi-floor structures made of brick and colored in various shades of gray and beige. All residences had well-kept lawns and two-car garages. A few trees and a full sidewalk lined the streets. And to my joyous surprise, a bicycle lane was installed on the major road into the subdivision.

"They put that in there because studies have said it slows down traffic," Charles explained.

"It looks great!" I replied.

My friends had moved here from California three years earlier, and I was impressed with their living situation. I've heard the pejorative term of "McMansions" that belittles homes like these—"cookie-cutter homes" placed one after another in a boring suburban layout, and based on the typical American appetite for bigger and better … and funded by debt. But I liked the neighborhood, and I would surely take advantage of that bicycle lane if I lived here. I was happy that my friends had such nice accommodations for themselves.

Inside, their house seemed like new. Their sizable dining room looked as though it was never used. Much of the first floor was made with quality wood, polished and pleasant to the eye. Their living room had a fireplace, big-screen TV and two huge couches. The kitchen was warm, inviting and open with an eating area. Nice furniture populated each room. At the same time, their home was far from a lifeless museum. Signs that a teenager and two five-year-olds lived there were evident throughout. Toys were scattered all around and made the house come to life.

I said "hi" to Araceli, Charles' wife and to their three kids: daughter Rachel, and the younger twins Carter and Sydney. Everybody seemed hurried and preoccupied. It was a Friday afternoon, an ordinary weekday for them. Araceli told me we'd have dinner in an hour—enough time for me to take a shower and get settled.

Charles carried my bike up the stairs and into the spare room. It was cavernous with nothing on the walls and only a bed and night table, but this too, felt inviting and comfortable. I felt the soft new carpet beneath my feet and admired the brand-new ceiling fan above. The bed was large with lots of pillows and a stylish comforter on top.

A hot shower restored my senses. The soap was real—a white bar that became creamy and gooey on my skin. Most motels offered a hard, chalky bar that barely liquefies with use. It's like cardboard soap, unyielding to even the hottest shower. But not today: I scrubbed my body conscientiously, and then soaked my hair in peppermint-scented shampoo, which I found in a copiously-filled toiletry dish for guests.

Refreshed, I returned downstairs to the kitchen. A bowl of salad and bread sticks were already on the table. Charles brought out our drinks. The kids drank water and the adults were served iced tea. Rachel had gone out, and so it was Charles, Araceli, their two young tikes and me. We waited eagerly for the lasagna to be ready, while Araceli worked hard behind the counter.

"So tell the kids what day are you're on," said Charles.

"Day thirty-six," I replied.

He leaned down to his children and said, "See kids? Steve's been out riding a bike thousands of miles."

The five-year-olds didn't know what to say; their dad had put them on the spot. Sydney gazed at me with her head tilted and a shy grin.

"Really?" asked Sydney.

"On a bike?" asked Carter.

"That's right. He started in California, where your grandparents live. Remember how long of a drive it was when we visited them?"

Both kids seemed in awe, and then, they began to squirm in their chairs. Sydney played with a toy while Carter turned his spoon upside down and spun it over and over again.

Charles turned to me, "So do you know what you did on each of those thirty-six days? If I threw out a random number like seventeen, could you tell me where you were?"

"I can," I said with a gleam of pride, "New Mexico and riding with my friend, Dave."

I handed him my digital camera. "You can see pictures from everyday if you like. That's probably the only way that I remember stuff."

Araceli opened the oven and smoke came out. Then she placed an enormous tray of lasagna on the table. She kept apologizing. She said the lasagna would be too hot and it was a "last minute thing." I'm insecure as anyone when it comes to hosting and cooking for others, and so I understood her view. I had to encourage her. She had no idea what I had been through in five weeks, mainly eating out or munching on convenience store snacks.

"Do I need to remind you I'm a bachelor who doesn't cook? This looks delicious. Also, thank you for that dish for guests in the bathroom. That peppermint shampoo was amazing!"

She smiled modestly and said, "I think we need to host you more often then."

I had more to add. "I've eaten okay on my journey, but there's something exquisite about homemade food." I reached my hands out to the tray of lasagna, oozing with heat and steam. "It's the taste. It's how it fills your stomach. It feels like home—'homemade' they say."

"And right now, home is wherever you are. You and your bike," chimed Charles.

"That's a song!" I replied, "It goes, 'Home is wherever I'm with you.' It's close enough."

My eating was like a replay of when I was at Sean and Glenda's house. I chowed down piece after piece of lasagna. They had so many bread sticks too. Araceli encouraged me to keep eating. Throughout my visit, she was constantly offering me food, coffee, snacks, and even the kids' candy. I liken it to my Italian background, where it seems a tradition for mothers and grandmothers to offer guests as much food as they want. Her generosity was a sweet sign that she cared. As we carried on with our lasagna feast, I thought fondly of Sean, Glenda and Leyna in Texas. They were the blessing to me on Day Twenty-Two, exactly two weeks earlier.

Araceli asked, "So is there anything you want to do?"

"Yeah, sleep," I said in all seriousness, although I knew it would sound humorous.

They asked if my guestroom was to my liking. Of course, it was.

"Really, I don't need to do much," I turned to Charles, "All I need is for you to take me to a bike shop tomorrow. I need more inner tubes and I'd like to have the back tire looked at. That's about it. Otherwise, I'm very okay with lying around."

I sat slumped. Tiredness was getting to me right at the kitchen table.

Charles was delighted at the thought of going to a bicycle shop. "We'll do that," he said, "I've been meaning to look at their new bikes myself. Just know if you want to do or see anything in Memphis, we can do it in the afternoon. There's Mud Island River Park or Graceland. I still haven't been to those places!"

"What about the Civil Rights Museum? I wouldn't mind that."

"I've been there and that's a good choice. We can do that," said Charles, as he reached for another serving of lasagna.

Araceli jumped in to our conversation, "Let him sleep. Don't push him. Look at this man."

By now, I had both of my elbows on the table and held my head. I was torn. Part of me demanded that I lie horizontally throughout tomorrow, yet the other part wanted to see whatever Memphis had to offer. After all, I'd never been to this city before.

Araceli thought for a moment and said, "I am trying to process how I'd feel if I biked from San Diego to here. I don't think I could do something like that, and certainly not in the succession of thirty-six days like you have. I think it would kill me."

I looked toward her and knew that she was sincere; her face expressed both admiration for me and a concern for my physical welfare.

Charles added, "It's like you're from another world right now. I can't even imagine."

"Put it this way. Right now my full-time job is to ride my bike everyday. That's all," I explained, "Also I can eat as much as I like. There are no worries about gaining weight or counting calories or that kind of thing. By the way, can I have another piece of lasagna?" I inquired, as I helped myself to more. They both laughed and said it was.

Charles asked, "Speaking of food, do you like barbeque? We'd like to take you out tomorrow night. You're in Memphis and you've got to have barbeque. The smoked ribs at Corky's is really good. It's so tender that the meat slides off the bone when you pick at it. Or the brisket. Pretty much everything is excellent."

"I'm all for it!" I said.

As dinner was wrapping up, we noticed thick snowflakes had begun to fall and within a short time, about three inches of snow covered the ground. We admired the snow through the window, and the kids' ability to behave at the dinner table diminished with their wonder at the whitening world outside. They were so excited and begged if they could go out and play. Their mother helped bundle them with their hats, gloves and coats, and they ran outside in the snowy backyard. They attempted to build a snowman, but it was more a large mound of snow. Charles and I moved to the living room and watched them play through the window.

Charles pondered out loud, "Remember, snow is a big deal for us. We never got any in California, and in Memphis, we might get two or three snowstorms like this, but that's it. It's probably good that you're here with us all warm, instead of stuck in a motel room in Winona."

"I'm so glad to be here. You've got a great set-up," I said.

Charles turned his eyes away from the window and faced me. "It's been a while since we last saw each other. You haven't changed much, and I say that as a good thing. But I'm in a whole different ball game. Once I married Araceli, I immediately became a husband and stepdad. And then when you have your own kids, it's crazy. I have a friend who says, 'Having kids ruins your life in the best possible way.'

He's right. When you become a father you lose your right to be selfish. If your children don't come first in your life, you will fail," Charles paused for just a moment, as if wanting to pick the right words. "It's not about me anymore. I never imagined the idea of watching a kid's movie with Sydney on a football Sunday and not caring because it was for her. It's a weird, intense love that you simply can't describe until you feel it. Nieces and nephews are awesome, but even they don't prepare you for parenthood. Everything your child does or says takes on much more meaning than anything that anyone else in the world has to do or say."

I said, "No question, you have my respect and admiration. You've changed, and I say that in a good way too. I'm a single guy. No kids. No significant other. No nothing. I don't have that life experience that you have."

"I hope you're okay with that. You're on your own journey. Maybe someday you'll become a father, or maybe you won't. Becoming a father is better than you expected, and it's a lot more work that you expected. And there's no handbook for it. My twins have different personalities. One form of discipline works with one child, but not the other. You know how you swear you'd never say something that your mom or dad said to you? It can be frightening," said Charles, with a hearty laugh.

"Well, maybe I'm here to encourage you, buddy. It's funny. Sydney looks just like you. She has the curly hair like mine. And Carter looks more like Mom. By the way, do they get along?"

"They do. So far they have the same friends, which is helpful."

I laughed. "My brothers and I had our moments. I was the middle kid." I sort of giggled about what I was about to say next. "We put our mother through hell sometimes. I know I did."

We kept watching the twins play in the snow. Other neighborhood kids joined them, as well as an older child who helped them make a more respectable snowman. Charles decided to join them and I stretched out on a couch in the living room. My body reclined with ease on the partially worn couch with plastic toys in the creases of the cushions. I pulled out two and placed them on the floor.

In the evening, Araceli suggested to Charles that he help me do laundry. Using a washing machine instead of hand washing my clothing in a motel sink was a treat. I showed them my extra shirt, pants, socks, hat, and gloves—the extent of my spare clothes. I held it in a crumpled ball in my hands.

"Where's the rest of it?" asked Charles.

"That's all I have with me, besides what I'm wearing."

"My goodness, you're tough," he said.

I laughed. Charles made me feel tougher than I ever felt before.

It was only eight p.m., but my overworked body demanded that I get ready for sleep. The soft guest bed was a sanctuary to my aching muscles. I sifted through the myriad pillows where my head would lie. It was a project removing them, selecting which to discard to the floor, and which to keep on the bed—some for my head, one between my knees and one to squeeze. I wrapped myself up in two thick blankets and got cozy. With the lights out, I lay on my back, staring at the ceiling, with the only sound of the vent humming. Right then, I decided my friends could make this room into a bed-and-breakfast.

The kids made some noise in the hallway as my hosts prepared them for bed, but it didn't bother me. Nothing would distract me from sleeping. My body was so out of it. Even if I only biked twenty-eight miles that day (Greenwood to Winona), the exposure to the cold while exerting myself had done a number on me. If anything, the family noise energized my very being. As I was drifting ever so slowly from that 'land of in-between' of wakeful sleepiness, I was conscious of the loneliness that sometimes creeps into my life. The truth is, I need more people around me. As a single man, it seems like I do everything alone. I live alone. Make important decisions alone. Sleep alone. Eat meals alone. I don't have any kids that occupy my time, my dedication, my soul. Yes, right now, I wouldn't want it any other way—I was fulfilling a dream. However, I knew I needed to soak in the interaction with my warm friends in this bustling household. Like an exhausted child who might need to hear the familiar and comforting voices of family as he or she is falling asleep, I realized that tonight I was that child.

***

The next morning, Araceli whipped up pancakes, eggs, bacon and orange juice. After that, it was a lazy start to the day with me hobbling around the house for about two hours. Once in a while, my hosts noticed me grunting and wincing as I got up, sat down or walked upstairs.

"Are you sure one day of rest is enough?" asked Charles, after I toppled onto the living room couch.

"Yeah, I'm all right."

Maybe I wasn't, but I'd grown accustomed to my bosom buddy—muscle soreness.

At midday, we made it to a bicycle shop. There were hundreds of new bicycles inside: beach cruisers, mountain bikes, road bikes and childrens' bikes, together with every accessory a cyclist could need. They even had some antique tricycles and beside the counter, a unicycle.

Charles raised the unicycle and declared, "Now this is what you need. You're cheating with two wheels. I want to see you go across the country on this!"

"I'll do that if you can ride across this shop on that."

"Uh, I'll pass," he said, with a laugh.

An employee greeted me as I stood with my bicycle beside me. He looked like an expert bike mechanic with his apron and tools in this shirt pocket. He had short white hair with thick-rimmed glasses, and he was trim with muscle definition in his arms. It was obvious that he was in shape.

After I explained about the four flat tires a couple of days ago, he crouched down and inspected the tire.

"It looks reasonably new. You just bought it?" he asked.

"Yep."

"It looks fine."

"That's what I thought."

He gazed up to us, "You said you were biking in Mississippi, right? If I had to guess, I'd say it was the roads. I remember I once biked for days in Louisiana, heading to New Orleans, and I had the same problems as you. And Louisiana isn't much different than most of Mississippi—flat after flat on horrible, crumbling roads. I've been there!"

I breathed a sigh of relief and said, "At least I know it wasn't me."

He topped off both of my tires with air using their floor pump per my request, and I bought more inner tubes. On this journey, a bicycle shop was a refuge. They fix bikes and sell supplies, and it can be a place for refreshment. On this day, I needed to vent and had a friendly bike mechanic in front of me.

"The hard part about flats is you rarely know *why* you got it," I explained, "Sometimes you know if the culprit is still sticking into the tire, but most times, you have little or no data. Then, if you get a second flat on the same day, you wonder if you didn't fix the previous flat correctly. Sure, it might be obvious if you get a flat within minutes of riding, but what if you go ten miles down the road? That's where the madness sets in. You don't know if you got it because you didn't fix the previous flat right, or did you just have bad luck and something different punctured it?"

The mechanic clearly understood and said, "You're right. It can be a dilemma. Half the time, you probably won't see what caused the flat. Sometimes you'll find it. Sometimes you won't. The questions to ask are: did you make sure nothing was still lodged in the tire? Or did you get sand inside the tire while putting the new tube in? That can puncture a tube. Did you insert the tube in a way where there was a crease or ripple in it? You need to be diligent and precise."

By now, I knew all his points. I just had to vent some more.

"You know what these flat tires are like? It's like taking a test in school, and all you get back is the grade, but you don't get specific answers to the questions. You don't know what you got right or wrong. I fix a flat and then seven miles later, I get another."

"I got his calls," Charles chimed in, "He was walking on the highway after his fourth flat of the day."

Then I added, practically yelling, "And I ask myself, 'Am I going crazy? Did I fix it right?!'"

"Believe me, every cyclist has these moments. You're not alone." He turned to Charles, "Now you said you were interested in riding more and buying a bike? I don't want you to be discouraged. Sometimes people get fed up after getting a few flats and they turn to a different sport. It's a shame."

"Yeah, don't be discouraged by this conversation. It's so worth it," I said.

"I know," said Charles, "Flats sound like a pain, but it sounds like it takes only a few minutes to fix, right?"

We agreed.

The store was quiet and the mechanic had time to chat with us more. My presence had him reflecting about his own multi-day bicycle tours. He said he was once on a semi-pro cycling team and he had competed in ironman triathlons. Now that he was older, he had become more interested in leisure, long-distance touring like I was doing. He said he once biked the entire Natchez Trace Trail which begins in Natchez, Mississippi and ends in Nashville, Tennessee, and he dreams of biking across the country someday.

"My youngest child is in high school. Once he goes away to college, I'll probably retire and I hope to go. Maybe I could convince my son to go with me."

Then he keyed in on me, treating me like a superstar. "This riding makes you tough, doesn't it? I remember when I did the Natchez Trace Trail. Me and three other guys went eighty to one hundred miles each day. At first you have concerns about the weather or being in good shape. Then after about a week, you get into a groove and you say, 'I'm going. I don't care about anything. Whatever comes up, I can handle.' You find yourself mentally and physically stronger."

I grinned and said, "I think you're right. But I'm only going about sixty miles a day."

"That's still a lot," he said, "And you're carrying more stuff in these panniers."

His words about being stronger rang true, and I felt encouraged. Sometimes it's hard to know if you're changing, because you're too close to yourself to notice. Sometimes it takes someone else to point it out.

"You said you're from Colorado?" the man added, "I competed with a lot of people from the western states. We lived for many years in Maine, and I trained as much as I could. But the truth is if you're a serious professional runner or cyclist, you train in the West. You've got the open spaces and mountain passes, and elevation is on your side. Sure, we have mountains on this side of the country, but you can't do much training in Appalachia or the Northeast. Part of it is the culture. Bicyclists in Colorado or Utah get more respect—I've seen it—they're revered almost."

I laughed. "I think you're right."

"It's different in Tennessee. Once I was biking about twenty miles east of here, and a couple of rednecks in a truck slowed and came beside me. They pulled out their shot guns. Then they were laughing and it was obvious they were drunk. I was real scared. Another time I had a beer bottle thrown at me. There's a lot of stuff you can't control, so I've got to tell you to be careful, okay?"

"I will," I said appreciatively.

Then his face grew stern and he leaned in toward me. He said, "Bicyclists don't get a lot of respect in the South. There's a guy who works here who got hit by a car on two separate occasions in Atlanta. Each time the car sped off, a hit and run."

"That's terrible," I uttered.

By now, Charles had wandered away from us and was examining new road bikes. Another salesperson was assisting him, as they discussed the advantages of different kinds of bicycle designs. My friend was sounding serious about buying something. I joined them and encouraged Charles to buy a used bike first and prove to himself that he's dedicated to the sport. That way, he wouldn't run the risk of wasting money and having an expensive toy collecting dust in his garage. Charles listened to me as he was enjoying looking at the many bikes. The image of him riding with Carter and Sydney on their smaller bikes felt so good to me.

Then suddenly a twinge of fear went through me, and I didn't want Charles to take on road biking. I'd rather he have a mountain bike and ride on trails, not roads. That was safer. The mechanic's talk about the dangers had clouded my mind. I shuddered at the thought of Charles getting hit by a car.

***

In the afternoon, Charles gave me a driving tour of Memphis. While stopped at a traffic light near downtown, he pointed to a restaurant in a rundown building with a sign above reading "BBQ."

"Smell that?" he asked.

"No."

"You don't?" he said with surprise, "That's the sweet smell of barbeque. That's one thing I've appreciated about living here."

We went to a park that lined the Mississippi River with good views of the downtown skyscrapers. Charles pointed out the Pyramid Arena, a venue that was used for indoor sporting events for years. It was also nice to see the river again. Eventually we visited the National Civil Rights Museum, which is also the site of the Lorraine Motel where Martin Luther King Jr. was shot and killed in 1968. The museum maintains the exterior of the motel as it was in its day. We wandered among exhibits that document the civil rights struggle and history of black Americans.

We took our time and read practically everything. For one prolonged period, we drifted apart into different sections of the museum, and I couldn't find Charles. Then I texted him, and he texted me back with his location. I chuckled audibly over the conveniences of modern technology, and then immediately was embarrassed because the people around might think I was crazy for laughing for no obvious reason. Near the end of the tour, we rejoined and came to the motel room that Martin Luther King Jr. and his peers stayed at on the fateful day he was murdered. The sacred site was in the décor of the era, including the bedding, furniture and wall fixtures. Everyone was quiet and reverent. The air was thick with emotion.

As we were driving home, Charles said, "You know, I'm glad you're here. I don't usually go anywhere. You gave me an excuse to get out of the house."

"That's great, but don't feel bad. You have responsibilities."

"Yeah, but that's only part of it. My dad traveled a lot. He worked for the Navy. Since he wasn't around much, I feel the need to be home all the time with my kids. I know most guys go out even though they're married with kids. I guess I prefer living vicariously through other people. Like you and your bike trip."

I smiled and said, "Yeah, if I lived here, I'd get you out more. I've always wanted to visit that Civil Rights Museum. I'm glad you moved to Memphis to get me there."

"So was it worth it? What did you think of it?" he asked.

"Honestly, I already knew much about the history of the civil rights movement, and the exhibits seemed like a refresher course."

"Me too," said Charles.

"But I'm so glad I went." I added, "No question the motel room at the end was special. I've stayed at many old motels that didn't look much different than the one we just saw."

Charles paused for just a split second, and then we both laughed.

I added, "There is one thing I learned. Usually there is a gap in history as far as what is taught about the movement. It goes from Selma and the passage of the Voting Rights Act of 1965 and then skips over to the death of MLK three years later. But I didn't know about the March Against Fear in 1966.

I thought in silence about what I had learned. James Meredith made history when he enrolled as the first black student at the University of Mississippi in 1962. Despite the civil rights accomplishments that were happening, Meredith asserted that he still felt intense fear as a black man over traveling and living his daily life in the South. Bravely, he decided to do a solitary 220-mile walk from Memphis to Jackson, Mississippi to make a symbolic stand. At the beginning of his march, Meredith was shot by a sniper and hospitalized, and civil rights workers continued the march on his behalf. The march grew into the thousands and was estimated to be 15,000 strong at its end three weeks later.

I said, "I'm not saying my bike ride is equivalent at all, but imagine walking in a hostile environment for weeks. Add in some problems with loose dogs and roads with little shoulder and that would be a doozy."

"I hear ya," Charles said, "I still worry about you. Speaking of minorities, you're a unique person in your own right. You're riding a freakin' bicycle across the continent. Do you see any bikes on this road right now? No. Most people drive cars."

"True," I said, appreciating the thought, "But come on, you're the minority, at least a racial one. You're officially a black man, an African-American. Right?"

"Yes, I am," he said.

I shifted toward him in my passenger seat for emphasis. "So what did you think of the museum? That's more interesting to me."

Charles gave it some thought, and then replied, "About discrimination, I felt like I was shielded from a lot of racism. I grew up middle class in a navy town in southern California. I went to Catholic schools, and there weren't many black kids in private schools. So basically, I spent my childhood years with white children and some Mexicans. The schools weren't big and I knew most of the kids. It was low pressure. If there were conflicts or someone was misbehaving, they were dealt with quickly. To be honest, I felt more comfortable around whites and Mexicans than I did black people, only because I didn't have much contact with them. But after high school, my dad wanted me to go to his alma mater, which is Southern University in Baton Rouge. Ever heard of it?"

"Southern! I've heard of it only because of college basketball when they make the NCAA tournament as the fifteenth or sixteenth seed."

Charles laughed. "That's right. Go Jaguars!"

"By the way, I passed Mississippi Valley State two days ago," I said, "That's another school that pops up in the news when they make the tournament. Earlier this week they were the number sixteen seed against UCLA and they lost 70-29. I saw some of the highlights. I always cheer for the underdog in those games. So anyway, what was Southern like?"

"My college experience was different. The student population was 99.8% black, and all the professors were black. It was a good school. People were friendly, and I got a great education. But even then, I've never been—what's the word?—very race conscious. Maybe I'm naïve, but I just didn't see much racism or feel it much. But my dad grew up in New Orleans. He's seventy-five and was born in the 1930s, so he was down there during the time of separate drinking fountains and segregation. I've never talked to him in detail about that, and I've been meaning to. Once he kind of mentioned that he wanted to buy a house in Port Hueneme or Oxnard and I don't remember the full story. I don't know if they wouldn't give him a loan or wouldn't show the property to him, but all I know is he didn't get the house. He wouldn't say much more."

"You should ask him," I said.

"I should," he said, "There's one more thing to add. After school, I moved back to California for a few years and met Araceli. When I got this job offer in Memphis, we weren't sure what to do. We were open to moving, but we'd never been to Tennessee. I remember Araceli and I were sitting at the kitchen table, and she told me, 'If anybody is racist against our kids, we're leaving.' I completely agreed with her. My kids come from a bi-racial family, because Araceli is Hispanic. But the kids don't have any problems. They're doing as great as five-year-olds can be. And they're pretty much growing up as I did."

"They're great kids, for sure," I said.

"But you know," Charles said, taking his right hand off the steering wheel and using it to gesture, "This has me motivated. I really should ask Dad about the old days. He tends to be quiet about those things."

"That's just like a dad," I interjected. "I know it's a sweeping stereotype, but our parents' generation did not talk about hard things. I really think it's generational."

"You might be right," he said, "I'll give you an example. My dad's dad—that would be my paternal grandfather—he left my grandmother for some kind of long distance job, and apparently he never came back. My dad has never mentioned my grandfather, and my mom pretty much told us the little information she knew."

"Wow," I said, "We have a lot in common. I have a story that's similar to yours."

I shifted back to my normal position in the my seat and gazed out the window, watching nothing in particular. It helped me put my thoughts together.

"Really? Let me hear it," he said.

"My dad was about fourteen when his dad died of some kind of health problem. That was in the 1950s. I can't remember my dad ever talking about his dad. Nothing was ever said about his death or what he was like. My dad has never shared memories of what things were like for him as a kid—nothing. As for my grandfather, I have only vague facts about him."

"So we both have dad's dad issues, don't we?" quipped Charles.

"We do," I said, "But about not talking about things. Are we any better? I'm not so sure. Our parents had an excuse, at least. They were born around the time of the Great Depression and World War II. You just didn't whine. They were dutiful and hard workers. You didn't air out your dirty laundry to others," I said. Then I added with laughter, "And people rarely saw therapists, either."

"Speaking of which, I'm sure I'll screw up my kids somehow. They'll probably have a similar conversation about me in another twenty years." Then Charles turned to me and added, "You can be their therapist someday."

We both let out a hearty laugh, and then I interjected one thing.

"By the way, you are a good Dad," I said reassuringly.

"Why thank you."

"We all make mistakes," I said, "especially with our families. The key is to never quit."

We continued on the highway back home. An upbeat song was on the radio and we grew quiet. Both of us were enjoying the tune. It was a peaceful gap in the conversation. When the song ended, Charles turned to me and said, "You know, I'm so proud of you for following your dream. I respect that. I've driven my family to California a couple of times; I know how long it is, and you've biked it. I still have a hard time wrapping my mind around that."

Once we got back to Charles' house, I immediately reclined on the living room couch and stayed there for the remainder of the afternoon. His piece of furniture was becoming my faithful companion. If only I could snap my fingers and have access to it at any moment on the roadside!

In the evening, the family took me out for barbeque. Rachel was out again, but Carter and Sydney joined us as we dined on the most celebrated food in Memphis. Charles had hyped barbeque so much that I almost expected a letdown, but there would be none. We went to a place named Corky's and all had a good time. I acted especially goofy with the five-year-olds. I'd put my face close to theirs and then shake my head violently with my long curly hair flying all over, while saying, "I'm crazy!" The more I did it, the more the kids loved my silliness.

Before we ordered, Charles leaned forward across the table and said, "We've learned a lot about barbeque since moving to Tennessee. The culture is very different here. In Memphis, barbeque is a meat. In most of the country, if you say, 'I'm having a barbeque,' it means you're grilling. And you could be cooking burgers, hot dogs or whatever. Here, barbeque is pork, and it's prepared in many ways."

I ordered a set of ribs basted in a special dry sauce with sides of baked beans and crunchy potato chips. The meal was exquisite, and my stomach was practically bulging when done. It was probably the best barbeque I've ever had.

The next morning, Charles and I awoke at five a.m. so he could shuttle me back to Winona. We had to leave early so he would have enough time to return to Memphis to attend church with his family. The city was engulfed in darkness, but the light of sunrise emerged as we entered northern Mississippi. There was still some snow on the ground, but its cover lessened as we traveled south until there was none. The sun peaked over the trees lining the highway, promising a warm day.

Charles and I didn't talk much. We were both tired. I did thank

Charles a few more times. All too soon, Charles pulled into the very gas station in Winona where I was sitting two days ago. We both got out, and he lifted my bike off the rack and placed it down.

"All right, this is it," he said.

"Thanks for the hospitality," I said.

I didn't know what else to say. Saying good-bye can be so awkward. We hugged, and I thanked him one more time.

Next thing I knew, Charles drove away. I watched his vehicle and waved at the last moment before he entered the interstate on-ramp. Again I was alone with the bike, ready to take on the familiar rhythms of the road.

CHAPTER XVI

SPEEDING THROUGH THE SOUTH

Keep away from people who try to belittle your ambitions.
Small people always do that, but the really great make you
feel that you, too, can become great.

Mark Twain

*H*ighway 82 had beautiful roadside scenery beyond Winona. Fragrant magnolias blooming with pink flowers flourished on the lawns of country homes. Other trees were awakening to spring's call with green buds highlighting their branches. It promised to be a warm and sunny day, and before I had biked far, I stopped to apply sunscreen. That's when I noticed a group of deer eyeing me from the edge of the forest. I remained still, whispering to them as I grabbed my camera to photograph them, but even the movement of twisting my body and reaching into my pocket was enough to spook them. Once I got the bike moving forward, they scampered in a mad rush to safety, but through the trees I could see they had stopped and were staring at me as if wondering whether this strange creature was a friend or foe. I called to them affectionately, "Hey guys!" They didn't move.

The black tape on my handlebar had loosened and frayed from gripping it so tightly these past weeks. And my new bike had become dirty; it was far from the shiny spectacle when I walked it out from Landis Cyclery. Grease covered the bottom of the frame nearest the chain, and splotches of dirt and mud were caked directly behind the front wheel. When new, I had sworn to myself with the greatest of intentions that I would keep this bicycle clean, but so far I hadn't. I had this rationalization: many friends love driving their monstrous, four-wheel-drive, high clearance vehicles over primitive mountain trails. It can be a matter of pride to leave their vehicle filthy and mud-splattered. Perhaps I should feel the same about my Trek 1.2.

This morning, the bike felt heavy and sluggish. It fought me. With each of my pedal rotations, it pushed ahead. I wasn't in the mood to pace yet, and so I let it coast. With deliberate exaggeration, I pedaled slowly and became aware of every muscle used. My gluteals, quadriceps, calves and hamstrings were all working. I noticed how the shoulders, arms and wrists also worked for balance. I stood up and pedaled hard. The bike swayed back and forth as I pushed my weight from side to side. Together, we were dancing. I gained a speed of nineteen miles an hour, and then reverted to the saddle with shoulders hunched. The bike had cooperated. It was waiting for me to initiate. Even one day off seemed to do wonders for my strength. The bike and I—both of us were ready to take on the remainder of Mississippi.

Near Mayhew, I was staring down at the pavement when I came upon a tree limb sprawled across the shoulder. Too late to stop or swerve, with a jarring thud I rode over it head-on. In that split second, I expected to catapult onto the pavement and have a punctured tire. Thankfully, neither happened.

At Starkville, the road engineers had transformed this relaxed four-lane highway into an interstate design, with turnoffs that had deceleration and acceleration lanes. Forest surrounded me with no way to know if there were services off the exits. When the signs read Columbus, I'd gone eighty miles and exited at the first opportunity, hoping to see lodging emerge soon. However, the wall of trees continued unbroken. I must have been still on the outer edge of town. Itching to get off the bicycle, I kept riding, knowing I'd run into something soon. After turning on another back road, eventually I arrived on Main Street. I pulled onto the sidewalk to scan the busy drag, hoping to see a motel. At least it felt like the ride was over. Downtown Columbus seemed pleasant enough with shops to browse, a bookstore and old church steeples. I stood at an intersection and wasn't sure what to do. I probably should have asked someone, but there weren't many people around. Then I decided to continue east on a business route, knowing I would ride parallel to Highway 82 and figuring that I'd find something. About a mile ahead, I took a chance and stopped at a dumpy motel. The clerk was friendly and professional, and the fee was only thirty dollars with tax included, the cheapest rate so far of this trip. My finances were dwindling at this point, and I told myself I could make do with less than lavish.

The furniture in the room was old and crummy, like the junk one would see in a thrift store. There was a flimsy table that looked like it would break if I sat on it, and by the window were two rickety wooden chairs. The floor was covered in a thin and worn gray carpet. It appeared as though the room's original design had glass for much of the door-side wall—a common design for motel rooms in the 1950s and 1960s. Now cinder blocks were stacked around a small window. The dead bolt and lock on the doorknob were sturdy, but there was a distinct gap of air below. The lone bed was small and the sheets were clean. One of the two pillows didn't have a case. The massive antique television sat on an old dresser with scratches. The remote control was missing the battery cover. I inspected the bathroom: it appeared fine. After doing this assessment of the room, I laughed nervously. I'd just have to make the most of it.

Stepping back outside in search of a meal, I noticed two people in grungy clothes sitting in front of their door; it looked like they must live there. Near the lobby, I was greeted by a heavyset woman with stringy brown hair and a gray t-shirt stretched across her front. She must have been pregnant with how her stomach pushed out, but it was hard to know for sure.

"I saw your bike. What are you doing?" she asked.

"Biking through. I'm going across the country."

She took a big drag of her cigarette, and then said with a smile, "My roommate has a bike. He doesn't ride it much these days. It just sits in the living room like an ornament."

"Are there any places to eat if I walk up this way?" I asked.

"No. Just a little grocery store. But there's a Church's Chicken about a mile ahead. I love that place."

And then she proceeded to tell me all about the chicken they serve and the dinner combinations on their menu. She rambled about their biscuits and how their food was better than other fast food restaurants.

To be honest, our interaction seemed a little odd. I couldn't quite put my finger on it, but it was one of those conversations where the more I conversed with her, the more I felt uncomfortable. She gave me so much eye contact. Was she flirting with me? Or was she seeking cues that I'm a drug user … like her? She asked more questions about who I was, and this time I was vague. I didn't want to fuel this exchange in anyway. She asked where I was staying, and I felt the dilemma of wanting to be socially graceful, yet avoiding saying anything that will continue the discussion.

"I'm staying over there …" I said, pointing in the direction of some rooms.

Then I excused myself and hurried to the nearby grocery store. When I returned, the woman was gone, but I felt negative vibes about this place. There were other people standing idly on the end of the business property, appearing suspicious. I took a deep breath, knowing shady things probably happened here, and I thought that maybe I made a mistake to stay at this motel. I was thankful that I didn't have a car parked out front—a giveaway that someone was staying in my room. And if I went outside, I feared that I would be too friendly or that I'd risk bringing attention to myself. My mind ran with the possibilities of receiving an unexpected visitor. It was only four p.m., but I decided to stay in my room for the remainder of the day. I had enough food for the evening, and I lay down and watched television, trusting no one would bother me. Sure, I felt holed up in this dingy room, but it would be night soon.

Then, only fifteen minutes in, I was using the bathroom and heard a knock on the front door. (I was on the toilet.)

Was it the spooky woman? Did she bring her roommate with the bike?

"Hold on," I shouted. I hustled as quickly as I could to make myself clean and presentable, but it took time. Whoever was there knocked again. "I'm coming!" I shouted louder.

As I got to the door, I made a fast decision: whoever is on the other side will receive the meanest, dirtiest expression. They will know that I do not want to be disturbed. I stood up straight, tightened my cheek muscles and put on my most serious face. I whirled the door open and in front of me was an elderly black woman, just five feet tall with silver hair and squinty eyes. She was frail and harmless, like my grandmother, with poor posture that made it so she couldn't even raise her head high enough to see my stern face.

"I forgot one of your pillow cases," she said.

I let her in. She was a maid.

"I'm sorry. I meant to put this in here earlier," she added, as she placed the pillow inside the case with an explanation about how the mistake happened. My heart melted.

"Thanks. I appreciate it, ma'am."

"Is everything else about the room okay?" she asked.

"It's good, thanks."

When she left, I let out a hysterical laugh, resolving that worrying about this motel was no longer allowed. I was a grown man and could handle a night in a shabby motel. I told myself I'd talk to friends on my cell phone. Take a nap. Or pray. Whatever. Just think happy thoughts. That evening, I did unwind, and the motel was as quiet as anywhere else, although I sure as heck didn't leave my room when it got dark.

The next morning, my final experience in Mississippi was wild. I rode eight miles east of Columbus and approached the cloverleaf on-ramp that would reconnect me to Highway 82. Right there was a rundown house with dogs in front, all unleashed. Suddenly a beastly brown dog, much of it disheveled in grass and dirt, sprinted across the street toward me. A car slammed its breaks, screeching to avoid it. I was ahead and riding quickly, but this dog was intent on the chase as he barked. I turned back and yelled at it, not showing any fear as it continued its pursuit. In another tenth of mile, I turned onto the on-ramp and thought I was free and clear. I took a deep breath ... only to hear the jingling of the dog's collar. The mutt was running across the grassy area of the cloverleaf! I shouted in mockery, "Is that the best you got?" Inside however, I was very alarmed over this canine that looked underfed. *Does this dog want to munch on my legs?* I pedaled harder and decided if this got ugly, I'd use my carry-on pump for self-defense. A bash to the head could do the trick. But soon the dog, outpaced, gave up on me. It was gone for good.

I returned to Highway 82. Only a half mile ahead, I stopped to catch my breath and regain my bearings at a sign for the Alabama state line. I was disgusted at how any human could allow their dog to run loose and be a nuisance to their neighbors, but I also knew there would be humor when this story would be told in the future. What a way to leave Mississippi—hounded out of the state!

***

Beyond the town limits of Gordo, Alabama, the back tire went flat. Similar to the tallying of my days, I also numbered my flats. This was my tenth overall—two in the front, eight in the back. At least this one happened on a pretty section of road with rolling hills and forest. Not long after I had the back wheel in my hand, a green SUV pulled over beside me. The driver lowered his window.

"I'm here if you need some help," he shouted, alone in the driver seat, "I'm a cyclist. I know what it's like to be in your situation."

Those were words I liked. The man's name was Glenn, and we shook hands. Immediately, I noticed his muscular shoulders and his aura of a bicyclist who spends many days hunched over on a bike. He was middle-aged, dressed casually in jeans and a sport shirt. He appeared confident and bold without a trace of shyness. I leaned my head through the open window in the passenger side door. To be in the shaded confines of his SUV, protected from the elements, was a welcome change.

"Like I said, I've had flats," he said, "It's humbling to be on the edge of a road, fixing a tire, and you've got cars and trucks passing you. You know everyone has to be checking you out, pitying you, and they're saying, 'I'm glad I'm not that poor dude!'"

We belted out laughter at the same time.

"You get it!" I said.

"So do you need help?"

"Not really. It's just a flat."

I knew he wanted to help, and maybe if I had said "yes," he would have been overjoyed. But I couldn't let this man fix this, while I sat on my butt and watched. This was my dirty job, like changing the soiled diaper of one of your babies. He was interested in my journey though.

"We've got to talk," said Glenn, "I said I could help you, but maybe the tables are turned. I think you can help me. I've always wanted to bike across America. Since I was sixteen, I've daydreamed about doing it. I remember reading an article in a magazine about a couple who went from Seattle to Boston, and they met all these friendly people. Sometimes they stayed with strangers or camped on people's farms, that kind of thing. I should have gone when I was younger," he said.

"Aww, you've got to do it," I said with warmth. "You look in better shape than me."

He waved his hand in dismissal, "You're too kind. I've been in great shape at times, but not now. I do ride a couple times a week. As for doing a trip, my family and work responsibilities are too great to get away for long. Not now, not with my kids. They need me. I am fortunate that my wife is supportive of me going someday, but realistically, I could only get two weeks off for vacation."

"I'm thinking about riding it in portions," he added. "I could take off one to two weeks each summer and do it in pieces. If I rode hard, I could go 500 miles in a week, maybe more."

"That's a great idea," I said, "If you come through Colorado—that's where I'm from—I could ride with you. Or better yet, I could be your support vehicle. That would be fun."

His eyes gleamed and said, "We need to keep in touch. So how long has it taken you?"

"Five weeks and four days."

"That's not bad. You're not that far from the Atlantic."

Then, I remembered something that I wanted to encourage Glenn about.

"If you do the southern route like I'm doing, the entire ride is shorter. I'm projecting it'll be about 2,600 miles for me, from San Diego to the Georgia Coast. I think it's 3,000 from L.A. to New York, and it's near 4,000 from Seattle to Maine. See, I'm doing the lazy route—it's practically the shortest distance between shores."

He refused to accept my humility. "Don't knock your ride," he said. "Did you hear me? You're biking across the continent. It's something to be very proud of."

I smiled and agreed.

"Where are you headed today?" he asked.

"Tuscaloosa."

"You don't have that far to go. Only about twenty miles. Maybe less from here."

I had to interject, "Although I'm thinking of riding farther to Centreville if I feel good. I'd stay at the one motel in that town."

His eyes opened wide. "I grew up in Centreville and know that area well. I know exactly where that motel is. It's in Brent, the next town over. Centreville and Brent are up against each other. That's in Bibb County, although there isn't much there. Then where after that?"

"Highway 82 all the way to the beach. It'll take me near Brunswick and I'll finish at Jekyll Island." I pulled out my paper map from my back pocket.

"Can I see that?" he said.

He studied my map in his driver's seat, while I continued to lean inside his vehicle. It was so nice to rest. I could have stood there all day. Glenn flipped the map upward and downward, taking time to orientate himself to it. Then finally, he pointed to a stretch of Highway 82 in central Alabama and said, "This section is not good for road bikes. There's little shoulder all the way to Montgomery. A buddy of mine rode that once and he said there's loads of semi-trailer trucks on weekdays. It scared him. And years ago, I thought about riding it all the way to the beach, the very route you're taking, but I didn't because of the dangers. I'm just putting it out there."

I didn't like what I heard, but I wondered what would be an alternative.

"Here's a route I suggest," he said, " If you want to get to Dawson, Georgia, take Highway 82 to Maplesville but then divert by traveling east on Highway 22 through Clanton and then head toward Alexander City. From there, you can bike on Highway 280, a safer four-lane road through Auburn and Phenix City, before reconnecting with Dawson."

His suggested detour would require about three days of riding—the same number of days as I planned, with a few extra miles. I didn't know what to think, but there was no doubt that he cared, and I appreciated that.

Soon, Glenn needed to leave.

"I live in Gordo and I'm headed to Tuscaloosa for a meeting, but I'll be coming through later," he said, as he gave me his business card. "If you need any help, call me, okay?"

"You bet," I said.

The card read that he was a pastor of a Baptist church. Now this was good public relations. After Glenn was gone, I fixed the flat with ease.

Back on the bike and riding, I thought about Glenn's advice about diverting that section of Highway 82. No doubt, he seemed like a sharp guy, but in the past, I've found taking advice from locals has its risks. Sometimes their sense of distance is off, or their standard of what is safe or unsafe is different from mine. Then again, he did offer specific information about the road's lack of shoulder. The debate went on in my mind for miles, and as I entered the edge of Tuscaloosa, I decided to stick with my planned route. My lodging had already been planned in Alabama, namely in Centreville, Montgomery, and Eufaula, and I didn't want the hassle of finding motels in new places.

In Tuscaloosa, Highway 82 became McFarland Boulevard on the north side, a busy corridor with shopping malls, restaurants and a plethora of businesses. I biked through, stopping for lunch, and then continuing. On the northeast side of the city, the road made a distinct ninety-degree turn south and suddenly, I found myself riding on a bustling highway with speeding cars and trucks. Of course, I stayed on the shoulder, but with acceleration and deceleration lanes for cars to get off this crazed road, I had to stop and wait for a gap in traffic large enough to cross every one. I continued to a bridge that spanned the Black Warrior River. Traffic rushed by at swift highway speeds. The shoulder narrowed to half a car's width with patches of gravel. I winced as the bike's wheels rumbled over it. Part of me wanted to get a photo of the river, but the busyness of the highway had me too distressed to stop. *Just get through!* Thankfully on the other side of the bridge, the traffic calmed. My cyclometer read sixty-five miles when I saw a group of chain motels on the far end of Tuscaloosa, but I passed them all. I was determined to make it to Bibb County.

The road reverted to two lanes into the country. As the road relaxed, so did I. It felt good that I was now playing with the house's money. Having passed my conservative goal, every mile I claimed would be extra points. I passed farms and a stray liquor store. Beautiful overhanging branches shaded some of the road sections. At eighty miles, I rested. I stretched my arms and breathed life into my tight pectoral muscles and shoulder. I rolled my neck in slow circles and twisted my hips.

Ninety-one miles now. The motel in Brent, at last.

On the front porch of the motel lobby, I pretended that I was southern by sipping sweet tea while sitting on a rocking chair. An older couple walked by and greeted me, and I responded in kind. I sat there for an hour, enjoying the evening.

By 7:30 p.m., I was on the verge of dozing off even with the television on while under the sheets of a king-size bed. Eighty-five miles yesterday. Ninety-one today. The sloth in me wished I could rest more: to not have the nagging feeling of a clock ticking away until I'd be back on the bike … in just thirteen hours.

***

As I biked out of town the next morning, my body was aching. My left shoulder blade was hurting, and the back of my neck was filled with knots, craving a massage. Coupled with the dark and gloomy aftereffect of overnight rain, I was grouchy. My mind flooded with memories that usually make me bitter when I dwell on them.

A high school teacher once gave me a C- for a quarter. I expected a better grade and asked her for an explanation, but she never gave one. I was a teenager without strong social skills, but now I would have chained myself to her office door in protest until she gave me an answer. Years later, a college professor once openly laughed at my answer to his question that he posed to the class. While my answer was off, it was by no means laugh-worthy, and I regretted not doing something about it. Then my thoughts went back to bullies and childhood fights. A kid in the fifth grade. A bully in the seventh grade. Another in the tenth grade. My list of grievances continued with unscrupulous bosses and backstabbing friends over the years. All this pent-up irritation brewed in me as I toiled on the bike. Sure, I knew how fruitless it can be to feed anger and resentment, creating a monster within. Yet my anger helped me to ride better. This ugly cognitive mess came to a climax when I took things into my own hands. I gave a tongue-lashing to my enemies. I shot some of them dead. I kicked my professor in the face, and he bled badly. Then a quiet voice in my conscience asked, "What … are … you … doing?"

Even though I was alone, and surely no other human knew the rash of insanity in my mind, I felt terrible to be so grouchy. Right there, I stopped and put the bike on its side. I put on my thicker gloves to warm my hands and ate some dried banana chips. The short break was enough to snap me out of my funk. I knew better than to fight battles that don't exist or are long gone. They steal your peace and ruin the possibility to enjoy the moment.

Highway 82's shoulder narrowed to nothing. The pavement ended directly beyond the white line. Now this was a pressing concern that focused me on the the present. I stayed as far to the right as possible, knowing motorists would need to show care in passing me. The road swept through rolling hills in the Talladega National Forest—nothing like the mountains in the western USA—but enough to give a hearty workout. All vehicles passed courteously.

Two hours later, I arrived in Maplesville. With twenty-five miles under my belt, I took a break at a general store that sold pickles floating in a barrel. Ah yes, Alabama! And in the country. Next door I entered a Subway restaurant where I reclined in a booth. The place was empty. I removed my helmet and gloves and stretched my legs.

That's when an employee noticed me and said, "You made it here already?! I passed you when I was driving to work." She was young and pretty with silky blonde hair tucked underneath her visor.

I grinned and stretched my arms out. "That didn't seem fast to me."

She was disbelieving. "Really, I'm surprised you made it that quick. You've covered quite a distance. I drive here from Brent and its long enough by car."

Her encouragement put a big smile on my face. I thought about the guy at Mississippi Valley State and wondered if he and this girl were angels from the same spiritual battalion. Her name was Amy. She seemed the type of girl who could charm anyone and be the life of the party. Her deep southern accent was endearing too.

"Do you want anything?" she asked.

"Honestly, no. Can I sit here for a while?"

"Sure, stay as long as you want," she said, like a good hostess, "So what are you doing?"

For whatever reason, I didn't want to say that I had been going across the country. I'd let her think I was local.

"I'm riding to Montgomery."

"That's an hour drive from here. When I passed you I thought, 'Does he have a car?'"

I laughed. "Thanks so much for thinking that."

"So? Do you have a car?"

"No."

"Do you need a ride?"

"Well, no …"

Her eyebrows rose. "You don't seem like you're from around here."

I broke into laughter. "You're right. And I love your accent by the way."

She put her hands on her hips and joked matter-of-factly, "Down here, we say the rest of the country talks funny."

I loved her witty response and said, "There are many parts where people have strong accents that sound worse than anything: folks in Maine, Boston, Brooklyn."

Then I told her who I was, where I was from, and what I was doing.

"Bless your heart!" she shouted.

By now, I had grown tired of the attention my ride was giving me. I wanted to know more about her.

"I have family in Florida and plan to move this summer. I can get a job as a waitress and live with them. The main thing I want to do is go to school to become a graphic designer," she said.

"There's a huge market for that."

She said confidently, "I've done some web design, but I want to create magazine layouts and do advertising work. I don't want to be making sandwiches for the rest of my life."

My legs were entirely horizontal in a booth, when I stood up and twisted my waist back and forth.

"You must be tired," she said, shaking her head with sympathy.

And then a song, "Superstitious" by Stevie Wonder, played on the overhead speakers. I said, "Yeah, but it's like this song. You just have to go with it." I swayed to the beat and raised my arms in a modest dance, while she giggled in amusement.

Onward I continued on Highway 82, which continued to have no shoulder. Many more tractor-trailers were using the road, which I thought was strange for this part of central Alabama. According to my map, Interstate 65 was relatively close and connected Birmingham and Montgomery. It seemed most drivers would want to take that route over this. However, this road did seem to be a reasonable choice for those traveling between Tuscaloosa and Montgomery. Perhaps truckers knew that there was less highway patrol, or maybe there's a weigh station they wished to avoid. Whatever the case, there was more traffic than expected.

Two tractor-trailers passed me, each moving way over. Then another came flying in the opposite lane. Another mile ahead, semis going in opposite directions approached, with the truck behind slamming its horn, terrifying me. The driver must have been ticked at the tight squeeze play, with him needing to slow. And then, the road returned to peace and quiet. After two more miles, I began to ascend a long and gentle upgrade, and soon heard another 18-wheeler coming from behind. The trucker blared his horn from afar. Then, as he passed, I got sprayed with water coming out of its side. I was shocked, unsure if it was a form of antagonism, an honest mistake, or just the unpleasant consequence of not having a windshield like the rest of my fellow travelers in petroleum-burning vehicles. As the truck went ahead, I waved, hoping I could "kill him with kindness" as they say, but I felt humiliated. And here—a special effect sound should fall from the sky if this was a movie—I thought of Glenn's advice. He had recommended that I detour at Maplesville, and right then I knew he was right. Foolish me. I could say with certainty that this was not a bicycle-friendly section of road. There was no shoulder, and all I could do was stay to the far right of the lane. All I needed was one stupid-texting teenager to wipe me out. I said a prayer and dealt with it. I reminded myself that if there's legitimate danger, just pull over. It's not worth risking my life.

In the next hour, more tractor-trailers passed. I waved each time with my left hand as they were coming from behind, even though I was surly and bitter. I was angry—over the road conditions, the horn-hitting trucker and myself too. I tensely waited for another loud horn to scare the crap out of me.

In Billingsley, I stopped at a convenience store. I browsed inside and a sixth sense told me that I wasn't welcome. Nobody greeted me or seemed friendly, another thing to contribute to my mood. Outside, one big semi-truck after another roared by. As a kid, I loved how cars and trucks often resembled a person's face from the positioning on the headlights, front grill and bumper. On this day, those trucks' faces seemed meaner than usual. I am not an anti-trucking person, and in fact, thousands of trucks had passed me safely. I have friends in the trucking industry, and I was fortunate to not have had any disturbing run-ins since the one in eastern Arizona.

As I sat on concrete in the front of the store, I found myself thinking this was becoming a not-so-enjoyable day. Then my conscience spoke to me. *By the way, weren't you a rude driver when you were younger?* Many memories that I'm not proud of came to mind. Injustices. How I've wronged people. How I've hurt them. Acts and deeds I'd be embarrassed about if anyone knew or rehashed them. I sensed this had something to do with all the horrible negative thoughts I had earlier. My conscience was right and put things in perspective. I told myself that if there's trouble with others on the road, I had to remember that God has forgiven me for things far worse. That encouraged me.

I decided that I needed to make a connection, something to loosen me up, and so I sent a text message to Veronica. She's that friend who grew up in this region, but has since moved to Atlanta as an adult. I last connected with her by phone in Arkansas and was due to contact her.

"I'm in Chilton County," I texted, "Lots of trucks on Highway 82. Narrow shoulder. Ugh!"

Veronica's reply came back within seconds, "Chilton County is the worst place that ever happened to me. It's like the Bermuda Triangle. Don't get sucked in. Keep going!"

I laughed heartily. Although I didn't have the details, her sympathy felt good. Again, I thought of Glenn's advice and found a bright spot. At least this experience might be a good story to tell—as long as I survived.

I remounted and got back on the road, knowing I had to toughen up and handle whatever came my way. Then the "Superstitious" song that I heard in Maplesville began to ring in my head, and I pedaled hard, keeping pace with the upbeat melody. With the first oncoming trucker, I waved confidently, and I saw him give a full wave back. On the right, I passed a parked utility vehicle with two men working on something. The guy lightly tooted his horn, his arm raised with a fist as if he was cheering me on. "Go! Go! Go!" he seemed to be saying. I smiled. Maybe not everyone was against me.

Beyond Plattsville and into the outskirts of Montgomery, the road engineers of Alabama finally had mercy on me. It widened to four lanes through an industrial area with plenty of shoulder. I breathed easier, proud of my perseverance. My map indicated that Highway 82 served as a beltway for the west and south sides of the city, and my plan was to find a motel on South Boulevard. Somehow though, I missed a turn, and I thought I was still on Highway 82 as I passed the Maxwell Air Force Base. Soon, I was in an urban and congested part of the city. I grew concerned, unsure of where I was. Then, beyond a traffic light, my road became a single lane that ahead would split with turnoffs for interstate highways. If I continued, I only had choices between I-65 to Birmingham and I-85 to Atlanta.

"What the heck is going on?" I shouted in anger.

I turned back on the shoulder and biked against traffic, not caring if a cop had seen me and would want to give me a hard time. In fact, I would've screamed to him about the confusing roads in Montgomery! I stopped and studied my map insert of the city, and even knowing that I was near those two interstates, I still couldn't figure out where I was. For the first time since Day One in San Diego, I was hopelessly lost.

I biked in and out of streets and felt like a lost puppy. Eventually I returned the way I came and went to the entrance of the Maxwell Air Force Base. A guard at the entrance gave me directions, informing me that I was about three miles from South Boulevard. After I thanked him, another man in full military gear who overheard our conversation, spoke up, "This is a dangerous neighborhood. You don't want to be out here at night!" He said it with authority and care.

Yes, sir! Maybe I should have given him a salute.

At least, I knew where I was now. When I got to a motel on South Boulevard, my extra riding in Montgomery gave me a tally of seventy-four miles.

Showered and relaxed in my room, I called Veronica to inform her about all that happened.

"You biked through my neck of the woods!" she said, "I grew up in Clanton and I know exactly where you were. I know all those roads."

"Really?" I asked.

"That's right. My Dad had his own delivery business and I would go all over with him in his truck. I know where practically everything is in Alabama."

"So what about the part about the Bermuda Triangle?"

She laughed. "You've got to believe me. I grew up well and I take nothing away from my upbringing or the region, but I had to get out of there when I got older. I'm so much happier in Atlanta."

"I understand."

"So how far did you ride?"

"Seventy-four miles."

"You go. You're speeding through the South!" she exclaimed.

I thanked her and grunted as I turned on my side. "And I went ninety-one yesterday. Not bad, huh? By the way, I know I'm not giving you much notice, but I think I'll make it to Albany on Thursday," I said.

"I can't make it," she said with sadness, "Work is hectic. I just can't take a day off and drive that far."

"It's okay," I said affectionately, "Just think of me tomorrow. I think you're the only person I know from Alabama, and I have one more day in this state."

***

After riding seventeen miles beyond Montgomery, a sign told me that Eufaula, my destination, was seventy miles away. I didn't flinch. Biking eighty-seven miles didn't seem like a tall order anymore. I passed a construction site with men who were working on a culvert with shovels. I waved, and they waved back. I felt so much more upbeat from yesterday, and no doubt some of it was from the sunny weather.

From what I could gather, the equine industry is prevalent in southeast Alabama. I passed many ranches with horses grazing, many of them on grassy grounds lined by white wooden fences. There were beautiful horses in white, brown and black. The scenes were so pretty that I stopped frequently to snap pictures.

At a lone roadside store, I took a break. Inside was one man running the place, and I was the only customer. There was no music as I walked around, and the silence felt uncomfortable. Near the front, I saw an array of beef jerky and felt compelled to break the quiet with real conversation.

"One of my dilemmas is I see great stuff like this, but I can't eat it because I'm on a bike. I've got to stay at least somewhat healthy. I can't put anything in my stomach that will slow me down," I explained, and then added, "Then again, I could buy it and bring it with me, but I'll be honest: I don't have much self-control. I'm sure I'd eat it right away, and then I'd regret it."

The man said something quietly, but I couldn't understand him. I grabbed a sports drink in the freezer and approached the counter.

That's when he said something more clearly, "Usually the bicyclists come on weekends, but they cause problems being in the way of truckers."

I was taken aback, not knowing what to say. Today was a weekday, but I hadn't seen many tractor-trailers on this section of road. In fact, it was fairly quiet. I shrugged off the comment and pressed on to be friendly.

"This area sure is pretty," I said, figuring that complimenting someone's home region would build rapport.

"Sure is," he said.

His tone of voice sounded curt, but sometimes it's hard to really know someone's intent.

Outside, I gulped down liquids and ate some crackers. Standing and pacing was so pleasant, as other muscles needed to be worked from sitting in the saddle for so long. I thought about the sour man in that store and laughed. He reminded me of that toxic personality that everyone has to deal with at one time or another. Nearly every day, I had experiences in convenience stores, and I had met some interesting people, but this one was a dud. I brushed it off.

My ride continued through Union Springs and Three Notch. I stopped at a sign about an Indian treaty boundary line created in 1832 that ceded much of the land to the United States. There were also dogwood trees with spectacular bright white flowers, with a few blooming in pink. I biked well, stopping a few times to snap pictures, and making good time.

When I arrived in Midway, I had biked sixty-five miles and needed a longer break. From the road, the town didn't seem like it had much. I passed some houses, a church and a fire station. On the left was one convenience store, and I rolled beside the entrance. A young man stood out front. I couldn't tell if he was of high school age or older, but it seemed that he was just standing there. Didn't he have something better to do? The fear of another bike theft crept up on me. This seemed like a teeny-tiny southern town ... I shouldn't have been too concerned, right? I locked my bike beside the entrance and assertively said "hi" to the guy, making eye contact with him. I wanted him to know that I was tough, or at least that I would react strongly if he touched my bike.

Inside, the cashier greeted me and said, "You don't need to lock anything around here. People would stop coming if it wasn't safe."

I smiled and should have asked if he'd buy me a new bicycle if he was wrong. Still, this man was probably the owner of this business, and I let myself relax, knowing he was probably right. I purchased my snacks and went outside, and that guy was still standing there in front of the store. It was a quiet scene. There were no cars on the road or in the parking lot, and it was just the sounds of birds chirping. I looked him over, probably longer than I should have, idly trying to gauge his age. When our eyes locked, I said, "Hey buddy."

That's all it took. The ice was broken, and we chatted.

"San Diego? You started in California?" He was shocked and wanted to tell someone. "They should put you on TV!"

I laughed and shook my head. "No, a lot of people have done this."

"Are you staying in town? We could have you come to our high school and speak."

Just then, two of his friends approached and acted like they had nothing else to do. Again, we got into a rundown of what I was doing.

One guy asked, "Are you having fun?"

I paused for a moment, struggling to find the right words.

"That's not an adjective I'd use," I said, "Memorable. Tiring. Adventuresome. Those words fit better."

"Come on," he said, "I'm sure you've had fun."

His question challenged me. Sure, I've had fun moments and being outside this store with these young men was quickly becoming one. But my bike trip, as impressive as it was to them, had been a series of monotonous rides, day after day. Perhaps looking back at our greatest triumphs, we may think of our effort with joy, but as we worked for it, the time, effort, money and sweat probably didn't seem like fun.

"No, it's not fun," I said, "Not most of the time."

When I think of "fun," I think of riding a rollercoaster or playing miniature golf boisterously with friends. It's playing cards with your buddies all night, peppering the darkness with laughter. Fun usually doesn't require much effort, but what I had been doing was tough. It was a demanding mission that required that I be on my toes at all times. The day-to-day physical demands were grueling, but of course, it was worth it.

"So do you guys bike much?" I asked.

"No, we don't do anything like that," one guy said shyly.

"Well, I see you're a basketball player."

One of them wore a shirt that read, "Who Did It? Bullock County High School 4A State Champions 2008." They told me about how good the high school basketball team was that year with pride in their voices.

I tried to encourage them about cycling as a sport, but they weren't persuaded. By then, the store became busier. Another guy walked up after pumping fuel in his car, and my three new friends boasted about me.

"This guy! He's going across the country!" one exclaimed.

They made me feel like a star. I stood there with my hands on my hips and took it in, knowing I wouldn't always be this popular.

Then, an old and rusted pick-up truck that seemed on the verge of breaking down parked in the lot. The driver got out and entered the store, and the teenagers went to tell the man in the passenger seat about me.

"He rode here from Montgomery today and he's still going. He's gone two thousand miles."

I waltzed over to the truck and greeted the man. He was older, with a baseball cap and a bushy goatee. He said he was heading to Eufaula.

"We can put your bike in the back if you want a ride. With the three of us, we can squeeze in."

"No, I can't do that." I said, "I gotta keep this honest."

"You'll be riding through Barbour County. We've got some pretty countryside," he said.

"It's definitely pretty. I've seen so many dogwoods—that's what you call them, right? The trees with the bright white flowers on them. They're amazing!"

His eyes gleamed with mine. "They are. And you'll like Eufaula," he said. He recommended a Cajun restaurant and told me about a spot on the edge of Lake Eufaula that is best for viewing the scenery.

Then the three teenagers were carrying on. One was making fun of the other, teasing over some incident from when they were small children. I sensed my presence ignited something in them. With so much laughter and activity here, I was so happy. I thought of my earlier experience at the lone mart, and the difference here was like "night and day." If there was ever a nationwide contest for the friendliest retail store, perhaps this place in Midway would win. My soul sang as I said good-bye and went on my way.

Ahead in the wooded lands of Barbour County on that quiet two-lane road, I stopped, for no obvious reason other than something inside told me to. With the bicycle on its side and my feet on the edge of the road, I took in the surroundings with all of my senses. The chirping of the birds. The slight breeze. The sunlight intermittently breaking through the upper branches of the forest. The smell of more dogwood trees in bloom, fragrant and wonderful. Everything seemed to be coming alive. My heart told me to pay attention. This was a moment that I'd always remember. Experience it fully. Enjoy it. I was near the end of Alabama and would only have one more state to go. Surely, this was the end game. The fourth quarter.

Hours later, when I arrived in Eufaula, I had biked 337 miles in four days. It was only three-and-a-half days ago that Charles dropped me off in Mississippi, but by now, my friend seemed like a distant memory.

Eufaula is located on the west shore of Lake Eufaula, a body of water that acts as the border between Georgia and Alabama. It's a town with southern charm with many historic Victorian-era homes. I had dinner at that Cajun restaurant suggested to me, enjoying beef brisket with brown gravy and corn-on-the-cob chowder soup. I walked around and from the main avenue, there was a broad enough opening that I could see the lake in the distance. Georgia, the final state that separated me from the end, was across that lake. I was thrilled over my progress. Later that night, I bought a plane ticket to fly back to San Diego, scheduled for one week ahead.

CHAPTER XVII

Keep Pedaling East

Say that I starved;
that I was lost and weary;
That I was burned and blinded by the sun ...
but that I kept my dream.

Everett Ruess

The next day, I biked with enthusiasm on the bridge and causeway across Lake Eufaula. The shoulder was wide enough that I could gaze at the water, the sunlight glistening over it, without worry. Many boats were in the distance of this attractive body of water. The closest boat had a man fishing on an elevated seat, a fun undertaking on a beautiful morning. I waved in his direction, but he didn't respond, probably because he didn't see me. I crossed the lake and rode through the village of Georgetown, Georgia and with just four riding days to reach the Atlantic Ocean, suddenly I felt an urgency to reflect. Would I miss this ride? Should I have done things differently? Did I enjoy this trip enough? And there was that one nagging question that kept surfacing: was I any different? I didn't know.

For years, I had lived in the dreaming stage of biking across America. Now the actual doing stage—just six and a half weeks long—was nearing its end. And then I would enter the last phase, where the journey would be in the past and I would forever look back on it. That seemed like scary territory, considering how my memory has played tricks on previous recollections. Memories of good and joyful times have been clouded; in other instances, my retrospection omits details that belie just how difficult a time really was. Already, even with the ride not over, I could do a playback of scenes, and the hard times were softening and blurring with the good ones. The bicycle tour was becoming like a massive quilt that contained patches of all my experiences. Or even better, the adventure was resembling a water color painting where the shades of emotion sloppily mesh into one another. This grand piece of artwork was uniquely my own. It was a masterpiece—something to hang on my bedroom wall that I'd set my eyes on every morning when I awaken.

I wanted to remember this trip as it was and so I did more note-taking near the end. Often, it felt like I was lecturing myself.

Don't forget all the monotony on the bike.

The aches and pains.

The lonely roads.

The motels.

And the convenience stores—all different, but good heavens, all the same.

It has been a valiant journey, hasn't it? I'm convinced that I'm living proof that anyone can bike across America or ride a long distance over many consecutive days. This bicycle campaign had become a friend that I had gotten to know well. It was so many things. Cycling cross-country is the constant whirring sound of passing cars. It is riding by home after home, and wondering who lives there and what they're about. It is wanting to be done with the day's ride, even though you just started and know you should try to enjoy it. It is flat tires. It is roadside litter. It is bumps and cracks, and sand and gravel. It is peeling off your sweat-drenched jersey each day and scrubbing yourself in the shower.

It is being at the mercy of road engineers who likely didn't take into account someone traveling by bicycle. It is sore shoulders and burning leg muscles. It is loneliness. It is perseverance in spite of the loneliness. It is being content with yourself.

***

My first day in Georgia would be the most difficult, as two mean truckers, a loose dog and a flat tire would give this poor cyclist a meltdown.

I was riding up a hill in Quitman County, when a tractor-trailer passing in the opposite direction slammed its horn. The noise rattled me and was unmistakably rude. Although I had waved at so many cars and trucks, even some that antagonized me, I couldn't play that game here. I turned back and raised my right arm with my hand open, to communicate, "What was that for?" Who knows if the trucker saw my gesture? The offense lingered with me for miles. I just couldn't shake it off.

In Cuthbert, a dog ran from a home all the way onto the road. It was small and harmless, but it got me more edgy. Then, past the town's east side, I was back in the country on a wide shoulder with two eastbound lanes beside me. I was so far to the right that no motorist could possibly be annoyed with my presence ... except the obnoxious driver in the semi coming from behind. At the point of passing, his horn roared at length, the thunderous noise terrorizing me.

Instantly, I thought it may have been the previous jerk ten miles back, as the truck had the same red front and gray trailer like the previous one. Or maybe it was a buddy of his, and they were making a concerted attempt to heckle the cyclist in red who was riding through. As the semi sped ahead, I focused on the logo and saw the name of the company on the back. It read, "Southern Ag Carriers." I was so thankful to have good eyesight!

Too fired up to let this go, I called 911 with my cell phone. When I got the dispatcher, I was hot and angry. "A truck on Highway 82!" I shouted, "That's where I'm at. He slammed his horn for no reason just to intimidate a bicyclist. I was totally on the side of the road and he had plenty of room to pass. He had no business doing that!"

The dispatcher wasn't alarmed. In fact, I got nowhere with her. She asked a few questions, but didn't do anything. Sure, it'd be dubious for a law enforcement officer to come out and do anything constructive, but her lack of sympathy wasn't appreciated. Afterward, I learned that an infraction did take place. According to Georgia state law (O.C.G.A. 40-8-70 [2010] Section 1), vehicles are prohibited from the use of an "unreasonably loud" or "harsh sound," and furthermore, it forbids the use of a horn when it is unnecessary to ensure safe operation.

I kept thinking about it as I continued riding. Truly, I wasn't that enraged, but something was at stake. If these truckers did this to me, they've probably done it to others. With the name of the trucking company, I could make a complaint, and maybe make enough noise that it would deter them from doing this to the next cyclist. Directory assistance helped me find the company headquarters and within minutes I was speaking to a woman in charge of taking grievances about drivers. At least this time, I had someone who showed empathy and listening skills. We built rapport within seconds, and I vented everything to her.

"Your driver was out-of-line! I was all the way to the right and he had plenty of room to pass, and it wasn't a love tap, like a 'beep beep' but a prolonged 'hooooooonk.'"

I laughed, amused at my imitation of a truck's horn.

"I'm sure it didn't sound friendly," she said.

"No, it didn't!" I shouted, "And it's worse when you're riding a bike and your whole body shakes from the startling noise."

"Wait, did you say you're on bicycle?" she asked, surprised.

"That's right."

She showed interest in some of the details of the trip, and the more questions she asked, the more I smiled. It was hard to remain angry for long. Then she got back to doing her job.

"I'm so glad you're okay," she said. "Your safety is the most important thing. Our policy is clear that our drivers must show the utmost care and respect to others. We take every incident seriously and follow up on all of them."

"That sounds good," I said.

"Did you see a number on the back of the truck?"

"No."

"It'll be tougher to track it," she said, but she followed up with a variety of questions, trying to narrow down which truck it may have been.

"We have so many trucks and I can't make any promises," she said, "but I'll do my best. The most important thing is that you're safe. I'll get back to you if I can track the driver, or issue a warning, or if I have more questions."

I could tell this woman was genuine and a professional, and she was helping me cool off.

"Honestly ma'am, I'm not that upset anymore. Most truckers are fine. It's rare that something like this happens," I said.

The fact that she was doing something made me feel better. And at this point, it really didn't matter whether anything came of my complaint. It was just nice to be heard. When our conversation ended, I got back on the bike and continued.

Today's ride would be a short one, only forty-nine miles to Dawson, and I was getting close with only twelve miles to go. Soon the shoulder on this two-lane highway narrowed to eighteen inches. The riding became stressful. Many more vehicles passed as the day ensued, but the bullying truckers from earlier had me on edge. And then, two miles west of Shellman, the thing that I dreaded would happen one last time on this journey: a flat tire. Again in the back wheel. The eleventh overall, ninth in the back.

I knew I should have been tougher, but this flat, coupled with the tensions of the day, contributed to a meltdown on the side of the road. I didn't cry or scream, or do anything drastic. In fact, I just stood there calmly, pitying myself. I wanted to curl up in a tight little ball. Or maybe disappear. Or just leave my body and fly away. Yes, I was way at the end of this bicycle tour—something I should feel so good about—but that didn't matter at this juncture. I felt humiliated. Southwest Georgia was proving to be quite a bicycle-unfriendly region, and I didn't feel welcome.

I escorted my bike toward the edge of an onion field and leaned it against a sprinkler system. I paced a bit, stretching my arms and gazing at the sky, and found myself thinking deeply. To be this close to the end, quitting was a ludicrous option, but somehow I needed to pull myself out of this gloomy state. I prayed. I didn't know what to say to God, but the only thing I uttered was, "I'm tired of this."

Eventually I got to the task of fixing the flat, and even with all my experience, I still felt uneasy about the job. I worried that dirt or gravel might inadvertently get inside the tire. And I still had apprehensions about mistakenly looping the chain as I sought to wrap it around the back cassette. When you're nervous, there is always something that will bother you.

When I resumed to riding, I knew I'd be okay, but my emotions were shot. Within the first mile, my cell phone alerted me to a text message. Usually, I ignored my phone while riding because it was a hassle to stop, grab my phone and respond, but this time, for reasons unknown, I did. And it was meant to be. The text was Jason, that friend and former co-worker who last encouraged me while I was in Graham, Texas. It read, "Keep pedaling east. The ocean awaits."

It was a perfect message. And at the right time, too. It made me roar in laughter, and I shouted, "Thanks Jason. That's great advice— I'll keep going east!"

***

A pizza in Dawson got my mind off things in the afternoon. And azalea bushes with bright pink blooms around the motel grounds gave me something to photograph and enjoy. I slept well that night.

The next day for the first time I tried boiled peanuts at a roadside stand in Sylvester. They were cold and soggy. Later I learned they need to be served hot—freshly boiled and seasoned—the very opposite of what I had.

In Albany, I made one final visit to a bicycle shop. I bought tubes and a new back tire. The older one, bought in Greenville, was already showing signs of wear. The young man who ran the shop had lived in Colorado, and with that we connected warmly. He moved to Aspen to live the adventurous life of a ski bum, but returned to his hometown to be closer to his family. He said he wasn't surprised that I was cycling across the country.

"People have come into the shop who've said they're doing it," he explained. "And honestly, some of them are weird. There was this enormous man with a goatee—he must have been about 300 pounds—who was riding a mountain bike that was too small for his size. He was riding west and handed me a slip for his cause. It was strange."

"I'm sure people think I'm on the eccentric side too."

"No," he said, "You're the first normal person I've ever met to bike across America."

That made me chuckle. I had no idea how to respond.

As I biked through Albany, I passed the headquarters for Southern Ag Carriers. I considered paying a friendly visit to the woman who had taken my complaint, but I kept going. Yesterday's episode was all "water under the bridge" by now. I finished in Tifton, with only 125 miles to the end. After dinner, I wandered around town, buzzing with joy and anticipation. By now, being so close to the Atlantic, even if I had gotten another seventeen flat tires, I could have handled them without a drop in my attitude.

The next day, the humidity thickened and the temperature rose to eighty-five degrees in south Georgia. Thick forest lined the route as I rode through towns with unique names such as Enigma, Alapaha, Willacoochee and Axson. The riding was easy, as Highway 82 became flatter than anywhere so far. If anything, there was probably a slight descent as I came closer to sea level.

Another seventy-five miles brought me to Waycross, and my stay would mark the eve of the final ride. This town is on the north side of the Okefenokee Swamp, a 438,000-acre wildlife refuge and wilderness area that extends into north Florida. If I had a car or knew someone who would give me a tour, I would've loved to have explored the wetlands, seen the headwaters of the Suwanee River and searched for alligators. Then again, could I have taken a day off knowing I was so close to the completion of my dream?

After dinner, I stopped at a Dunkin Donuts near the motel. This is one of my all-time favorite places for coffee. I sipped on an extra-large blueberry-flavored coffee (with cream, no sugar), its wonderful scent and steam oozing from the top. I casually paced on the sidewalk and enjoyed my drink, not knowing how I would react when I'd arrive at the beach tomorrow. I've seen some professionals who have won major cycling tours, hold a glass of champagne during their final ceremonial rides. With my beverage in hand, the version I imagined seemed dorkier. If I could find a Dunkin' Donuts shop, maybe I'd buy a cup of coffee and sip it periodically as I cruised to the finish line.

Eventually I settled in front of my motel room. It was too nice to sit inside on a night like this. Tall palm trees rose above with splashes of pink in the background from the sunset. Then, I realized that the motel had its hot tub open, even though the pool was closed. Immediately I took advantage of it. With everything but my head submerged in the hot, bubbly water, my sore muscles got some well-needed therapy. I sat there like a vegetable, gazing up at two nearby palm trees as it got dark. The occasion felt so special. I was proud of myself—beaming over what I had accomplished—but then the question hit me: would I feel sorrow tomorrow?

CHAPTER XVIII

THE LAST DAY

This is not the end.
It is not even the beginning of the end.
But it is, perhaps,
the end of the beginning.

Winston Churchill

*T*he last day had arrived.

While I wish I could give an embellishing description about the start of this final day, I can not. In fact, I had difficulty getting out of bed. Sure, there was expectation brewing inside my mind and heart, but the physical side—ruled by my aching muscles—had its own agenda, and that was to sleep in. Even with all the distance I'd covered, there was still a feeling of dread each morning, knowing that it was up to me to move forward. No one can pedal for me. The energy required must come from within. And biking sixty-one miles, however easy I made it seem to this point, is still sixty-one miles and no leisure outing.

Yet, once I had showered, checked-out and went outside with

the bicycle, I couldn't allow myself to remain groggy. Like when you're feeling satisfaction from putting the final pieces into a massive jigsaw puzzle, I too, was on the verge of completing a crowning achievement. No, this was no ordinary ride. As I rode out of Waycross at sixteen miles per hour, I began to feel electric currents of excitement. Passing each mile of the countdown, something in my soul was stirring toward delight, and then I realized how absurd it would have been to lie in bed like a sloth, postponing this glorious final ride.

As I rode on Highway 82, I noticed how this journey changed my appearance. By now, my arms and legs were well-tanned with distinct tan lines on my upper arms, ankles and front tips of my fingers. My calf muscles were more defined. My cycling shoes were new seven weeks ago; now they had scratches and scuffs, and the right one even carried a mud stain that would not come off. My red jersey was a deeper red; now it was badly faded. Still, the greatest difference I noticed was in my stamina. Despite the aches and pains from constant riding, it felt like at any moment I had Hulk-like strength to go for a run or play in a tackle football game. When I walked, my strut felt strong and athletic.

The route went through thick forest with only an occasional home breaking up the tall, stately pine trees. Besides the sound of cars passing, all seemed peaceful. Pedaling sandwiched between roadside tranquility on one side and the roar of speeding, petroleum-burning machines on the other was something that I'd miss. It is a paradoxical combination and yet so typical of biking cross-country. Suddenly a flock of birds flew across the road, their wingspans wide. Then three more followed. From my distance they appeared to be swans, or maybe great blue herons, so striking and graceful. Quickly I grabbed my camera, hoping more would appear for a picture, but I had no such luck.

I stopped for breaks in Nahunta and Waynesville, feeling bubbly and talkative at convenience stores. Each time I told someone about how special this day was, but there were no magical interactions with locals. It's funny—sometimes when you try to force it, nothing noteworthy happens, but when you least expect it, the wildest experiences can occur. For example, I made no attempt to set up what would transpire next.

After crossing into Glynn County, I was almost hit by a car. A minivan pulled up from a country road. Usually while passing drivers who stopped perpendicularly, I made eye contact with them. This time, I didn't. After riding by, I heard the sound of a motor unusually close. Suddenly in my peripheral vision, I saw the car had turned onto the highway and was heading directly at me.

"Whoa!" I shouted.

In that split second, the car kept coming.

"*Whoooooooooah!*" I screamed, even louder.

The driver stopped with a screech. The front fender ended up inches from my side.

"I'm sorry!" the driver cried out. She was a young woman, perhaps a teenager and new driver. From her tone of voice, it was obvious that she felt horrible and hadn't seen me. Immediately, I turned toward her and gave a friendly wave as she passed and joined the eastbound lanes. I couldn't see her reaction as she drove ahead, but I didn't want her to feel guilty about this. I'm certain that I'd be especially hard on myself if I were in her shoes. And I hoped I didn't sound too angry. My response was only a split-second reaction to a situation that triggered self-survival—scream, yell, do whatever to get the driver's attention. With the incident over and the girl well ahead, I breathed a sigh of relief. In my five-year history of bicycling, that was the closest I'd come to having a collision with a moving hunk of steel. Still, it was the type of day where not even a scary encounter with a car could get me down.

As I continued east, there was more evidence that the ocean was near. The smell of the salty ocean breeze. Billboards for beaches and vacation attractions. Even the homes and cars were becoming nicer and more upscale.

Then, I biked past a sign that read:

I-95   4
Brunswick   12
Jekyll Island 16

After 2,449 miles, my journey had been reduced to sixteen remaining miles. Highway 82 finished its course in Brunswick, and I passed under Interstate 95. Now I was on a different road, and the terrain changed one last time. The sizable Brunswick River was adjacent to the route, and for a while I saw more boats tied-up on docks than cars. I checked my cyclometer: I had gone fifty-five miles, and as usual my body was ready to be done. After all these physically-demanding rides, I longed to get some lodging, sleep, and then awaken the next morning without the pressure to go.

Only six miles separated me from the Atlantic Ocean, and I was bursting with energy like an elated child on the last day of school. I was a happy, gleeful hobo on two wheels. And yet, the more I thought about the end, there was that other feeling that I couldn't deny—melancholy. It's true that there were a plethora of moments when I dwelled and fixated on reaching the end, but now, with the ocean less than an hour away, I knew I would miss this tour. Suddenly, I wanted to travel back in time and do it all over again.

As a senior in high school, I remember how I wanted the academic year to be over. I mostly hated the high school experience— the peer pressure, the cruel ways that kids are to one another, the pimples and of course, the schoolwork itself. I remember the feelings of anticipation and jubilation during the final weeks. However, when graduation became a reality, I felt sad that an era had ended, and I began to miss people—schoolmates, teachers and even classes that I hadn't liked much. The same was happening with this bicycle journey.

Shouldn't I celebrate? Shouldn't it be like the ways that college-level and professional sports teams whoop it up when they win a championship? Athletes run onto the field when the victory is final. They carry on and spray champagne on each other in the locker room. After all, I was about to accomplish a dream that I could "hang my hat on." For the rest of my life, I could list this feat on my resume with pride. And no one could ever say that I was "all talk and no action." Oh yes, I did it. I kept at it. And I overcame.

Maybe what I was feeling is similar to what a successful married couple feels when they reach an anniversary like twenty years. Do most couples become euphoric on the specific day when they hit the milestone? I don't imagine so. Their joy is probably a more deep and profound delight, one that gives them strength and wisdom through life. There is a common saying that "happiness is in the journey, not the destination," and I believe it. There is a trap in the psyche of humanity that insists that contentment will come through accomplishments. Or when we arrive. Or when we have that thing that we long for. "As soon as I turn eighteen, things will get better ..." "As soon as I'm in a relationship/get married/get divorced ..." "As soon as I make [enter the amount of money] ..." "As soon as I bike across America ..." Yes, within the hour, my dream would be fulfilled, but the culmination would not be captured when my wheels hit the ocean's water. The magnificence of this feat happened day after day—each time I chose not to quit and to face adversity with courage.

My biking continued a little longer in coastal Georgia. I hit my last pothole. I maneuvered around roadkill—a dead raccoon. I averted more litter. And then I guzzled most of the fluids in my water bottles. It would all be for the last time.

Four days later, I would catch a plane that would take just five hours (with a layover in Houston) to return to San Diego. The thought of traveling so quickly to where I had started was astonishing. That night, I'd have dinner with Jae and Krista, laughing, conversing and showing them my pictures. It would feel like I had never left them.

When I returned home in Buena Vista, Colorado, I received so much adoration from friends and neighbors, but soon I'd revert to everyday life. I'd regain my weight and return to moderate fitness. My energy level would decrease. And I wouldn't sleep as intensely. Sleeping was far more rewarding while biking across America.

Three months from this day, my father would be diagnosed with pancreatic cancer. The disease would spread quickly and he'd die five months later. When I learned about his diagnosis, I was overwhelmed with emotion like any son would be, but another part of me was unsurprised. I remembered God's words about becoming my father, and who knows, maybe the message was at least partly given for this reason.

One year later, I'd view the bicycle trip like a wonderful fairy tale. In fact, I'd joke that I was "living in the past" as I viewed my photos with fondness. Sometimes I would get depressed, wishing I could do it again, and I would miss the pressing questions and uncertainties of each day. *Will I make it? Will I get a flat? Will I encounter any interesting people?* Eventually, I'd laugh over the not-so-pleasant experiences of having my bicycle stolen, being stranded in the desert from mechanical failures and run-ins with semis. Most of all, I would miss being challenged, where I was forced to face my fears, defy the odds and do whatever it took to ride to the next town.

Three years later, I would be fortunate to go a second time on a similar route across the southern USA. On that expedition, I would relish the days more, although it wasn't very different from the first. I'd have nine flat tires, instead of eleven. More people would ride with me for segments of the trip, and I'd use social media to draw more attention to my journey and the charity that I promoted.[1]

After this adventure, I do not see American towns like I previously did. Now I view them from a cross-country perspective. I assess the layout of roads and notice the locations of motels. I ask myself, "If I was biking through, where would I stay? Where would I eat? What would I think about this place?"

The ending seemed anti-climactic. I forgot to stop somewhere to carry a cup of coffee with me to the beach. Ahead was a towering suspension bridge that led drivers to Brunswick and St. Simons Island, but I turned right for Jekyll Island. This was the final destination. For months this spot on my map had been an abstraction, a mystery, but now I was only four miles away. I stopped one last time to take photos and drink fluids. I called close friends, but only reached voice mails. I had already accepted that there would be no cheering crowds and no one waiting for me at the beach, but I thought maybe I could rope someone into the experience. It just wasn't meant to be.

Jekyll Island is one of a handful of barrier islands in Georgia that can be reached by car, and I biked on a two-lane road with relaxed

---

1   You can view my photo journal of that 46-day tour on www.bikeacrossamerica.net.

traffic. Most motorists were here to enjoy this scenic coastal destination, and no one seemed impatient or in a rush. The road went through marshlands untouched by human development and alive with aquatic wildlife. Hundreds of ducks played in the water, while seagulls squawked overhead.

Three miles later, there was a bridge with a sharp ascent entering Jekyll Island. My legs tore into that hill. I gripped the handlebar tightly and pedaled without breathing hard or showing any strain. I had one final dance with my bike—this wonderful new bicycle—and I thanked it for being such a faithful companion. Now, my physical conditioning was as robust as ever. I was as fit as I'd probably be for the rest of my life.

Jekyll Island was formerly a state park and today conservation is its main focus. There are just a few homes, restaurants and lodging options in the laid-back setting. There are bicycle trails, walking paths, a water park, and of course, beautiful beaches.

Once I got on the island, I was just another bicyclist among many. Most rode casually on beach cruisers or wide-tire bikes. Some were families with the kids following behind on smaller bikes. It didn't take long before I could see the ocean through a break in the trees, and I could not have finished on a prettier day. A sunny blue sky. A refreshing ocean breeze. And palm trees all over. The euphonious crashing of waves—ah I remembered that sound on the Pacific coast—captivated me as I entered the parking area for the beach. Throughout my journey, my vision had been dominated by the road ahead, but now before me was a sea of blue water extending to the horizon. I rode on a wooden pedestrian bridge to the edge of the sand, but the surface was so soft that my wheels had no traction, and so I waddled with the frame between my legs until the sand got harder. There was only one-hundred feet between me and the water. It was all about the end right here.

I gained speed, but pressed my brakes abruptly when I had an idea. I stopped, dropped my camera and other valuables into a pile, and then charged ahead. My front wheel split a small wave and I rode until the water was high enough to stop me. I planted my legs knee deep, and did a graceless tumble off the bike, yelping from the impact of the water's coldness. Within seconds, I felt rejuvenated and splashed around with laughter. Then, I realized I still had my helmet on. I unstrapped it, tossed it on the shore and dunked myself fully.

Stay connected with Steve through his website, www.stevegarufi.com, and on the following social media pages:

Facebook: www.facebook.com/stevegarufi

Twitter: www.twitter.com/stevegarufi

YouTube: www.youtube.com/kisscactus (personal)
www.youtube.com/bikeacrossusa (Bike Across USA)

Pinterest: www.pinterest.com/stevegarufi

Cover design and layout by Susan Dunn in Buena Vista, Colorado.
www.susandunndesign.com